Advance Praise for

TESTING EDUCATION

"Finally, we learn directly from a teacher what happens when joy and creativity are drained out of education by misguided and harmful education policies."

—Nancy Carlsson-Paige, author of *Taking Back Childhood: A Proven Roadmap for Raising Confident, Creative, Compassionate Kids*

"Reflecting on her own long and varied career in our public schools, [Kathy Greeley] bluntly catalogues, through the stories of her students and colleagues, what has been lost, and what harm has been inflicted on a generation of students and educators. We should all heed her call to create what our communities deserve and high-stakes testing has denied: 'strong, rigorous, engaging, loving, inclusive, democratic schools.'"

—Max Page, president of the Massachusetts Teachers Association

"Greeley gives a rare insider's look at the devastation wrought by corporate ed reform. Spanning a nearly forty-year career in urban schools, *Testing Education* is a searing exposé on the damage these policies continue to inflict. This is a must-read for people interested in understanding what public schools have consequently lost—and how to rebuild them into vibrant democratic institutions."

—Deborah Meier, coauthor of *Beyond Testing: Seven Assessments of Students and Schools More Effective Than Standardized Tests*

"THIS is the book I've been waiting for! As a veteran teacher, I know the joy and magic that's possible in a classroom, and I know that the current context in public schools has made it all but impossible to make that magic. Kathy's warm, insightful writing reminds us of what's possible and provides clear analysis of how testing mania has caused public schools to veer wildly off course."

—Karen Engels, 4th-grade Cambridge Public Schools teacher

T0273995

"A powerful read that provides a firsthand account of 'what we had, what we have lost—and what we must regain' as we reclaim our best practices from the policies and mandates of a corporate driven agenda."

—Deb McCarthy, vice president of the Massachusetts
Teachers Association

"I loved this book. Greeley is an excellent storyteller with a compelling tale about the marvelous possibilities of teacher-led schools. It will interest educators, parents, policymakers, and anyone concerned about the health of our education system."

—James Nehring, author of *The Practice of School Reform: Lessons from Two Centuries* and professor of leadership in schooling at the University of Massachusetts Lowell

"[Greeley's] story is not self-indulgent. It is not romanticized. It opens the sociological imagination in profound and complex ways. More importantly, in 'answering with her life,' she provides a powerful example of what must be done."

—Ricardo D. Rosa, coauthor of *Capitalism's Educational Catastrophe: And the Advancing Endgame Revolt!*

TESTING EDUCATION

TESTING EDUCATION

a teacher's memoir

Kathy Greeley

University of Massachusetts Press

Amherst and Boston

ISBN 978-1-62534-783-1 (paper); 784-8 (hardcover)

Designed by Sally Nichols
Set in Freight Pro
Printed and bound by Books International, Inc.

Cover design by Sally Nichols
Cover photo by Olinchuck, *Back to School*, stock.adobe.com

Library of Congress Cataloging-in-Publication Data
Names: Greeley, Kathy, author.
Title: Testing education : a teacher's memoir / Kathy Greeley.
Description: Amherst : University of Massachusetts Press, 2024. | Includes
bibliographical references and index. |
Identifiers: LCCN 2023046462 (print) | LCCN 2023046463 (ebook) | ISBN
9781625347831 (paperback) | ISBN 9781625347848 (hardcover) | ISBN
9781685750534 (ebook) | ISBN 9781685750541 (ebook)
Subjects: LCSH: Educational tests and measurements—United States. |
Education—Standards—United States. | Education—Curricula—United
States. | Public schools—United States.
Classification: LCC LB3051 .G66699 2024 (print) | LCC LB3051 (ebook) |
DDC 371.260973--dc23/eng/20231101
LC record available at https://lccn.loc.gov/2023046462
LC ebook record available at https://lccn.loc.gov/2023046463

British Library Cataloguing-in-Publication Data
A catalog record for this book is available from the British Library.

To Len,
a true visionary, leader, and friend

"Education is not the filling of a pail, but the lighting of a fire."
—William Butler Yeats

CONTENTS

A NOTE

I considered naming this book "Boiling Frogs." It is said that if you put a frog in a pot of boiling water, it will immediately jump out. No frog in their right mind would just sit in a bubbling cauldron and boil to death. But if you put that frog in a pot of cold water and gradually heat it, the frog will happily sit in the water . . . until it is too late.

Over the last twenty-five years, our public schools have been in a slow boil. The change has been gradual, almost unnoticeable, at least to some, but just as deadly. If parents had been asked in 2001 to send their children to schools as they are today, I believe there would have been instant and mass rebellion. No parent would have subjected their children to the excessive testing, the extreme focus on "data," the standardization and scripting of curriculum, the cruel and developmentally inappropriate demands on students, including the elimination of recess and free play. No, they would have jumped right out of that pot.

But some people understood. Especially teachers. This is one teacher's story of how we got to the boiling point.

TESTING EDUCATION

WHY WRITE THIS BOOK?

It was Monday afternoon and nobody really wanted to be there. What other profession besides teaching holds staff meetings after a full day of work? On a Monday, no less. People are tired and often a little cranky. Everyone was especially apprehensive this day because we had a consultant coming. Our school had been through many changes over the years. We had been forced to move from a diverse, multiracial neighborhood to a majority white and affluent one. A few years later, we had to give up our K–8 model for one without a middle school, so our 6th-, 7th-, and 8th-grade comrades left. We then became home to the city's Sheltered English Immersion program and a separate strand of self-contained special needs classes. Subsequently, because of intense curriculum and testing demands, we stopped having multigraded classes and went to looping[1] instead. However, again because of increased curriculum and testing demands, we then had to give up looping and went to single-grade classes. Since our move to the more affluent neighborhood in 2001, the school had had five different principals (six, if you count the substitute one who filled in for four months). Our school had changed so much we weren't sure who we were anymore. The consultant was hired to help us figure that out.

She immediately got people on their feet, asking us to organize ourselves into chronological order according to how long we had worked at the school and then break into groups. I was in a small group of teachers who had started working at the school in the mid-1980s to early 1990s. We were the true veterans, the elders. There were some folks in the second half of the 1990s, a bigger group in the early 2000s. But I was quite surprised to see how many people were in the category of working at the school for only one year, or even less.

The consultant then handed out chart paper and markers (there are always chart paper and markers at these sessions) and asked each group to record what stood out to them about their "era." My group dove in with excitement.

"Remember when we used to have assemblies with the whole school and we all did that play in Creole?"

"Remember when the one-twos [first and second graders] did the giants unit?"

"Remember when we had the Design Lab and worked with MIT?"

"Remember the shadow project?"

"Remember when the eighth graders did their Graduation Review Panels?"

"Remember when kids would visit each other's classrooms to share their work?"

We were all laughing in such delight as these memories rolled on that we didn't notice that the other groups of teachers were looking at us.

"You guys are having an awful lot of fun," someone called over.

"Yes!" we answered. "School used to be fun!" These memories energized us.

When it came time to share out, we went first. School used to be so different, we explained. There was so much joy! You would see kids sprawled out in their classrooms, working together, designing and making all sorts of things, sometimes even spilling out into the hallways. It felt like a real community, and there wasn't the stress about testing and "getting through" curriculum. We had time to explore subjects deeply. Students produced complex and beautiful work. Teachers had a voice, a real voice, in running the school. We were encouraged to experiment, try new things. We felt respected and supported. People worked really hard, but we loved it. We were all a bit giddy and a little breathless as we shared our experiences of so many years ago in the school.

But as each group reported out, moving through the timeline to present day, the energy shift away from joy was palpable. There was talk of state and district testing, constant assessments, fear of failure—of not reaching their students and of losing their jobs. People talked about ever-changing curricula and the burnout of constant "initiatives." They talked about exhaustion and not knowing how long they could stay in a job like this.

How did this change happen?

I started teaching in 1979. The first half of my career was exciting. I had opportunities to learn, grow, experiment, create. Although I had a rough start, I eventually became part of an innovative school where I felt respected and valued by my students, parents, colleagues, and principal. There, I got to use my brain, experiment, make mistakes, find solutions. In addition, I got guidance, encouragement, and support. I also struggled mightily, did a lot of crying, felt in over my head at times, and saw need, as well as opportunities, for improving schools and preparing teachers to do this really hard and exhilarating job of teaching children.

Our students learned how to read and write, understand math, practice the scientific method, and think critically. They produced plays, wrote and illustrated books, painted murals, built model bridges, did in-depth studies of the natural world around them. They worked in internships in their community at places like a bicycle repair shop, a plumbing business, an architectural firm, learning about both work and their city. They learned to be peer mediators. They went camping and climbed mountains. They also learned how to work with each other, understanding and valuing the diversity of their community. They developed their voices, to speak out about their beliefs and convictions. Our students did amazing things they hadn't believed they could possibly do.

But undercurrents were threatening our vision of education. I was aware of them, but felt protected living and working in my bubble of "progressive" Cambridge, Massachusetts. Then came the

MCAS exams (Massachusetts Comprehensive Assessment System), one of the early high-stakes standardized tests, and a lynchpin of the Massachusetts Education Reform Act of 1993. The first tests were given in 1998 to public school pupils in grades 4, 8, and 10. By 2003, when passing the test became a requirement for graduation from public high school, the state was testing students in grades 3, 4, 5, 6, 7, 8, and 10.

From the beginning, these tests faced strong resistance across the state. Teachers, parents, administrators, university professors, and others argued that they took away from instructional time, incentivized "teaching to the test," and reduced complex student assessment to a single score. But the impact that the MCAS and the movement that was promoting such standardized tests had on our public schools was much more insidious than we could have ever imagined at the time.

Twenty-three years into the twenty-first century, "education reform" has radically changed every aspect of school life. We no longer have time for producing plays. Or building model bridges. Or community internships. Or camping trips. With the implementation of high-stakes standardized testing, schools have continually narrowed the curriculum to focus on math and literacy skills—often dropping the arts, world languages, social studies, and even science, particularly in low-income neighborhoods, where these subjects are already under-resourced. We increasingly spend time "assessing" students by giving them standardized tests to prepare them for more standardized tests. Enormous amounts of time are spent analyzing test data, which, at least in my experience, tell teachers a fraction of what they already know about who is struggling and who is excelling. We not only have statewide curriculum frameworks with massive numbers of standards to meet, more and more we have scripted, standardized "teacher-proof" curricula to go along with them. We have "pacing charts" telling teachers what page they should be on in the textbook on what day of the month. Recess and free-play time are being eliminated, even from kindergarten classes, so we can "cover the curriculum." We are told over and over that our schools are failing and the only way to fix them is with restrictive and punitive policies for schools and teachers, standardized curricula and assessment, and ever-more privatization.

Teachers experienced these draconian policies firsthand. In 2014, Suzi Sluyter, a highly respected kindergarten teacher in Cambridge quit her job after teaching for twenty-five years. Her letter of resignation was published in the *Washington Post*.[2] In it, she stated:

> In this disturbing era of testing and data collection in the public schools, I have seen my career transformed into a job that no longer fits my understanding of how children learn and what a teacher ought to do in the classroom to build a healthy, safe, developmentally appropriate environment for learning for each of our children. . . . I have watched as my job requirements swung away from a focus on the children, their individual learning styles, emotional needs, and their individual families, interests and strengths to a focus on testing, assessing, and scoring young children, thereby ramping up the academic demands and pressures on them.

Suzi's letter resonated deeply with me. She was describing what is now "normal" for teachers: mandates and initiatives and reforms and "innovations" and data and spreadsheets and on and on and on. I too had watched this take over the life of the schools I worked in.

When I began my career in 1979, "education reform" was not on the political radar. No statewide curriculum frameworks existed. There were no Common Core State Standards, no high-stakes testing, no teacher tests. There was no AYP (Adequate Yearly Progress), SGP (Student Growth Percentile), or CPI (Composite Performance Index). No schools had been "turned around." There were no charter schools. There was also no internet, so no online "academies" or CBI (computer-based instruction). Huge inequities did exist between urban, rural, and suburban schools, and people had fought many battles, led by groups like the NAACP, for equitable funding.

The main issue facing schools in the late 1970s was racial integration and broader concerns about equity. Even though the U.S. Supreme Court had ruled against legal segregation in the landmark

Brown v. Board of Education case in 1954, many communities in both the North and the South were still fighting over the Court's decree that separate schools were inherently unequal. Opposition to integration was intense. In Virginia, a "massive resistance" campaign, led by U.S. Senator Harry Byrd, closed schools and even school districts for years. In Boston, violent battles had ensued over court-ordered busing in the early 1970s. White working-class mothers pelted school buses carrying Black children with rocks and bottles, hurling racial epithets at terrified ten-year-olds attempting to go to school. White families abandoned the public schools in droves, while Black parents fought to get basic resources for their children.

The Civil Rights Movement affected other educational policies, too. With President Lyndon Johnson's Immigration and Naturalization Act of 1965, increasing numbers of immigrants and refugees from Asian, Latin American, Caribbean, and African countries were coming to the U.S. This resulted in a spike of students attending schools who did not speak English, particularly Black and brown children. In 1968, the first federal bilingual education act was passed and, in 1973, the U.S. Supreme Court ruled in *Lau v. Nichols* that the lack of support for students with limited English violated the Civil Rights Act of 1964. Under *Lau*, schools were obligated to assist non–English-speaking students to overcome linguistic barriers.

Another battle for equity was fought by parents of children with special needs. Before Congress passed the Individuals with Disabilities Education Act (IDEA) in 1975, millions of children had been denied "appropriate access" to public education. Some were warehoused in seriously substandard, ability-segregated classrooms, while others were excluded from school altogether. The IDEA guaranteed that all children with disabilities would be provided with a free and appropriate education to meet their unique learning needs.

Schools were changing. At least, the demographics of public schools were changing.

As people fought for greater equity and access *to* schools, some people were also looking to make changes *in* schools. Historically, public schools had promoted cultural homogeneity. Students were taught to conform to, not question, the status quo. But the social upheavals of the 1960s and 1970s were challenging that approach. Inspired by progressive thinkers like John Dewey and Francis W. Parker from the earlier part of the twentieth century, some educators started to question the traditional structure and values of public education. If they were going to teach such a diversity of students, maybe teachers needed diverse ways of teaching them. Maybe children didn't all learn in the same way or at the same pace. If students were coming from different cultures and backgrounds, maybe they—and their teachers—needed to learn how to understand and value differences, how to work collaboratively rather than in competition, how to think critically about the world around them.

It was during this period that Deborah Meier opened her alternative school, Central Park East, in New York City; that Ted Sizer started his groundbreaking research on U.S. high schools that would lead to his seminal book, *Horace's Compromise*; and that a group of parents came together in Cambridge, Massachusetts, to start a child-centered school called CAPS, the Cambridge Alternative Public School.

But as progressive ideas and experiments in schools were flourishing, a reaction was starting to build. Public and social services were undermined in favor of privatization; public housing was under attack; white flight and redlining sent cities and rural communities spiraling into debt. Public schools were experiencing significant budget cuts; teachers were being asked to do more with less. The gap between rich and poor was beginning to widen.

The first major salvo of the attack on public education came in 1983. A federal report called *A Nation at Risk: The Imperative for Educational Reform* sounded alarm bells that America's public schools were failing:

> Our nation is at risk. Our once unchallenged preeminence in commerce, industry, science, and technological innovation is being

overtaken by competitors throughout the world. . . . [T]he educational foundations of our society are presently being eroded by a rising tide of mediocrity that threatens our very future as a Nation and a people. . . . If an unfriendly foreign power had attempted to impose on America the mediocre educational performance that exists today, we might well have viewed it as an act of war. . . . We have, in effect, been committing an act of unthinking, unilateral educational disarmament.

It was later documented that much of the report's data were flawed.[3] Public schools were not failing so much as struggling, with shrinking funds, to meet the needs of an expanding and diversifying student population, especially in urban areas. But actual facts never stand in the way of people with a particular political agenda. Educators grew wary as politicians and others latched onto the report to pursue their own purposes. President Reagan praised the report for its call for prayer in the schools, school vouchers, and the abolition of the U.S. Department of Education. The document, however, had never even made mention of such recommendations.

A Nation at Risk launched the modern "education reform" movement, driven by a corporate model of change, setting off waves of new policies at the federal, state, and local levels for the next thirty-five years. There were calls for school vouchers, charter schools, merit pay for teachers, increased testing, and nationalized curriculum. The most sweeping change occurred in 2002, when President George W. Bush signed the bipartisan No Child Left Behind Act (NCLB) into law. NCLB called for increased accountability in exchange for more funding. Most significantly, it required schools to test students annually, measuring their adequate yearly progress (AYP). If any subgroup of students failed to show growth, the state could eventually shut that school down. Even if students who had scored in the "proficient" or "advanced" range failed to increase their scores from year to year, a school could be considered failing because it was not "showing growth."

There was tremendous resistance to this standardized, one-size-fits-all testing approach from teachers and parents. But the business leaders and politicians who were pushing this "data-driven" reform dismissed their challenges; in particular, they attacked teachers and their unions as the root cause of failing schools. Don't trust teachers, the "reformers" cautioned. They are only interested in protecting their jobs.

NCLB had set a goal of 100 percent proficiency for all students in the country by 2014. In 2006, 29 percent of schools were labeled as "failing." By 2010, that number had risen to 38 percent. By 2011, several states had school "failure" rates of over 50 percent. Arne Duncan, Secretary of Education under Barack Obama, darkly predicted that soon over 80 percent of U.S. schools would, under NCLB, be labeled as failing. But that was the issue. Schools were being *labeled* as failing when, in fact, they were not. Again, parents and others began to protest—especially as white suburban schools started appearing on the list of failing schools.

Eventually, President Obama abandoned NCLB and replaced it with an equally onerous initiative called Race to the Top. RTTT tied school funding to teacher evaluations, adoption of the Common Core State Standards, expansion of charter schools, and the "turnaround" of "failing" schools.

At first glance, at least some of these reforms appear reasonable. Having clearly articulated standards seems like common sense. We need to assess students to see if they are learning and if the school is doing a good job. Teachers need to be well-educated, "highly qualified," and evaluated. Parents should feel confident that they are sending their children to a good school. But when we look more closely at each of these "reforms" and the actual impact they have had on public schools, a different picture emerges.

A number of people have written critically about these "reforms" of the last few decades. Diane Ravitch, who initially championed the "standards" movement, blasted her former colleagues in her book *The Death and Life of the Great American School System: How Testing and Choice Are Undermining Education* (and later in *Reign of*

Error and *Slaying Goliath: The Passionate Resistance to Privatization and the Fight to Save America's Public Schools*). Noliwe Rooks wrote about the particularly negative impact of these reforms on children of color in *Cutting School: Privatization, Segregation, and the End of Public Education*. Eve Ewing told the story close up and personal in *Ghosts in the Schoolyard: Racism and School Closings on Chicago's South Side*. Todd Farley exposed the testing corporations in *Making the Grades: My Misadventures in the Standardized Testing Industry*. Numerous other books and hundreds if not thousands of articles have been published in educational journals as well as in the mainstream press condemning this effort "to remake public education in the image and likeness of for-profit corporations in a competitive marketplace."[4]

But at least one important voice has been missing from the debates about educational reform. That of teachers and others who have worked on the front lines of our public schools. People like Suzi, and me, who were old enough to witness the "before" and "after" of the education reform debacle. When I have shared some of the projects my classes used to do, many teachers have responded, "Wow, I wish we could still do things like that. How did you ever find the time? What about preparing for the [insert your state's standardized test here]?" The tragedy is not only that schools no longer provide this sort of education but that educators can't even envision it anymore.

I have worked with many talented, highly motivated teachers who care deeply about their students. But I recently realized that many of them have only known schools as they are today, stuck at that far, data-driven end of the spectrum. For newer teachers, having hours of standardized testing is the norm. Expecting kindergartners to be able to read is the norm. Giving homework to first and second graders is the norm. Teaching third graders how to write a literary essay (typed on the computer) is the norm. Scripted curriculum is the norm. Jumping from one seeming silver bullet to another is the norm.

But it doesn't have to be.

I wanted to write this book for them and for anyone else who is interested in children, how they learn, and the survival of public education. I want to share a vision of what schools can and should be—without top-down, corporate-driven "reform" initiatives. But I also wanted to write this book for the people who have not experienced firsthand and thus do not understand how these changes have pummeled our public schools. I want to offer those people a closer look, a more intimate account of the profound impact—no, the damage—done by these initiatives.

When I retired in 2018, after nearly four decades of work in the public schools, I had both witnessed and experienced an unimaginable and deeply disturbing transformation of our public schools. How did this change come about? And why? How had we lost our way so badly? That is what this book is about. Not from a policy or educational history perspective. There are many excellent books that describe that far better than I can. But I lived through this change at the ground level, in the trenches, as a classroom teacher, coach, and administrator. I experienced it. I want people to know what this history *felt* like: what we had, what we have lost—and what we must regain.

This is my story, my experience as an educator in a time of tremendous change. I don't know if it is typical or unique. Maybe it is both. I hope it can contribute to a dialogue about what real change can look like in our public schools.

CHAPTER 1

TEACHER EDUCATION
1979 — 1980

I was only fifteen when Martin Luther King and Bobby Kennedy were assassinated. But they had already made a powerful impression on me. As a child of the 1960s and 1970s, I wanted to contribute to my community, work for social justice, change the world. After finishing college in the Midwest in 1975, I moved to Boston without any real plan about just how I would do that. Healthcare seemed important, so I eventually got a job as an assistant in a clinic next to one of the public housing projects in Cambridge, Massachusetts. But it turned out that I really didn't like being around sick people. The smell of antiseptics made me nauseous and I grew faint at the sight of blood. I had to find another way to "serve the people." If not health, maybe education? The combination of the intellectual content, the human interaction with young people, the sense of belonging to a community, and the mission of preparing children to live in a democratic society seemed like a much better fit for me.

So I decided to become a teacher.

At that time, teaching was not a particularly respected profession (nor is it now). When I told a friend that I was going to be a teacher, she said, "A teacher? Why would you want to be a teacher? You are so much smarter than that." She was not alone. In later years, at parties and other social gatherings, when I would say I was a teacher, the conversation would awkwardly stall for a second and then someone would change the subject to talk about their new law practice or business enterprise. Clearly more interesting subjects than shaping young children's minds.

In 1979, to teach in a public school you needed a college degree and teaching certification. I had the first but not the second. To me, the certification process was an annoying hoop to have to jump through. What would I learn in an education program? It was well known that education departments were a joke. After all, if you knew your subject matter, how hard could it be to teach? I had no sense of the art or craft of teaching. I felt, like much of the public at that time, that anyone who had a college degree and who liked kids could walk in off the street and be a good teacher.[1] But, in 1979, the Massachusetts Department of Education mandated that public school teachers be licensed. Luckily, the Boston area had a plethora of education schools and certificate programs. Given my attitude about teacher training, I looked for a program that had the fewest requirements.

I decided to apply to Tufts University for a master's in education degree, or MEd. In the Tufts program, in addition to getting an MEd and a teaching license, graduate students interned at Medford High School, for which they received a stipend. The program would begin in the summer, with five interns taking a full course load. In the fall, we would teach in an alternative program, called the "School Within," and take more courses at the university in the afternoons. Medford High's assistant principal and a Tufts advisor would supervise us. Then, the following summer, we would finish our classes. I liked the idea of the hands-on experience, and, given that I had no money, the idea of earning a stipend was especially appealing. I took out a loan to cover my additional expenses.

During the summer of 1979, I met the other interns and attended classes. According to my Tufts transcript, I took three courses: Techniques of Counseling, Problems in Teaching Reading, and Advanced Educational Psychology. While these courses may have been interesting, I honestly cannot remember anything that felt helpful in preparing me to teach social studies to tenth and eleventh graders. I wondered when we would find out what specific course we were supposed to teach.

About two weeks before school started, I was beginning to get nervous. With no guidance about curriculum or instruction from Tufts, I decided to visit Medford High School on my own. I found my way to the windowless Social Studies Department office and shyly stuck my head inside the door. The man at the desk in the office was absorbed in papers.

"Excuse me?" I interjected.

He looked up at me, annoyed.

"Hi!" I said brightly. "My name is Kathy Greeley and I am one of the new School Within interns." His eyes narrowed, but that didn't slow me down. "I came by to find out about the curriculum I should be using," my voice trailing up into more of a question than a statement. "I'll, uh, be teaching social studies."

"Don't even bother," he said. "We don't care what you teach. Do whatever you want. Those kids aren't going to learn anything, anyway. They could care less." I was shocked.

"Uh, okay," I stammered. I wasn't sure what to do. "Well, would it be okay if I borrow some of your textbooks?" The room was lined with big, fat textbooks of all different sorts.

"No, you can't take any of these books. Those kids will just destroy them."

Those kids, again. Which kids? I wondered. What is so wrong with them?

After my unsuccessful visit to the social studies office, I decided to check out my classroom. I found the room and the door was open. It was an odd-sized room, shaped like an L. It had a large chalkboard on one wall, a smaller chalkboard on another wall, no windows. It had fifteen or so chairs and three tables that would seat about six kids each. That was it. There was no teacher's desk or chair, no bookshelf, no books, no reference materials, no maps or globe. No paper or pencils. Not even chalk or erasers. It was an empty L-shaped box. It was going to be my home for the next year, along with eighteen tenth and eleventh graders.

I went home in a panic. School was about to start. I didn't know what to teach, much less how to teach it. I didn't have any materials.

I didn't know what to do. Many teachers I know have this night-mare, or some version of it, before school starts. They are stuck in front of their class on the first day with no plan. Or maybe no clothes. But this wasn't a dream. This was real. It was long before the internet, so there were no "Teachers Helping Teachers" web-sites or online curriculum to borrow. What was I going to do?

Then, to make matters worse, a few days before school started the four other interns quit. Evidently, they knew something that I didn't. Actually, I was also realizing that our "teacher preparation" had been utterly inadequate, but I thought I was smart enough to jump into teaching without any training. Even more, I really needed that stipend. I was going to stick with it. That meant that on the first day of school I would be meeting the School Within students on my own, at least until Tufts could recruit new interns to the program.

The School Within was a program for "reluctant learners." "Reluctant learners" were students who had had so many absences, disciplinary infractions, or course failures that they were one step away from dropping—or being pushed—out of school. It offered a work-study schedule each day. Students came to class from 8:00 a.m. to 12:00 p.m. They took English, math, social studies, and sci-ence before going to a job for the rest of the afternoon. This was supposedly a kind of vocational program. But these were not train-ing jobs, like learning to be an electrician, auto mechanic, or beauti-cian. The School Within kids were working at McDonald's or Burger King or ringing up groceries at the local Star Market.

As I wondered what I was going to do with "those kids," I knew that I had to find something to hook their interest. *Okay*, I thought, *if they are all working, maybe we should learn about working*. Work-ing! That's it! We would start by reading Studs Terkel's classic *Working: People Talk About What They Do All Day and How They Feel About What They Do*. The challenge was which story to begin with. Should it be the one by the sex worker? That would get their atten-tion. Should it be the grocery store clerk, something the kids might identify with? Or should it be the store owner, so they could get a glimpse of their boss's life? Should it be the teacher? No, that was a no-brainer. What about the gravedigger? Or the carpenter-poet? Or the lawyer? Each story held a person's life on its pages.

In the end, I don't remember which story I picked. I also don't remember much about the first days of school. I do remember being extremely nervous and the kids greeting me with not only a distinct lack of enthusiasm but with something bordering on antagonism. They knew they had been labeled second-class citizens and they had been stuck with a teacher who didn't have a clue about what she was doing. They knew the other interns had bailed. They had giant chips on their shoulders, which seemed to me appropriate. One of the girls had been in the School Within the year before.

"Where are our old teachers?" she demanded. "I really liked our old teachers. Why do we have to start all over again with someone new?"

I tried to explain how the program worked, but the resentment in her eyes was clear.

"We are going to do some 'exploring' together," I said, trying to sound confident. "I want to share one of my favorite books with you."

Did they have to take notes? No. Was there going to be a test? No. They just needed to listen. They gathered around, relieved that they didn't have to do anything, and I started reading. Within a couple of paragraphs, they were enthralled. They frequently interrupted with questions, and at the end of the first story, they begged for more.

We spent about a week just reading the stories and talking about how people felt about their jobs. They had interesting insights about the stories and were very tuned into issues about class and power. Why should one person make so much more money than another person? Isn't digging a ditch or clearing garbage just as hard work as sitting at a desk? These were lively discussions that had a sense of urgency. After all, these were up-close-to-their-lives kinds of questions.

This led us into a study of labor history. We looked at the beginning of the Industrial Revolution in America, in our very own backyard. We learned about Eli Whitney and interchangeable parts, the Lowell mills, Frederick Taylor and "scientific management," Henry Ford and mass production. We created our own assembly line to test out how fast we could create airplanes (paper ones). We role-played conflicts between labor and management. As students took on different roles, they could see that these issues were complex, not simply black and white with good guys and bad guys.

We started exploring work in our community, visiting some of the kids' worksites. One day, we took a field trip to the General Motors factory in Framingham to see how they built cars on an assembly line. We walked through the factory and watched workers actually assembling an automobile—bolting car doors to the chassis, welding the roof onto the body, installing the windshield and other glass. We had a chance to talk to the foreman and a couple of workers. The students conducted themselves beautifully and asked a number of thoughtful questions. It was a wonderful experience for them, and for me.[2]

We delved into the labor movement itself. Using *Labor's Untold Story* by Boyer and Morais, students started to read about people who had organized and fought for their rights from the beginning of the Industrial Age. The Pullman Strike and the Bread and Roses Strike of 1912 fascinated them.

"Why haven't we heard about this before?" they wanted to know.

"I'm not sure," I replied. "I didn't learn it in school, either. But I did learn how to learn it on my own. You can, too."

But, I have gotten ahead of myself. In summarizing this story, I've made it all too clean and simple. It is true that, over time, a cohesive curriculum emerged that engaged and challenged students. But the reality was that I went home and cried on my boyfriend's shoulder every day for the first two months of school (he would later become my husband). He was also in a teacher training program, but at a different university and at a very different kind of school. We worked together to develop lesson plans, but we were like the blind leading the blind. We did not have a clear plan with long-term learning goals. We had not yet learned about Wiggins and Tighe's backward design or Project Zero's Teaching for Understanding. We were scrambling day to day to first figure out a plan and then find the resources to carry it out. We'd spend three or four hours developing a one-hour lesson plan. Actually, I'm not even sure we could have called it a "lesson plan" because we didn't know how to write one; we still had not learned anything about that in our university courses.

Furthermore, the kids were not easy. They were testing me, as kids do. It takes time to build trust, even with the easiest kids. And these were not the easiest kids. They wore their mantle of perceived failure with proud defiance. Given the hours at the high school, the classes at the university, the workload of the academic courses, and trying to come up with something to teach every day, I was exhausted.

By the end of September, Tufts had recruited four new interns to the program. We now had English, science, math, and special education teachers. They were even less-prepared than I had been, coming in after school had already started. We shared two classrooms between the five of us. The English teacher joined me in my L-shaped box, the science and math teachers had a bigger room on a different floor of the building, and the special-ed intern floated between. Again, with no support or guidance from Tufts or Medford High, the five of us did our best to form a team. We would come together to talk about the kids and to support each other.

One early morning in mid-October, as I was setting up for the day, the science teacher came in. I was surprised to see him; he didn't usually stop by in the morning. His face was tight and drawn.

"Are you okay?" I asked.

"I need you to come up to the science room," he responded.

"Okay," I said. "What's going on?"

"You'll see."

He was silent as we walked up the stairs together. When he opened the classroom door, I was speechless. Everything had been trashed—chairs turned upside down, pencils broken, papers and books strewn all over the floor. I felt like someone had sucker-punched me in the solar plexus. We eventually found out who had done it and confronted the student.

"Why did you do this, Jamal?" Jamal was one of two African American males in the class. He was a tall, handsome, young man. I thought he had liked me, or at least my class. I thought he would trust me enough to talk. But he looked at me with disdain and just shrugged his shoulders. That day, I cried in school, unable to hold it in until I got home.

I couldn't understand what had provoked Jamal to act with such anger and violence. Maybe it was a test to see how we would react. Maybe it wasn't personal; maybe it was just rage at having yet one more inexperienced white teacher who did not know or understand his life. But it begs the question of how we prepare teachers to teach students who don't look like us, or who don't come from the same culture or class background.

What I hadn't known at the time was that, two years earlier, there had been some serious racial unrest at the high school. Black students were in the minority at Medford High, only about 15 percent of the overall population, the rest of whom were predominantly white. I'm not sure what triggered the fights, but Black students had been locked in certain classrooms to "protect" them from large groups of white students threatening them. Fifteen years later, a similar incident would effectively shut down the school for days. Clearly, the community had not addressed racial tensions within it. A *Christian Science Monitor* article published December 12, 1992, quoted a Black student: "There are white teachers here who make racial slurs and treat black kids differently. Everybody knows this, but how are you going to take that out of some teacher's head when it's been there for forty years?"

How many teachers work in neighborhoods where they know its history, or even its present? How many teachers, especially those who work in urban areas, have ever walked further afield of their school than the parking lot or the Dunkin' Donuts where they grab their coffee? What if every new teacher to a school had an orientation that included a day or even half a day walking around the community, talking to the people in the shops (if there are any) or just seeing what the physical space is like? They could see where their kids come from, what the housing is like, what they go home to every day. They could see what their playgrounds are like or if there are any playgrounds. They could see if there are stores with fresh vegetables available or if their students live in a food desert. In a few hours, they could have at least a beginning understanding of the community they are working in. And what if teachers also learned some of the history of that community? My knowing about the race riots at Medford High School may not have prevented Jamal from trashing the classroom, but it would have given me some valuable insights into my students' lives.

As part of my program, an experienced mentor teacher was supposed to supervise me. My mentor teacher from Medford High School was the assistant principal of the school. He was friendly and jovial, but I don't recall him ever setting foot in my classroom. Whenever I tried to talk with him, he was too busy. It wasn't long before I stopped trying. I sometimes wondered if he even knew who I was.

I was also supposed to have a university advisor, someone from Tufts who observed my practice and gave me guidance. My Tufts advisor visited me twice during the year. I remember meeting with him for feedback. Our conversation was brief.

"You're doing a great job, Kathy! Keep it up," he said. He had two pieces of advice though. "First, you really shouldn't Xerox so much. There are copyright issues, you know."

I replied that the Social Studies Department had refused to give me any books and I had no money to purchase them. If I didn't copy readings, the kids wouldn't have anything to read.

"Well, just try to keep the copying down," he said. "The second thing is, I don't think you should let students sit on the tables. If you are that informal, they won't respect you." He had watched my class as students had gathered around, some sitting on chairs and a few on the table with their feet dangling off. We had had a great discussion about some controversial topic.

"Uh, okay," I responded. "Anything else?"

"Oh, no! You're doing great!"

That was the extent of the feedback I got during my whole internship.

By the end of the first semester of school, the interns' frustration, including mine, had reached a breaking point. We had repeatedly requested support from the Tufts program supervisor, with no response. Finally, in early February, the five of us sent this letter to the head of the Education Department:

Dear Dr. P—:

We are writing this letter because after several months of working with the School Within, we feel it is time that attention be called to some of the serious inadequacies of the program.

The School Within is an alternative program at Medford High School that attempts to address the needs of the reluctant learner or potential drop-out. Tufts has sponsored the School Within for approximately seven years. In that time, one would expect that a solid smoothly-running program would exist that provided good training to the interns involved as well as a constructive academic and emotional experience for the young people from Medford High. Unfortunately, this is not the case.

We believe that much of the responsibility for the weakness of the program lies with the university and specifically with the program's supervisor, Dr. W—. While we don't doubt Dr. W—'s experience or knowledge of education, he has demonstrated little commitment or leadership to the program. This has been manifested in four major ways:

1. *Recruitment: Recruitment is at best haphazard. The program is not well publicized, and therefore receives relatively few applications, thus considerably limiting the selectiveness of the program.*

2. *Preparation: There is none. The summer is supposed to [be] spent in preparation, and yet there are no meetings or seminars scheduled. New and old interns are not afforded the opportunity to meet and discuss issues, problems, and experiences at the School Within. There is no written handbook or evaluation of the program. Thus, each year the new interns start from zero and are forced to "reinvent the wheel." In addition, Dr. W— has given little guidance in developing a schedule of courses for interns that prepare them and consider the special problems of teaching reluctant learners.*

3. *Supervision/Observation: To learn, people need feedback— criticism, praise, advice. This is especially crucial when new teachers, as in the School Within, have no role models to learn from. Dr. W— has observed classes at the School Within two to three times since September, and has made virtually no comments on our teaching.*

4. *Support: Everyone knows that one's first year of teaching is difficult, particularly when working with behavior problem youth. Support and guidance from an experienced supervisor are crucial to the learning process. For example, there should be weekly meetings planned that deal with issues such as discipline, attendance, motivation, drugs, sex, counseling, and child abuse, not to mention problems with specific students and inter-staff relations and morale. These have been proposed several times to Dr. W—, but he has failed to take initiative in organizing anything.*

We decided to write this letter, not because of any personal feelings against Dr. W—, but rather because we are convinced that the School Within has the potential to be a dynamic program that could effectively serve the needs of the community of Medford. We also believe that we deserve something—guidance, support, instruction—in return for $5050 tuition. We have expressed our criticisms and suggestions to Dr. W— numerous times and have only been frustrated by his lack of response.

We do feel that the program has been education[al] for us, trial by fire that it is, and somewhat beneficial to some students. However, by making others aware of problems from which the program is suffering, we hope that a better, stronger one can develop.
We look forward to your response.

We did not get a response.

In addition to not having support from either the assistant principal of the high school or my Tufts advisor, I don't remember having any contact with any other teachers at Medford High. In fact, the only other adults in the school that paid any kind of attention to me were the Medford police stationed in the hallways. I was rather taken aback to have police patrols, in full gear with guns and batons, in a school. I'm not sure if their presence was the result of the racial violence from a couple of years earlier, which continued to simmer under the surface, or what. I just knew that there had not been any police in my high school and that it felt intimidating. More than once, an officer stopped me, roughly demanding to see my hall pass. When I would explain that I was a teacher, they would look warily at me and let me be. But the lack of respect, the immediate assumption of guilt, the power differential between police officer and young person—all that was clear, and uncomfortable, to me. Our students felt that, too.[3]

Eventually, our study that had begun with some stories from Studs Terkel drew to an end. I'm not quite sure how long we spent on it, but it was probably close to three months. I know that no teacher now would feel they could spend that much time on anything, much less something that might not be in the required curriculum frameworks. But these young people had learned a lot. They were beginning to learn the importance of history to their own lives, and because of this connection to themselves, they were engaged. They learned to ask questions and seek information. They learned to take different perspectives and how to argue a point. They were learning how to learn. And they wanted to know.

Having finished up the labor study, I had to figure out what to do next. Again, I thought about the kids. What was important to them? What mattered to them in their lives? What was relevant to their own life experience? It didn't take too much thinking on my part. I knew what was next. They needed to understand the criminal justice system.

While not all my students were court-involved, many were. All of them had friends who had had run-ins with the police. Some of my students had been to Juvenile Court and had parole officers and/ or social workers. Kids would occasionally miss school for court appearances. So, the next unit of study? *Breaking and Entering: An Introduction to the Criminal Justice System.* This time, there was a clear narrative for the unit. We started by looking at the sociology and demographics of crime itself. What kinds of crimes did people commit? Who committed them? Who went to jail for them and who didn't? What was the difference between street crimes and white-collar crimes? What about sexual assaults and domestic abuse? Who received the death penalty and who didn't? We explored a range of issues through the lenses of race, class, and gender.

The curriculum then followed the storyline of an arrest. If you are arrested, what happens to you? What is the process? What are your rights? What are the police going to do to you? We talked about Miranda ("You have the right to remain silent . . .") and why the police have to tell you your rights. We visited the Medford Police Station and saw the booking room. We saw where fingerprints and mugshots were taken. We sat in a jail cell where the police took away the boys' belts ("Danger of suicide," they said). We talked about *habeas corpus* and the right to a speedy trial.

We visited a courtroom and saw a trial in progress. It was not like what they'd seen on TV; it was much less dramatic. The courtroom was drab. There was just a smattering of people sitting in the audience section. It was hard to hear people speaking. But I remember the uncomfortable feeling we all had about invading someone's privacy. We felt the weight of public accusation.

In mid-April, we tried again to advocate for better support from Tufts. Returning to our four key areas of recruitment, preparation, supervision, and support, we made twelve specific recommendations to Dr. P—, head of the Education Department, and Dr. W—, our program "supervisor." For example, we suggested that the program's interns be recruited by May so they could visit the School Within while it was still in session, thus familiarizing themselves with the program, the students, and the school. We suggested that interns learn how to administer certain diagnostic tests to give their students in the first weeks of school in order to better assess their students' needs. We asked that the program set up a formal schedule for interns to visit other teachers' classrooms at Medford High, as well as other alternative schools in the area. We asked that the Tufts supervisor act as an advocate and intermediary for the interns, including arranging up meetings with department heads, guidance counselors, and administrators either in the summer or in the first weeks of school.

Again, we got no response. While I felt proud of what we had accomplished that year, I knew I was a novice and that I had dragged my students along my own steep learning curve. It angered me and the other interns in the program that "those kids" were not getting the quality of education they deserved. If they were going to be in the School Within program, at the very least the program should be run responsibly with good supervision and quality preparation for the interns. We didn't want to see our kids be someone's guinea pigs yet again.

Toward the end of the year, we decided to try one more time. But this time we wrote to the president of Tufts and to the Medford School Committee. Again, we outlined our concerns, our efforts to get these concerns addressed, and the lack of response from the Education Department. Our goal was to ensure a quality program for both the next group of interns and the students with whom they would be working.

I can't quite remember how things played out after sending that final letter, but I do know we made some waves. One day on the Tufts campus during the summer term, I saw two new School Within interns. I approached them, saying, "Hi! I'm Kathy. I worked as the social studies teacher in the program."

They looked at each other and shifted uncomfortably.

"I thought you all might like to get together with those of us finishing up this year."

"Uh, thanks, but . . . well, we were told by the department not to talk to you."

"What?!" I was shocked.

"Uh, yeah. We'd like to, you know, but they made it pretty clear that we were supposed to stay away from you guys. You know . . . it's not personal or anything . . . we just don't want to get started on the wrong foot . . ."

I don't know what happened at the School Within that next year, but I do know that the following year the program was closed down. To be fair to Tufts, they eventually started a different secondary-education certification program that provided better preparation for its interns and continues to do so to this day. So I like to think that our efforts did, in the long run, pay off.

In the end, I met my goal of getting a master's degree and Massachusetts teaching certification. I felt proud of what we had accomplished together—both students and fellow interns. I had grown extremely attached to these "reluctant learners," and it was hard to say goodbye to them. And, while I hadn't learned much from my academic classes, I had learned a lot from the kids. I had discovered that they really weren't reluctant about learning at all. On the contrary, these young people were curious, thoughtful, and hungry to learn more about their world. "Those students" taught me to question the negative labels that people place too easily on children. It seems that when children don't fit our mold or expectations, we first ask what is wrong with them—rather than what might be wrong with us. It is easier to blame the victims.

There are many reasons why children become "reluctant" about school. It could have to do with traumas going on at home. Do we know that this boy's dad was just incarcerated? Or that this girl is being sexually abused by a family relative? Or that this one is hungry? Or that one is homeless? I have seen children struggle with school for all these reasons. Or it could be traumas that students experienced at school. Do we know that this child is being bullied? Or that a teacher has made racist comments? Or told a child they were stupid (I know this happens because it had happened to me)? Or they might just be bored and see no point to learning what we think they should learn.

It could be that some children need to learn in a different way or need extra supports, or they care more about their music or art or basketball because that is where they experience success. Do we seek to understand why students shut down, find school irrelevant to their lives? We need to question our own practice and our educational systems. We need to dig into reasons why we are not reaching a particular student or particular group of students. We need to take time to explore different, alternative approaches to learning that engage our multidimensional intelligences.

Which leads me to the second important lesson these "reluctant learners" taught me. Teachers need to be able to focus on the students who are in front of them, rather than simply on the content they are supposed to cover. It is critical to know your students and then develop curriculum that can connect with and inspire them. True, I was panicked when the Medford High Social Studies Department refused to help me, but they actually did me a favor. If they had handed me a curriculum guide or a textbook, I probably would have marched my way through it, dragging my "reluctant learners" reluctantly along. I would have felt obligated to "get through" the curriculum, and, even more disturbing, I would have thought I was doing a good job because of it. I would have "covered" the material, but I would not have taught my students very well.

Today, teachers face tremendous pressure to "cover" curriculum. They are laden with "standards" that must be taught. Increasingly, administrators give teachers "pacing charts" that tell them just how many days to spend on any one topic and when they must give an assessment. In some schools, teachers are expected to be on a specific page of the textbook on a specific day. It doesn't seem to matter if one, some, or several students do not understand the lesson. The focus is on getting through the curriculum, not building student understanding. It's like the joke about the chauffeur getting his boss to the train station on time:

The chauffeur has the car ready and waiting in the driveway. The boss is eating his breakfast. "We need to go in five minutes, sir," the chauffeur warns the boss. The boss nods and eats his toast. A few minutes later, the chauffeur says, "We need to go in one minute, sir," this time with a little urgency in his voice. The boss continues reading the morning newspaper, sipping his coffee. The chauffeur nervously looks at his watch. "We need to go now, sir, if we are going to catch the train." Again, the boss nods but doesn't move. The chauffeur is now very anxious. "Sir, we must leave now if you are to catch your train." Again, no response from the boss. So, the chauffeur, in desperation, gets in the car, and drives to the train station so he can get there on time. Yes, leaving his passenger at home. As our curriculum has become more standardized, more focused on covering certain content, and more tied to specific timeframes as we try to jam more and more into kids' heads, teachers feel the pressure of getting to the station on time, often leaving at least some students behind.

This does not mean that we only teach what kids think they want to know (although some educators will argue that point of view).

But, especially when dealing with students who see themselves as failures or outsiders to the system—those "reluctant learners"—we need to make sure that they find themselves in the curriculum. If they can't see some relevance or purpose for learning what we are trying to teach, many students will just check out. Real learning begins with an interest, a motivation to find out, a question, a wondering, and a connection to self.

Let me share a personal example. Many years after my School Within experience, I was taking a class at Harvard University's Graduate School of Education. The class, taught by Dr. Eleanor Duckworth, was officially called "T440: Teaching and Learning," but everyone on campus knew it as the "Moon Class." One requirement for the class was to keep an ongoing journal about the moon. The only requirement was to regularly observe the moon and write or draw about it in our journals. In class, we would share our observations and reflections. I was thrilled with this assignment because I have always been a stargazer. I loved that I could just look at the moon and write about what I saw and thought. I declared to my seminar group that I was not interested in the science of the moon at all, that I just wanted to appreciate its beauty.

However, after a couple of months of watching the moon and hearing other people's observations, I found myself growing curious. Why did it tilt that way? Why did it look more orange at certain times? If there was a sliver moon in the night sky, was there a sliver moon in the morning sky, too? How did it connect to the tides? I was beginning to want to know what was going on up there. I listened carefully to the more scientific thinkers in my group. I took notes. I started looking up articles and getting library books about the moon. I became passionate about understanding lunar cycles.

While I am not claiming that my School Within students became passionate historians, I did see them become engaged and motivated. The scales of indifference, so familiar to many high school teachers, fell from their eyes. Not every day or maybe even every week. But I knew they were learning about something that mattered to them. Just as I had explained that I had taught myself about labor history because no one had ever told me about it in school, they realized that they, too, could go out and find out about their world.

Finally, I learned from my School Within students that teaching is really hard work and there is a whole lot to learn about how to do it well. After my experience with Tufts, I still felt disdain for education schools, but it made me think a lot about what *would have* been really useful to prepare me for teaching. In fact, high quality teacher preparation programs are essential to creating strong schools. In looking back at the letters we sent the university, I'm impressed with our recommendations. Some of the ideas we proposed are now routine for schools (e.g., regular observations of interns by university supervisors and a formal system for feedback and evaluation). Some education schools have implemented others, such as encouraging students to be dual certified in special education as well as in their subject area. Some of the ideas don't seem to have taken root yet, like regularly scheduled visits to other teachers' classrooms and other schools.

Although my first year of teaching was a trial by fire, I did survive. And through it, I forged key beliefs and understandings that would inform my practice for the rest of my career. My next challenge was to find a job.

CHAPTER 2

FIRST JOB
1980 – 1983

Unfortunately for me, I began looking for my first public school teaching job in 1980, the year that Proposition 2½ was on the Massachusetts ballot. Prop 2½ was an antitax initiative that limited property-tax assessments. It was part of the conservative pushback against social policies of the 1960s and 1970s. In Massachusetts, public schools had primarily been funded through property taxes. As support for Prop 2½ swept across the state (the referendum won two to one), school departments, seeing the writing on the wall, started trying to figure out how to cut their already limited budgets.

Most districts began with cutting such non-personnel items as office supplies, school materials like new textbooks, funding for staff development, and building maintenance. They reduced the number of "nonprofessional staff": teachers' aides, cafeteria workers, school crossing guards, and custodians. Many districts had to eliminate interscholastic and intramural sports, while some required parents to pay out of pocket to support their children's teams. They also jettisoned other extracurricular activities. Music, art, world language, home economics, and shop teachers were next on the chopping block, either reduced or eliminated altogether in many places. Reading specialists, guidance counselors, and administrators also got the ax. Finally, school districts were forced to cut even academic programs and teachers. This was known as getting "RIF'ed," RIF meaning "reduction in force."[1]

To make matters even more difficult, the burden of these layoffs fell disproportionately on younger teachers and particularly teachers of color. Nearly twenty years after the *Brown v. Board of Education* decision outlawed segregation, Boston schools, as in many cities around the country, remained very separate and very unequal. In the early 1970s, the NAACP (National Association for the Advancement of Colored People) sued the Boston School Committee for deliberate discriminatory practices including intentionally segregating schools. They also charged discrimination in hiring practices. Boston's teachers and administrators, in fact most school personnel around the state, were overwhelmingly white. In 1974, the U.S. District Court judge for the District of Massachusetts, Arthur Garrity, as part of his court-mandated desegregation plan, issued an order to racially balance faculty and administrative hiring. He required the city to hire 280 new teachers; for each white teacher hired, a Black teacher would also be hired. Other urban school districts also felt pressure to diversify their staffs and had made some effort to hire more teachers of color. But with the drastic budget cuts many urban areas were facing under Prop 2½, these "last hired" employees of color would become the "first fired."[2]

So 1980 was not a good time to look for a job in the public schools, especially for a newly minted teacher. I had wanted to work in Boston, but it was clear just how scarce those jobs were. I began to look around for other possibilities. I scoured the employment section of the newspaper each week (no internet then) and sent my resume out regarding any possible opening. I couldn't afford to be picky. By August I still hadn't had even a nibble. Finally, one day I got a phone call from the Robert White School in Boston, a "766 special needs" school. When they offered me the job the next day, I was ecstatic. My salary was $11,000 a year (this was at least half of what a starting teacher in Boston would make at the time).

The passing of IDEA, the federal Individuals with Disabilities Education Act of 1972, was an important milestone in public education. For far too long, school districts had pushed students with special needs not just to the back of the class but sometimes out the door and into the streets. In 1975, Massachusetts passed Chapter

766, a state law that guaranteed the right of all young people with special needs (ages three to twenty-two) to "an educational program best suited to their needs." While the intention was good, the implementation was mediocre. Public schools were not prepared to offer the kind of education that courts were mandating. This led to a profusion of separate schools that came to be known as "766 schools," independent—but publicly funded—for students with special needs.

The Robert White School (RWS) was a day program (some 766 schools were residential) located in the Erich Lindemann Center on Staniford Street in downtown Boston. The Lindemann is a heavy, imposing, futuristic building made of concrete with exterior walls that look like corrugated cardboard. It was originally built as a mental health facility but funds ran out before the building was finished. If you went up certain spiraling stairwells and opened a door, there was nothing there. Literally. There was just air. It struck me as ironic that a mental health center would have stairs leading nowhere.

The school was located on the third floor of the building. You could take an elevator up to our wing, but several students stopped at the first floor to get breakfast in the cafeteria, which also served patients who lived in various wards in the building. While some of the inpatients seemed fine, others were seriously distressed. A few sat, dazed, in a drug-induced fog; others could get easily agitated and an orderly would need to intervene. This was not suburban MacLean Hospital, where the more privileged people struggling with mental illness got high quality care. More than once, students asked me why the school was located in a building with a "bunch of mental people." Did we think they were mental? No, I assured them. But I did wonder if our society considered these young people as disposable as the patients in this building.

People from the Harvard Graduate School of Education had founded the Robert White School. It was a small program with about fifty students and a low teacher-to-student ratio. Students came predominantly from the Boston Public Schools, and the majority of them were Black or Latino, male, ranging in age from eleven to twenty years old. All were on an IEP, an Individualized Education Plan. Some had been diagnosed with serious learning disabilities; others had been kicked out of their public schools for emotional or behavioral problems. One student had punched his principal in the face. Another had been accused of rape. One of the girls was streetwalking. Nearly all of them struggled with reading. One student was so dyslexic, he could not read a text written for second graders. But he had developed such powerful coping strategies, it took months to find this out.

I was hired as a teacher-counselor, like most everyone else on staff. Even though Robert White was a school for special needs students, I did not have any certification or training in special needs education. Nor did I have any experience or training as a counselor. And I did not get any after I was hired. Each teacher was responsible for an academic area (mine was history and social studies) and for "counseling" a small group of advisees. We were expected to always be on-call, day or night, and to make home visits a few times a year. Many of the students were court-involved; teachers would have to leave their classes to advocate for their advisees on days they were in court. I remember getting calls at two and three o'clock in the morning during the week and on weekends from kids. Sometimes teachers debated whether it was a good thing to bail your kids out of jail in the middle of the night or if it was just enabling them. But the expectation from the school was clear: You show up at any time, 24/7.

Geoffrey Canada, renowned now for his founding of the Harlem Children's Zone and his advocacy for charter schools, was the principal of the Robert White. Most of the staff greatly respected Geoff. Everyone knew his background. An African American, he had grown up with a single mom in the South Bronx, one of the toughest neighborhoods in America at the time. While he had recently earned a master's degree from Harvard, he knew and understood the students at RWS in a way that many of the teachers, who were nearly all white and middle class, did not.

Geoff, who was just a couple of years older than I, taught me early on some important lessons about working with youth. I remember sitting with him in his office.

"Kathy, there are three things you need to know if you want to avoid problems in your classroom. First, you need to be clear. You need to let kids know what you expect and what the boundaries are. Secondly, you need to be consistent. You can't enforce your rules some of the time in one way or with one kid and other times in a different way with a different kid. They will pounce on you for that. Third, you need to be fair. Listen to them, find out their side of a story, give them space, never back a kid into a corner. Sometimes adults make mistakes. Sometimes kids break the rules. In the end, be fair. If you are clear, consistent, and fair, they will respect you."

Not only did Geoff share this good advice with his teachers, he modeled it for his staff in his own interactions with students. I would add one more thing to his list, though. Be calm. Geoff rarely lost his temper (except during basketball games—more on that later). Our students, most of whom had very unstable lives, knew they could count on Geoff to follow these rules. They trusted him.

I don't really remember what the guiding philosophy of the Robert White School was (or if there even was one), but the school did have a unique feature. It paid students to go to class. Students carried around a weekly voucher sheet. If they behaved in class, teachers would sign their sheet. If they earned a certain number of signatures, they would get a stipend at the end of the week (I'm not sure exactly how much it was—maybe $10 or $15). I hated this; most of the teachers did. Too often, kids would come begging you to sign off on their voucher. They'd make all sorts of promises about how they'd behave "next time" if you'd sign just this once. Some kids would get angry if you refused to sign. It was especially frustrating when you'd see kids leave school on Friday with their cash in hand and meet their dealer just outside the Lindemann building to score some drugs. But when the staff raised this with the Board of Directors, they flatly rejected any changes to the voucher policy.

Another interaction with the Board of Directors was especially memorable to me. There had been a number of violent incidents with kids. One fight I broke up by grabbing a kid from behind. As he let go of his opponent, we fell backward and he landed on top of me. Another student we'd had to hold in four-point restraint (they hadn't taught me how to do that at Tufts). The Board announced that they'd be running the next staff meeting, providing some professional development in how to deal with such violent situations. We filed into the staff room and they had cleared the room, with tables and chairs pushed to the side. Teachers were told to line up on one side of the room; the Board was on the other. Suddenly, they started grabbing the chairs and throwing them at us. To this day, I don't know what we were supposed to learn from that.

But that wasn't the only time when I felt my safety was in question. There were a few hairy moments when I was doing my home visits, too. All teachers were expected to do home visits to their "advisees." After the first home visit I made, I realized how incredibly valuable this practice was. It made a world of difference to see a student, a young person, in their own environment—not the school environment, which inevitably changed them. It helped us to better understand each of these individuals when we saw what their living situation was, who their parents (most had just a mom) and siblings were, and the neighborhood they went home to each day. I believe that home visits should be a practice for all schools as it allows for important insights into the lives of our students.

I was probably too naïve to be scared when I would visit Sean's family in the notorious Bromley-Heath projects in Boston's Jamaica Plain neighborhood. According to *The Boston Globe*, in the 1980s, "Bromley-Heath housing development was a terrible place. Garbage flowed. Crime raged. Even milkmen and furniture delivery crews refused to set foot there." I do remember feeling overwhelmed by the smell of urine in the hallways and the sight of a crumpled, nodding figure in a corner near the stairs. And I did feel some discomfort as people peered at me out of their windows and young men walking by made comments about "crackers" and "white bitches." But our families would protect us. Sean's mother would hang out her window and yell at everyone to leave me alone. That I was "cool." But when I visited Jane's mom (in a different neighborhood), I did briefly fear for my life.

Jane B. was a beautiful girl. She had huge round brown eyes. She was smart and bold as all get-out. She was fourteen or fifteen years old when she came to RWS and had been in a lot of trouble in her previous schools. I loved her spirit, but I struggled with her attitude on a daily basis. I knew her mom had mental health issues and there was no dad in the picture. I needed to make a home visit to connect with her mom. I'd parked my car on a street in Mattapan lined with small houses close together and walked down the front path. Mrs. B. opened the door and welcomed me in. As I sat on the couch, she asked me how I'd gotten there.

"I hope you didn't walk around in this neighborhood," she said. "This is a dangerous area. There are a bunch of crazies around here." She went on. "You shouldn't be walking around by yourself. Especially being a white girl. You really got to be careful. When I go out the house, I'm always sure to take this." She reached into her handbag and pulled out a very large meat cleaver and waved it around in the air. "You should get yourself one of these. You never know who you gonna run into around here."

I stared at the cleaver. Headlines in the *Boston Globe* flashed through my brain: "Teacher Hacked to Pieces in Mattapan." I thought about my mom and how sad she would be. I attempted a smile and explained that I had driven my car to her house.

"Oh, that's good," she said. "I won't have to worry about you, then." She tucked her protection back into her bag. I definitely developed a deeper understanding of Jane and her everyday life.

Although we spent some of our time in court or making house visits, we were, after all, supposed to be an educational institution. I had been hired as the social studies teacher. Once again, when

I asked what I was expected to teach, the answer was vague. The school didn't seem to have any expectations and I had a hard time finding out the Boston Public Schools' requirements. Given my new clientele, I thought I could use my curriculum on the criminal justice system that I had developed for my students in Medford. Kids were definitely engaged. They liked the idea that they had rights. In fact, I worried a bit that this knowledge could endanger them. The Boston Police did not have a great record working in communities of color. I invited Margaret Burnham to my class; she was a progressive attorney, whom the governor had recently appointed as the first female African American judge in Massachusetts. She spoke eloquently with the students about how to balance their Constitutional rights with the realities of street life in Roxbury, Dorchester, and Mattapan. They peppered her with questions and she answered every single one, patiently and respectfully. They all agreed, after she had left, that Judge Burnham was cool. They wished all judges were like her.

The old Charles Street Jail (now the uber-luxurious Liberty Hotel) was down the street from us, so I decided we should make a visit there. The jail was an imposing structure, a fortress peering out over the Charles River, made of large gray granite blocks. You could see the bars on the windows. I brought a group of students to the jail and, amazingly enough, the guards took us into the center of the cell-block. There were three tiers of jail cells that rose up around us with chain-link fencing along the walkways. It was extremely noisy. Men were yelling and clanging their bars and hooting at the few girls with us. At one point, one of my students, Louise, yelled, "Hey, that's my uncle up there!" She started waving happily, "Hey, Uncle Dave! How ya doin'?" They carried on a brief conversation until the guards intervened and shuffled us out. I left shaking my head.

Louise was one of the few students at RWS who intimidated me. When she looked at me, I could see contempt in her eyes, like she knew that I wouldn't stand a chance living in her world. She was a small, dark-skinned African American girl with a short Afro. She, like many of the students, was clearly very bright and I wondered what had happened to harden her so much by the age of sixteen. My biggest memory of her, besides the Charles Street Jail visit, was when we were celebrating someone's birthday. We had gathered in the Activity Room and there was a big sheet cake. I had a bunch of paper plates and was going to cut the cake up for everybody, but I didn't have a knife. "Oh, here," Louise said, and she pulled a knife with a seven-inch blade out of her boot. I was so astonished I just took the knife, cut up the cake, and then gave it back to her. I can't believe I didn't confiscate the knife. Nor did I tell anyone she had it. I was embarrassed that I hadn't taken it from her, and by the time I realized that I should have done something, it was too late. I always felt that she had done that to test me, to see what I would do. I failed that test, and she knew she had something on me.

Basketball ruled at the Robert White School. You had to twist kids' arms to get them to do homework—or even show up in class sometimes—but they were dedicated to basketball. We played in a league for 766 schools like ours, and, as a basketball lover myself, I joined in the practices and accompanied the team to games. Geoff was the coach, and he worked the kids hard. He expected them to be disciplined and to give their all. He was quite passionate, and during games, especially close ones, it was the one time I would see him lose his cool.

"What are you doing, Jenkins? Get your butt down that court!" he would scream from the sidelines. "What are you guys? A bunch of sissies? Hands up! Hands up!"

The players adored him. He was like a father to them. He gave them the tough love they craved and the attention they rarely got at home. He could play as well as the best of them and he taught them how to be better. I don't remember him ever missing a game.

After each game, Geoff would take the team out to McDonald's for a meal, on the school's dime. Kids were ravenous, of course, but it was more than just getting food. Going to Micky Dee's was a celebration. It was a reward for a job well done. The players were the big men on our very small campus. They were heroes to the younger kids. Teachers knew not to get into any disciplinary struggles, especially with one of the stars, on a game day. This bothered me. It seemed like the classic stereotype for Black men—you may not be able to read, but if you can hit an outside jump shot, you're all set. Some of the kids harbored dreams of big NBA contracts like Robert Parrish and Cedric Maxwell had (these two Celtics players lived across the street from the school in a luxury apartment building and we would occasionally see them coming and going). I remember speaking to Geoff about this. His view was that, through basketball, he could establish relationships and work ethics. If a student could see himself improve after shooting a hundred free throws, that could, hopefully, transfer to a sense of effort and efficacy in other areas, too. He argued that students needed to experience success and this was just a starting place—something that already mattered to them.

I could see Geoff's point, but I wasn't sure if we were moving kids beyond that starting place. At one point, I approached Geoff about bringing a theater group into the school for a residency program. Some of our students were quite artistic and I thought we could give them some of the same experience of success that the athletes were getting. He said the school didn't have the money. I asked about all the money that had gone to cheeseburgers and fries for the basketball team. "We don't have the money, Kathy," was the flat response. (I was able to write a small grant to fund the residency anyway.)

Boston at that time was a very divided city. While Judge Garrity's decision to hire more teachers of color in 1974 was not particularly controversial, his decree to bus students from poor Black neighborhoods like Roxbury and Mattapan to poor white neighborhoods like South Boston and Charlestown, and vice versa, had sparked a firestorm. The city had erupted in racial tension and violence. Buses carrying Black students were attacked by white protesters, who threw bricks, stones, eggs, and bottles while chanting racial epithets.

Boston's mayor mobilized riot police and, eventually, the governor called in the National Guard. While the biggest riots occurred between 1974 and 1976, racial tensions still roiled into the 1980s, always just beneath the surface, sometimes breaking through it.

The Robert White School was neutral territory. The downtown area did not belong to whites or Blacks. But I was shocked to discover that students had rarely, if ever, traveled outside their own parts of the city. Kids from Roxbury had never been to Dorchester; kids from East Boston had never been to Jamaica Plain, part of the same city. Some kids had never even been outside their own *part* of their neighborhood—for instance, kids in the Dorchester neighborhood hadn't been to other parts of Dorchester, like Fields Corner, Savin Hill, or Codman Square.

I wanted to expand these students' horizons; I wanted to expose them to parts of the world beyond the city. One beautiful spring Saturday, I took some of the boys from the basketball team to hike Mt. Monadnock in New Hampshire. These guys had never been outside the city before.

We were driving by a farm, when one of them got very excited and pointed to a field, "Look at the horses!" he cried.

I looked over and didn't see any horses. "Where, Tommy? I don't see any horses," I answered.

"There!" he pointed insistently. I looked again and saw about a half-dozen goats grazing. I tried not to laugh, but I did explain that the animals he was looking at were goats, not horses. The rest of the kids guffawed.

When we arrived at Mt. Monadnock State Park, my tough, swaggering teenagers did not want to get out of the car. "There are too many bugs here," they said. "It's too quiet here," they said. "There are only white people here," they said. They were clearly a little anxious. But eventually, they all piled out and we set off up the mountain. These young men were athletes, but they were not used to hiking. With lots of huffing, puffing, and even more complaining, they finally made the summit. And they were proud of themselves.

There was laughing and backslapping and joke-telling in the car on the way back, and palpable relief to be heading back to the city. It was getting dark as I hit the Southeast Expressway, looking for the right Dorchester exit to drop off my first passenger. But, somehow, I ended up taking a wrong turn. One of the kids said he thought we were heading toward South Boston. When we passed a street sign, he confirmed it.

"Kathy, you gotta get out of here," they urged. "They will kill us if we get caught here," one of them said.

My students, all Black, began to panic. "Relax," I assured them. "No one is going to hurt you."

The four of them flattened themselves on the floor of my car. I found it amusing that these big, tough guys were so terrified. But I was naïve. And I was white. At that time, I was not fully aware of the history of race relations in the city. I didn't understand the depth of anger and hatred that had been stoked there just a few short years earlier.

South Boston was Ground Zero for racist violence. It was the home of ROAR (Restore Our Alienated Rights), a virulently anti-busing group; and the South Boston Marshals, a racist paramilitary organization. In 1974, a Haitian man, who had mistakenly driven into the neighborhood, had been dragged out of his car and beaten nearly to death. Even if you were white, if you weren't a "Southie," you were the enemy. Michael Patrick MacDonald, in his memoir *All Souls*, wrote, "This neighborhood was very dangerous for anyone who was not from here, the west side, parts where the poorest people were." MacDonald said, "When we moved in [from Jamaica Plain] we were suspect. We were outsiders. We had all our windows broken out in Old Colony."

Nothing happened that night to the Mt. Monadnock adventurers. We eventually found our way back to Dorchester and everyone was returned home safely. But my own white privilege, I realized later, had indeed put these young men in danger; their fears were justified.

That wasn't the only time I learned a lesson about racism from the students at the Robert White. One time, we took a number of our students to visit a Boston TV station. They were filming a live talk show. The format was typical—a TV personality, an expert or two, audience participation. This show was about high school students and sex education. There were a number of other high school students there, nearly all of them white and clearly from the suburbs. The audience sat on three of the four sides of the stage. We were placed far off to the right. The host, a young, very blonde, very thin woman, would periodically make her way into the audience with a microphone to take questions or comments. Many students, including my own, were eager to contribute to the discussion.

In the first segment of the show, she concentrated her foray into the center section of the crowd. One of my students leaned over and said, "She ain't gonna come over here, Kathy."

"Of course, she will," I responded with confidence. Why wouldn't she? There was a commercial break and the TV host mingled among the students—the other students, I should say. But I still believed she would come over to talk to our kids. In the next segment of the show, she headed off to the left of the stage.

"See, Kathy," another student said. "She ain't gonna come over here. Just watch. She don't want to talk to us cuz we're Black." I dismissed these comments, as white people often do when Black people point out racist behavior.

There's another segment to the show, I assured them. "Third segment, she will come over to the third part of the audience." I still didn't believe that she could be so outrageously discriminatory against my students.

But she was. She went back to the center of the audience, even though several of our RWS students had their hands raised, quietly and politely. She took a number of comments from the white students, some with whom she had already spoken. Finally, with a glance in our direction, she said, "Oh, we are so sorry, but our time is up. Thank you, everybody, for being here . . . blah, blah, blah." She turned around and bounced back up onto the stage. The show was over.

I was livid. I couldn't believe she would diss our students like this. They had been right all along. I, on the other hand, was so sure that no one would discriminate in that way. Because in my world, people didn't discriminate against me for being white. I felt ashamed that I hadn't listened to my students. I felt complicit with what had happened. I knew the kids were watching me, waiting to see if I would do anything.

As we got up to go out to our van, I said, "Wait here." I walked up to the woman and said, "Excuse me, but I have to protest what you just did to my students."

She looked at me blankly, with a plastic smile plastered on her face.

"You called on all other parts of the audience but not my kids. You even went back to the same group of kids a second time. You refused to call on them because they are Black. That was incredibly racist and I am going to make a complaint to your manager."

She tried to protest, but I walked away. As I was heading to the parking lot, the cameraman came running out after me.

"You are right," he said. "I kept waving at her to go over to your kids, but she ignored me. She's done this kind of thing before. I think she is scared of them."

We did write a letter of complaint to the station, and we received a letter of apology from the manager. That was some vindication, but it couldn't take back the insult that my students had endured.

I often think that I learned far more from the students at the Robert White School than they learned from me. I was beginning to understand just how much young people of color, especially young men, were seen as suspect, as criminals, as someone to be feared by the white world. The young adolescents at RWS did, in some ways, present a menacing countenance to the world. They were angry. But I was often struck by their intelligent insights into a mean world, and I came to understand just how much they had a right to be angry, how they dealt with the indignities of racism and prejudice on a daily basis. They talked about "white ladies, like you, Kathy," crossing the road upon seeing them approach, shifting their purse onto the other arm.

"Why do they do that?" they'd ask. "It's like they think we're gonna steal something. They think we're all criminals."

I started watching people on the street, and indeed saw that what they said was true. I decided, when walking past a group of young men of color, to look directly at them and smile. Inevitably, I would see a hardness melt from their eyes. Many would give me a nod; some would even say hello. I still make a point of doing that, but I also still see white people crossing the road when they see a group of young men of color heading in their direction.

While there were a few excellent schools that were part of this 766 network, many, like the Robert White School, were pretty flim-flam. They relied on hiring staff like me who were young, inexperienced, un- or undertrained, idealistic, and willing to work long hours and weekends for little pay (at least for a few years), much like many Teach for America and charter school teachers today. We wanted to make a difference, especially for the kids who were most neglected by their society. Most of us were white and we thought we could save the world, if we just worked hard enough.

But, in spite of our good intentions, most of us didn't have a particularly good understanding of who our students were and what their lives were like. We didn't have any real analysis of racism and its deep intersection with class. Most of us knew little about learning disabilities or other kinds of special needs. At RWS, only one teacher on the whole staff had special education training. One teacher had been trained in teaching reading, a skill that every student desperately needed. Kids in schools like RWS needed experienced, highly trained teachers to help them gain both the academic skills and the life skills they needed to succeed in their world.

We also didn't have any training as "counselors." Again, young people, especially those of color, who lived in neighborhoods torn apart by poverty and violence, needed highly trained counselors to help them develop good coping skills and insights. They needed social workers who could help their families access the few resources that were available to them. They also needed positive role models. While Geoff Canada was a strong one, all the teachers were white. Our most vulnerable, most needy students should have gotten the best there was. But they didn't.

In spite of the American promise of "liberty and justice for all," these young people faced an unequal playing field every day. And, in the early 1980s, it was getting even more unequal. Ronald Reagan became President in 1981. Congress was slashing social programs in order to fund the biggest military buildup the U.S. had seen since World War II. It was the beginning of the crack epidemic and rising gun violence.[3] It was the escalation of the so-called "War on Drugs," when police started arresting thousands and thousands of Black and brown people, often for nonviolent crimes, leading to an explosion in our prison populations. My students were surrounded by poverty and despair. They went home from school each day wondering if they would be safe, wondering if there would be food in the cupboard, wondering if their mom would be sober, wondering when they'd see their dad or brother who was incarcerated again. When I asked one particularly talented young man what his goal was by the time he reached twenty-one, he said, "To still be alive." He was not alone in that sentiment.

I worked at the Robert White School for three years. Geoffrey Canada left at the end of my second year, heading back to NYC. His successor was not the kind of leader that Geoff had been. Harry had played football in the major leagues for a couple of years and somehow ended up in education. The staff did not have great confidence in him and had wanted one of the teachers to succeed Geoff, but the Board rejected the staff's preference. Unlike Geoff, who had been a father figure to many of the kids, Harry was the opposite. He used his size to intimidate people. He was unreliable and untrustworthy. He was frequently out of school. He claimed that he was out on "school business," but no one was really sure. The rumor was that Harry had purchased a sailboat, allegedly with school funds for our "sailing program." We never had a sailing program, and we never saw the boat. Maybe it was just mean gossip. But over the course of that year, the staff grew increasingly concerned about the leadership. We wrote letters to the Board, which it rejected. Finally, by the end of the year, nine out of the ten teachers submitted their letters of resignation. We'd had enough.

I had the additional impetus to leave because I was pregnant with my first child. My boyfriend and I had gotten married that fall because we wanted to start a family. I went into labor two weeks before the end of school and never went back to the Robert White. I even left all of my papers and materials at the school. It was June 1983. Proposition 2½ was in full effect. People with eight, nine, ten years of experience were being RIF'ed from the public schools. I didn't think I'd ever get a teaching job again.

CHAPTER 3

FINDING HOME
1984 — 1985

I loved being a new mom, but when my daughter reached eighteen months, I decided to look for a part-time teaching job. It was 1984, and openings (full or part time) were still few and far between, given the continuing impact of Proposition 2½. Then one day I got a phone call from an old friend. "Kathy," he said, "I know you are looking for a high school job, but I wondered how you would feel about teaching middle school for a bit."

"No way," I responded. "Those kids are crazy."

"Yeah, I know, but I heard about a job-share situation at the Graham and Parks School in Cambridge. It is right around the corner from you. There is a teacher there who wants to work part time, too, but she has to find a partner. I thought of you. Here's her phone number if you want to contact her."

The school was three blocks from my house. It was early December. My prospects for getting a high school job were grim. I decided to contact Roz. She explained that she taught English/language arts (ELA) and social studies to seventh and eighth graders. She was looking for someone to take over the ELA curriculum. We each would work one full day a week and three half days, leaving one full day off. The schedule was ideal for someone with a toddler at home. The only problem was that although I was certified as a seventh-through twelfth-grade social studies teacher, I was not certified as an ELA teacher. I did have a certification in reading, however, and that seemed to be good enough. I didn't know anything about teaching ELA. But I knew how to read and write so I assumed I would figure it out.

I applied for the job, even though it was for a part-time extended-term substitute, meaning I would earn just enough money to pay for childcare. It was worth it to me to be able to get back into the ring, so to speak. My plan was to gain some experience and get to know people in the Cambridge Public School system, and hopefully work my way into the high school.

The school was on a small, one-block side street in the Cambridgeport neighborhood bordering Central Square. The building, three stories high, was constructed in the late 1800s in red brick with the kind of big, light-filled windows that you would find in a factory building in Lowell or Lawrence. Classical Greek cement columns framed the entrance, with granite steps leading to the metal front doors. Asphalt blacktop surrounded the school like an apron. In the back of the school on one side was a parking lot big enough for about seven cars and, on the other, a small basketball "court" with two rusted hoops (no nets) about twenty feet apart. On either side of and across the street from the school property were residential buildings. The school building loomed out of proportion to the rest of the block, a monolithic brick box squeezed between row houses and two-family homes.

I remember walking up those stairs the first time. Unlike schools today, which are locked up tight like prisons to protect against potential school shooters or other criminals, the doors were open. I looked around for the main office, but was confused. Directly ahead of me, a low ramp led up to a half-sized gym. The Health Office was to the right and a Parent Information Office to the left, where a group of people were sitting and talking. They saw me standing awkwardly, wondering where to go.

"Hi!" said a woman in her late forties, brightly. "Do you need help?"

"Uh, yes, I'm looking for the office?" I replied.

"Oh, you have to go up to the second floor, and you'll see it in the middle of the hallway. It's glass; you can't miss it."

Interesting, I thought. I'd never seen a school where the main office wasn't the first thing you ran into. I wondered why they'd put the office on the second floor. When I asked about it, the principal, Len Solo, explained that he wanted the main office to be equally accessible to all students and teachers. Having the Parent Information Office on the first floor by the door was a deliberate decision that signaled the important role of parents and families in the school. This was just the first evidence of what a different kind of school Graham & Parks was.

I don't remember the interview process, but I did get the job. I'm sure there was not a lot of competition. Who would be willing to work for half of a substitute's salary, with no benefits? They were probably desperate to find someone. But I was desperate too. And I could afford it because my husband had gotten a decent paying job with health insurance at the Massachusetts Department of Education. Anyway, this was a temporary gig; I wasn't planning to be there long.

My negative feelings about middle schoolers were confirmed when Len walked me up to the third floor to see the classroom and meet the other seventh and eighth grade teachers. It must have been between classes because there was chaos in the hallway. Luckily, the corridor was carpeted to keep the noise down. Young adolescents were talking in small groups, gathered around rows of lockers. There was pushing and teasing and chasing and flirting. Amid the din, we heard a metallic banging. Len opened one of the lockers to find a small seventh-grade boy inside. He popped out and took off after a group of other boys. Len looked at me and said, "We are still working on our junior high model. We haven't quite figured out this age group yet." I wondered what I was getting myself into. However, after working with the kids at the Robert White School, I knew I could handle this. Cream puffs, I thought.

So I started my next phase of teaching at the Graham & Parks Alternative Public School in early December 1984.

"What makes Graham and Parks an alternative school? Alternative to what?" many people have asked me over the years.

My standard response was, "The kids don't sit in rows and they call the teachers by their first names."

While this was a somewhat glib explanation, these two practices did embody some profound underlying beliefs of the school. Graham & Parks had grown out of a school called CAPS, the Cambridge Alternative Public School, which had been started by a group of parents in the early 1970s. These parents, many of whom were educators themselves, wanted a more child-centered, hands-on approach to education for their children.

Visualize a "regular" classroom, especially in the 1970s. Most people picture a teacher either sitting at a large desk at the front of a classroom or standing just behind that desk at the blackboard. While the heavy wooden desk separates the teacher from her students, the students sit in neat rows separated from each other, presumably so they cannot look over at a classmate's paper and cheat. The teacher is talking (or writing on the board) and students are listening (or copying what is on the board). The room is very quiet, at least in a "good" class, as you only hear one voice at a time: the teacher speaking or a student answering a question. Everyone is reading the same book and has the same spelling and vocabulary words and the same math problems. Students read about history from a textbook and science from another textbook. What do you see on the walls? Depending on the grade, you see the alphabet in print and cursive, a poster explaining what a homophone or a metaphor is, maybe an illustration of the human body or a timeline of important dates in American history. There may be a few motivational slogans ("Shoot for the stars!" or "Practice makes perfect!") with cute cartoonish illustrations. Most likely there is a bulletin board that has students' latest tests hanging up, or it may have only the ones with a perfect score.

The founders of CAPS had a different vision. Coming out of the movements of the 1960s and 1970s for civil rights, women's liberation, Black Power, and gay rights, they wanted to create a school that was truly inclusive and democratic, a place where all stakeholders had a voice, including students. Inspired by John Dewey's views on democracy and education, the CAPS founders believed that the school itself needed to be a training ground for future citizens of the world.

One of Dewey's key beliefs was that we learn best by doing. If we want to live in a democratic society, schools need to teach children the skills of good citizenship. Children had to have opportunities to participate in decision making, develop tolerance for other people's views, and learn how to consider different perspectives. They had to feel empowered to ask questions, wonder about the world, and challenge the status quo. Rather than focusing on following directions and getting correct answers, as most schools had traditionally emphasized, the founders wanted to develop critical and creative thinkers. While they expected children to treat adults with respect, they also expected adults to treat children with respect. Rather than simply demand obedience, teachers would model the kind of behavior they expected from their children. Calling teachers by their first name was an intentional way of breaking down the traditional hierarchy of school and the authoritarianism of adults.

CAPS also understood that children learn in different ways and at different rates, something that people seem to have forgotten in the recent years of "education reform." While the school believed that all children could be successful, the founders understood that they would take different paths to the finish line and would arrive at different times. They wanted their students to be active learners, not passive vessels. They believed—again inspired by Dewey, Jean Piaget, Lev Vygotsky and others—that people learn by doing. Because of this, teachers needed to teach the *child*, not just the curriculum. They also believed that learning was socially, not just individually, constructed. Talking and problem solving with peers to make meaning of a poem, a math problem, or a science experiment would enhance everyone's learning. So, rather than have each student isolated from another, teachers designed their classrooms grouping kids around tables, havings meetings on a rug, or pushing desks together rather than apart. Rows were antithetical to the CAPS philosophy.

In many ways, CAPS was the original charter school. Its founding parents and educators from the community wanted to experiment with a new model for education. It was a public school open to all students in Cambridge. The school did not receive any additional funding from the district, but it had more autonomy over its budget. It also had more autonomy over the hiring process, including parent participation in the interviewing and selection of new teachers. Parents and teachers were also deeply involved in the school's decision making. Equal numbers of parents and staff, in addition to the principal, sat on the Steering Committee that made significant decisions about school policies. Finally, CAPS had considerable flexibility around curriculum, instruction, and assessment. One critical difference from current charters, though, was that CAPS remained "in district" and staff were part of the union, the Cambridge Teachers Association (now the Cambridge Education Association).

The Cambridge Alternative Public School had originally been located in St. Mary's Church in Central Square, a diverse and funky part of Cambridge. But in the early 1980s, CAPS merged with the Webster School, a struggling school in the nearby Cambridgeport neighborhood, to become the Graham & Parks Alternative Public School, named after Rosa Parks and Saundra Graham, a local welfare and housing activist. At the time, G&P was a K–8 school with about four hundred students. By design, the school was very diverse both racially and socioeconomically. Classes were multigraded, except for kindergarten; that is, each teacher had two grades in their classroom: grades one/two, three/four, five/six, and seven/eight. This was an intentional structure, rooted in the beliefs that children develop at different rates (so, a strong first-grade reader could be in a group with second graders), that they learn from each other (the older children model routines, good practice, and high-quality work for the younger ones), and that building a community is foundational to learning (children spent two years with one teacher).

The "junior high" had three seven/eight classes. There was a math teacher, another ELA teacher, and then Roz and me. Each teacher, in addition to their primary subject, taught a social studies unit. A part-time science teacher taught three days a week. We also had a small Haitian bilingual class that included grades five through eight at that time (it was later to grow to become a significant part of the school). Finally, a special education/resource room teacher rounded out the junior high team.

"What is the curriculum here?" I asked Len. "What do you want me to teach?" I understood that there was flexibility in the curriculum, but I figured there must be at least some kind of scope and sequence. I was wrong.

"That's up to you," Len responded. "We encourage our teachers to develop their own curriculum. In fact, we feel it is a strength of our school. People here have a lot of passion for what they teach. Their excitement inspires kids to learn."[1]

As a social studies teacher, I loved history and geography. At the School Within and the Robert White School, it had been easy to tap into my passion and share it with kids. As an ELA teacher, I wasn't so sure. I had always loved reading, so that seemed like a good thing to do with my new students. But I didn't know what else I should do, and I was probably too embarrassed to ask for help. So I did what most new, untrained, and inexperienced teachers do. I fell back on my own experience. What did I do in my seventh- and eighth-grade English classes? I tried to remember. We had spelling and vocabulary words. We analyzed poems (rhyming schemes and poetic formats, yuck). We wrote essays. I think we read a few books, but the only one I remember was *The Old Man and the Sea* (which I loved).

Luckily, unlike the schools in Medford and Boston, Graham & Parks did have materials and resources. There were multiple copies of books like *The Pearl* and *Julie of the Wolves*. There were some study guides the previous teacher had created and others that were professionally produced. There were anthologies of short stories and poetry, grammar books that helped me learn what a prepositional phrase was and when to use "who" and "whom," and notebooks with lessons on writing various kinds of paragraphs. I really wasn't sure how to put it all together, but I was ready to plunge in and do my best. I had the weekend to prepare.

No one told me that Roz and I were replacing a beloved and highly respected teacher who had become a staff developer in another school. Students had been excited to have Ann and were very angry to have to adjust to not just one but two new teachers. From day one, they gave us hell. They were constantly calling out or getting out of their seats or interrupting me. It was a daily game of Whack-A-Mole and a never-ending attempt to herd cats. One day I got so frustrated with one wiry little seventh grader, Miguel, I tied him to the string of the window shade behind my desk. He thought it was hilarious. So did the rest of the class. I'd kind of been joking, but it did keep him still for a while. Of course, this would not be a recommended form of discipline these days. In fact, I think schools have fired teachers for less.

I was struggling to establish some kind of order in the class. Finally, one day, after a few weeks, I couldn't contain it any longer. I sat down on top of my desk and started crying. The class suddenly fell quiet. They were alarmed.

One of them said in a small voice, "Kathy, why are you crying?" For once, they were all ears.

I wiped away my tears and said, "I have been trying so hard to do a good job here. I really want to be a good teacher for you. I don't know why you hate me so much."

They all looked shocked.

"We don't hate you at all!" they exclaimed. "We like your class!"

"Really?" I said in disbelief.

"Yes!" they chorused, with great sincerity.

"Well, I never would have known that from how people behave in here," I responded.

I don't remember the conversation that ensued, but I know there was one. We agreed to set up a behavior chart, visible to all, to monitor progress. It was quite rudimentary, but it did help to have a visual reminder of what we were working toward. I won't claim that they suddenly became angels and everything was la-di-dah after that one conversation, but things did get better. And I got some help.

As part of my daily schedule, in addition to my ELA classes, I would go to the classroom next door with my homeroom students to assist Steve, the math teacher. This arrangement was conceived as a practical solution to a challenging problem. Steve was teaching pre-algebra and algebra at the same time and had several different "ability" groups in one class. He needed help, someone to monitor the small groups when he was not with them, keep them on task, answer kids' questions, and generally keep things humming. My presence was helpful to Steve, but being in Steve's class was a god-send for me.

Steve was a master teacher. He loved math. His passion for it was infectious. But it wasn't just his excitement about equations and the Pythagorean theorem that made Steve such a great teacher. He ran a tight ship. I watched the same group of students who gave me such a hard time act completely differently with him. They listened to him. They paid attention. They did their homework. They wanted to please him. I realized that they weren't bad kids; they just rose to the level of what adults asked of them. Even with these squirrely middle schoolers, Geoff Canada's lessons still applied: Be clear, be fair, be consistent. That's what Steve was doing.

I finally had a mentor. In four years, I had never seen anyone else teach. But, every day, for the rest of that year, I got schooled in what good teaching looked like. I watched how Steve would set the tone for the class right away. Kids lined up outside his door and he greeted each one as they came in. If someone looked sick or depressed, he would offer them a cup of tea (he had a sink and an electric kettle in his room). If a student walked in upset or riled up about something, Steve would direct them to his "cubby" (a small study carrel) to take some space and calm down. No judgment, just "When you're ready, join us." I would see them put their head down on the desk, body tight and hunched over. But, gradually, their posture would relax. They would start turning their head and then their whole body toward the class. Next they would be raising their hand with an answer or a question, and Steve would just gesture for them to move back to their regular seat.

He spoke with a thick Brooklyn accent, which cracked the kids up. (Kids would ask him to say "beer" and "bear." They sounded the same.) Steve kept up a running banter with kids. He used humor as a class-management tool but seemed to know the line between affectionate teasing and ridicule. I never saw Steve denigrate or humiliate a student, nor would he ever back a kid into a corner. Students in Steve's class knew how deeply he cared about them.

They also knew Steve loved what he was teaching. He wanted his students to not only feel the same passion for the discipline but to also feel ownership of it. It was never good enough to just get an answer right. Steve insisted that you only really knew the math if you could explain it to someone else. (Over the years, Steve instituted a weekly writing assignment called "Explain it to Kathy.") Steve's classroom felt safe and relaxed, but students also knew that expectations for them were high.

I realized, however, that I could not be Steve. I was not a man (which I believe does make a big difference with kids). I did not have a funky Brooklyn accent. I have a good sense of humor, but I am not a particularly witty person. I didn't have a sink in my room to make tea for sick kids, either. I knew I had to find my own path; I had to be myself. But the training I got from assisting in Steve's math class was invaluable.

I had been at the school about two months when the first semester came to end. It was time for report cards. When I asked Len where to get the report cards from, he said, "Oh, at G&P, each teacher makes up their own report card, based on what you are doing. We call them 'progress reports' because we are really looking at what kind of progress each student is making. We don't use grades and there is no one kind of report card." I couldn't believe this. I don't remember what I'd done in Medford or Boston around report cards, but this was a "real" school, a public school. Didn't they have those little cardboard cards that fold in half, where teachers wrote an A, B, or C in the correct column? Some with a place for "behavior" or even "comments?"

I panicked. I hadn't thought about what *progress* students were making, much less how I would know that. I had thought I could just assign grades. An "A" to my strong students, a "B" for the pretty strong ones, and so on. I could label who was what. I tried to think of what I could put on my English Language Arts progress report. What had I been teaching? What had the kids been learning? I'd given some tests on the books we were reading together ("What is the theme of *The Pearl*?"); I could include those averages. I had been giving spelling and vocabulary quizzes. I could average those scores and put that in.

It is embarrassing to admit this, but I had not really thought that much about what my kids were learning. I was practicing the "empty vessel" model of teaching. That is, a teacher's job is to pour information into passive students' heads. Then we test them at the end to see if they "got it," whatever "it" is. Even as we read *The Pearl* or *Catcher in the Rye*, I wasn't thinking about developing the skills readers use to make sense of, analyze, and critique a piece of literature. I'd relied on teacher guides prepared by other people to figure out what was important to focus on and what "comprehension" questions to ask. If a student couldn't read the story on their own, I helped them get through it, but I had no idea how to help a student develop skills to become an independent reader. I did teach some vocabulary, but I seriously doubt that too much of it stuck with most kids. Each week kids had a list of ten words, usually from the book we were reading, at least, that they had to look up in the dictionary and then use in a sentence they would write. (One student wrote every single vocabulary word in a sentence that involved Bert and Ernie, the Muppet characters. His sentences always cracked me up, but I did wonder if it was a way of protesting a pretty pointless exercise.)

My "progress report" consisted of four categories: reading, writing, vocabulary, and class participation. I was terrified someone would challenge me and ask me to defend why I gave one student an A in reading and another a B+. Based on what? I didn't have answers for that at the time, but this experience triggered a lot of questions for me about the role and purpose of grades, progress reports, and assessments in general that I would continue to explore in depth, both for myself and with my junior high team.

If you know anything about teaching and schools in the 1980s, you will be struck by the word "team." At that time, teachers in most schools did not work in teams. They worked "independently," like separate eggs in an egg carton. In the traditional junior high model, classes were departmentalized. Teachers had a hundred or more students, students had five, six, or seven different teachers. Class periods were forty-five minutes. Teachers were not encouraged to talk with each other, and certainly were not given any official school time to do so. This structure made it difficult for teachers to know their students very well, much less think together about pedagogical issues. For students, the sense of community and cohesion that they had known in an elementary class was utterly gone.

At G&P, people wanted to change that. Knowing students well was a foundational part of the school's philosophy. Rather than diluting personal relationships or losing them altogether, as students transitioned from a self-contained class in elementary grades to a more departmentalized structure in junior high, G&P folks believed that young adolescence was a critical time to maintain and build strong connections to adults. Because we shared students, because we only saw a slice of each student's life, it was clear that teachers needed to talk together on a regular basis. Len, the principal, and Isabel Hanelin, G&P's staff developer, led weekly meetings with the junior high teachers during a common prep period. We would discuss concerns about various students, as well as common issues like hallway behavior, bullying, and homework expectations. But Len and Isabel also wanted to go beyond just talking about our kids. They wanted to involve teachers in building a developmentally appropriate program, addressing curriculum, assessment, pedagogy, and the structures that would support the needs of these young people.

Luckily for us, other people were also interested in the needs of young adolescents. In the mid-1980s, there was increasing concern about the number of student dropouts in the country. In response to this problem, the Massachusetts Department of Education created the Chapter 188 Essential Skills Dropout Prevention Discretionary Grant Program. Schools across the state were invited to apply for funding that would "address the needs of students at risk of leaving school prior to high school graduation." Research had shown that the roots of the dropout problem started in junior high (it probably starts in kindergarten) and the grant invited schools serving seventh graders and up to apply. We began to talk as a team about how we could use this grant.

Our theory was that if students felt more positive about being in school and felt more ownership over their environment, they wouldn't drop out so easily. We went back to Dewey and his ideas about democracy. If we wanted our students to feel part of a community, maybe we needed to give more time to building that community. If we wanted our students to act more responsibly, maybe we needed to give them more responsibility. If we wanted our students to be problem solvers, maybe we needed to guide them in solving their own problems.

Over a number of months and into the next year, we talked about possible programs and structures that would support these goals. We started holding monthly community meetings with all the junior high classes piled into one classroom. We had to move tables and desks, kids had to bring chairs, and it was very crowded (and at times smelly—junior high, after all). I don't remember the earliest agendas, but eventually we used these meetings to share student work, celebrate accomplishments, and debate issues. One time, for example, a number of girls came to me, upset that they couldn't play Double Dutch on the tiny playground in front of the building because the boys were always kicking balls into their jump rope. We brought the issue to the community meeting to let both sides air their grievances and to brainstorm solutions to the problem. We eventually agreed on alternating days of the week between jump rope and football. Because the community had addressed the problem openly and everyone had had a chance to weigh in, students easily accepted this resolution.

We debated starting a student government. We were concerned about the common pitfalls, especially that an election for student council was often simply an adult-sanctioned popularity contest. How could we avoid that? Should it be balanced by gender, by race? Should it be only for seventh and eighth graders, or should we include representation from the younger grades? When would it meet—during school or after? Who would supervise it? What would the student council do? How could it be more than a committee organizing bake sales? What if someone didn't do their job or abused their power? We brought some of these questions to our community meetings and decided to launch a new student council in the coming school year.

We also explored starting a school mediation program. Mediation was becoming increasingly popular in the adult world. Roger Fisher and William Ury of the Harvard Negotiation Project had recently published their bestseller, *Getting to Yes: Negotiating Agreement Without Giving In*. Rather than long, drawn-out, costly, and rancorous court battles, people were turning to mediation to get to "yes-yes" solutions. I had met a young man, Richard Cohen (now executive director of School Mediation Associates), who had developed a training module for a school-based peer mediation program. He had started working with our local public high school and was open to trying out the training with junior high students. Graham & Parks would be one of the first junior highs in the country to implement a peer mediation program.

I loved being part of a team that was trying to think deeply and creatively about developing a more effective program for young adolescents. For the first time (in my admittedly short career), I felt respected as a teacher. We shared a free flow of ideas in these meetings, without fear of judgment or censure. All ideas were considered and all people at the table had an equal voice. Even as a part-time extended-term sub, my opinion mattered. This truly democratic process profoundly shaped my view for the rest of my life of how schools should work. Len, as the principal, did not see himself as "above" the teachers. Rather, he had a different job. Our job was to teach and inspire children to be lifelong learners. His job was to find the best teachers he could and make sure we had the time, resources, and materials to do our job. He allowed us to make mistakes, and even protected us when we did. Which I discovered firsthand.

Because our school had no real playground, we would sometimes take our students to a nearby city park. While there was a large grassy area there for kids to play on, the swings were broken, the jungle gym was rusted, and the playground was littered with broken bottles and other rubbish. In an effort to get my students to see the power of the written word, I decided we would write letters to the mayor of Cambridge to advocate for a new and improved park.

The students wrote with passion. They detailed their complaints and offered specific ideas for change. We were very excited when we put all our letters in an envelope and sent them off to City Hall.

A few days later, Len called me into his office. "Kathy, I just got off the phone with the mayor. Did your class write letters to him about Dana Park?"

I nodded. I was proud that we were writing with a real purpose.

"Well," Len went on, "he was pretty pissed off. In fact, he was furious. He said the tone of the letters was not only rude and disrespectful, but the kids couldn't spell for s—t. He said, 'What kind of school are you running over there? And who is the teacher behind this?'"

I gulped.

Len went on. "I figured it was you, but I told him that it was not his business who the teacher was and that I stood behind students advocating for their community."

I mumbled my appreciation.

"But, in the future," he continued, "I suggest at least checking for spelling. It makes people take you more seriously."

Somehow, I managed to get through that first year. I worked hard, but mostly in a fog. I would teach in the mornings, pick my daughter up from her family daycare at one o'clock, when she would be ready for a nap. While she slept, I worked on my lessons for the next day. In the evenings, I corrected papers. My life felt very full. I couldn't imagine how people worked a full school day and still had a life. I figured that it would get easier as time went on. (It did not.)

I also knew I had to learn a lot more about teaching ELA. In the spring I had seen a flier posted in the staff room for a summer institute at the University of Massachusetts in Boston. It was a three-week course sponsored by the Boston Writing Project for K–12 teachers on teaching writing. This sounded perfect to me; it would definitely improve my English/language arts repertoire. I signed up with a couple of other teacher friends from Cambridge.

That July, as we were driving down to the UMass campus on the first day of the institute, I said to Chris and Robin, "You know, this better not be one of those 'do it with your students' kind of things. If they try to make me write, I'm going to drop out. I'm here to learn how to *teach* writing, not do it."

When I look back at that statement, I am horrified. While teachers can't be expert at everything they are asked to teach, especially in elementary school where teachers are responsible for all subjects, we absolutely become better teachers when we teach with and from experience. Luckily, the people at the Boston Writing Project knew that.

On our first day, we were asked to fill a piece of notebook paper, twenty-seven lines, with memories: I remember the day I broke my arm, I remember falling off my bike, I remember the day Megan was born, I remember . . . I was surprised by my list—some things I had not thought about in decades. Then we had to pick an early memory to write about. I chose one of a dance class my mother had enrolled me—a pudgy nine-year-old—in the hope that I would lose a few pounds. As I began to write, both the details and the emotions came flooding back to me. I could see that beige-colored leotard. I could feel my awkwardness and humiliation. I was surprised, and pleased, by how engaged I became in revisiting this memory and thinking about its impact on my self-image both as a nine-year-old and as an adult.

But then came the response group. The idea of reading this ditzy little piece aloud to other people terrified me. I dreaded the moment when I would have to read to the group. My hands were shaking so hard that I was having trouble reading the words on the page. My voice trembled. Even though the room was air conditioned, my armpits were slimy with sweat. It probably took me less than a minute to read—it was only one typed page—and then there was that silence, the silence that just makes you want to melt, implode, disappear. I'd been exposed. No one could think of anything good to say. They were probably searching for one half-decent phrase to compliment.

And then the comments came: "I really liked the part where you——"; "I liked that expression—," "The beginning of the story really grabbed me—" . . . People liked it? They had good things to say? They didn't think it was stupid? Before I knew it, we had moved into "Do you remember how it felt when—?" and "What if you made your closing line your opening instead?" and "Can you just clarify the sequence of—?"

I couldn't believe how I felt. I guess the word would be "validated." I had written something that people had actually found interesting. It had evoked memories of their own difficult years. They had appreciated the structure of the story, the craft. They had been curious to know more, which guided me as a writer about what else I wanted to tell. Their suggestions strengthened the piece. They were not sitting in judgment; they were engaging with me as a fellow writer, an equal colleague. I had never had that experience before in all my years of writing—in school, in college, or even in graduate school.

Half our day, five days a week for three weeks, involved time for writing or for sharing our writing with others. Mornings were spent exploring different pedagogical strategies, but I found that the most valuable lesson I was learning was in being a writer myself. I knew what it felt like to "not know what to write about," something kids would inevitably say when they were asked to write a story. But I also learned ways to push through and beyond to discover thoughts you didn't even know you had. I had a different understanding of asking students to share their work with others. I would tell the story of my beige leotard and sweaty armpits to every class I had for years to come, acknowledging for them that sharing your work with others is indeed scary, until you find how incredibly helpful it is to get real, respectful feedback. Above all, I learned the joy of writing. I couldn't wait to share that joy with my next group of students in September.

But there was a new twist in the plot. I was pregnant again.

CHAPTER 4
WINDOWS INTO STUDENT THINKING
1985–1989

I was four and a half months pregnant when I went back to school in September 1985. Still a part-time extended-term substitute, I continued to teach language arts and assist Steve in math. My students were doing more writing now and I brought a passion to that part of my class. But I honestly don't remember a lot about that fall. Being pregnant, having a toddler at home, and trying to be wife, mother, and teacher was all consuming. I do know that our junior high team meetings continued and we worked on a range of ideas for our seventh- and eighth-grade program.

My daughter Zoë was born at the end of January 1986. I decided to stay home with her for the rest of the school year, but when I went back to work in September, I was working full time. I had my half-time teaching position again, this time teaching two ELA classes and one social studies class. But I was also hired to facilitate our Dropout Prevention program, which the Department of Education had approved.[1] Our program would include developing the peer mediation program, a community outreach and apprenticeship program, beginning and end-of-year outdoor experiences, and a ninth-grade transition orientation. Additionally, a crisis intervention team would develop and coordinate academic and counseling services for at-risk students. During the last five months of the grant, I would work with other elementary schools to help them implement similar programs in 1987–1988. My title was the "school climate coordinator."

I hated that title, school climate coordinator. People didn't know what it meant. What do you mean "school climate"? Are you in charge of air conditioning? I am not joking; people would ask me that. "School climate" sounds like something separate from real school. It didn't seem to be about learning, or at least people at the time did not think that way. It felt like an add-on, something extraneous, even fluffy. But at Graham & Parks (G&P), we believed that the "climate" or culture of the school was foundational to helping our students grow into responsible, caring, well-educated adults. Because of that, the teachers were willing to invest their time and energy into implementing the different components of the grant.

Probably the biggest investment in time that year was our peer-mediation program. We recruited a diverse group of ten students to be trained as mediators. Rich Cohen (founder of School Mediation Associates) conducted three half-day workshops with the kids. They learned the basic theory of mediation along with hands-on training that included multiple role-play and feedback sessions.

Rich also helped us figure out how to implement this new program. Mediation, he explained, is a voluntary process. People cannot be coerced into doing it. The parties in conflict have to be willing to listen to each other and, if they choose, come up with a mutual resolution to the problem between them. This, too, cannot be forced. It is also important that the process be confidential. Students going to mediation have to trust that the mediators will not share their business with other kids in the school. Mediators have to act impartially, which can be hard even for adults to do. They have to be willing to put their own opinions aside to really listen to their "mediatees." The success of the program would rest on the integrity of these peer mediators. It also meant that the adults in the school had to be willing to step back and trust in the students to resolve their own conflicts. This can be challenging for a lot of adults, but at G&P, we saw this as part of our mission, especially for our junior high students.

As school climate coordinator, it was my job to supervise the program. It was challenging at first to get both teachers and students to remember to use it. It just wasn't on their radar screen. Numerous times I would hear someone talk about a student conflict, like gossiping or name-calling, and I would say, "That's a good case for mediation!" and they would say, "Oh yeah, right!" But the student mediators and I gradually started to shift awareness. It especially caught on as both teachers and kids saw its success. While the sessions themselves were confidential, students who had used mediation started talking positively about the process. That first year, we did over thirty different mediations. Nearly all of them were resolved successfully.

But the impact of the mediation program went beyond just solving interpersonal squabbles among students. The mediators themselves changed. They took their job very seriously, and they were learning important skills that they could carry into the rest of their lives. Something also shifted in the school climate. Not dramatically. There were still the normal issues associated with young adolescence. But with the peer-mediation program, the Student Council (which had started that year), monthly community meetings, and a few other changes in the junior high, there seemed to be a bit less of an "us versus them" culture.

Another part of my school climate coordinator responsibilities that year was to share our work at Graham & Parks with other junior high school programs in Cambridge. At that time, Cambridge had sixteen K–8 schools and one comprehensive high school, Cambridge Rindge and Latin School (CRLS). Although the ideas for the Hooked on Schools proposal had grown out of discussions at G&P, the district hoped to use this model to build stronger junior high school programs in all the schools. G&P would pilot the dropout prevention initiative and then begin to share our experiences with other seventh- and eighth-grade teachers. This gave me the opportunity to visit other schools, which was truly eye-opening.

The cultures in the other schools I visited that spring were very different from that of G&P. The other principals had not created any common planning time for junior high team meetings, and the teachers didn't really see the need to meet with each other.

"I teach math," said one teacher. "What do I have to talk about with the English teacher?"

"But you share the same students," I would say. "We need to think about the kids together. We only see a part of them, forty-five or fifty minutes out of their day. We are trying to think about what their experience is like, going from one class to the next. What is their whole day like?"

"My job is to teach math [or English, or science, or . . .]. That other stuff is not my business," was a common response.

I was also struck by how differently these other teachers related to their principals, and vice versa. One principal had scheduled a meeting for me with the teachers but didn't bother to show up himself. They didn't know who I was or why any of us were there. Another set up the meeting but had only told teachers that morning that they had to give up their one prep time of the day. Needless to say, there was a lot of resentment in the room. In another school, the principal did all the talking in the meeting. He clearly intimidated the teachers, who sat by silently. I wondered how those teachers could possibly start a student council where students could have a voice when they themselves were afraid to express an opinion.

I have watched a lot of "school reform" practices fail because people were only imitating the surface of an initiative rather than truly understanding the philosophy behind it. It is like seeing only the tip of the iceberg. Underneath the surface is the philosophy, the theory, the belief, and the commitment to supporting that practice. Without that foundation, the "tip," the innovative practice, will just float away. For example, the Small Schools movement that Bill Gates championed in the early 2000s pushed many large high schools to break up into smaller units. This was successful when teachers and administrators understood that the reason to have small schools is so that teachers and students can know each other well; that smaller school size enables positive relationships. It was not successful when people thought their work was done, rather than just beginning, when they formed these smaller-school communities without explaining why and creating the ongoing structures to sustain it.

Teachers, the people on the frontlines who have to implement these changes, are often not involved in the process of developing ideas or decision making. They are treated like foot soldiers who are expected to carry out commands without question or even real understanding.

What became clear to me was that the most radical change we were making at G&P was talking to each other. It was not our pioneering peer-mediation program or our beginning-of-the-year community-building outdoor adventure. Rather, it was bringing a team of teachers together on a regular basis to think about their students' needs. We would talk honestly and openly. We often disagreed and got into spirited debates, not only with each other, but with Len and Isabel too. We assumed, though, that we had to build consensus to make something really work. We knew we had to "own" the change, or it wouldn't happen, much less stick. I don't recall ever having a decision forced on the team.

My goal in these visits to other schools became not to explain how to start a peer-mediation program or student government, but to get teachers to talk together about their beliefs and ideas about teaching young adolescents. Sometimes this was greeted with resistance. It was hard for people to step back from their daily whirlwind of teaching to think big thoughts. But, gradually, at least in a couple of schools, people did begin to see the value of talking to each other, at least about their students.

While my work with the Hooked on Schools grant was moving forward, my academic classes were less than thrilling. I had developed better classroom-management skills, but I was struggling to inspire in my hormonally distracted students the same excitement and reverence I had for literature and history. That spring, I was teaching a unit on the Constitution. How could I get these twelve- and thirteen-year-olds to appreciate how revolutionary the United States

Constitution was for its time? How could I help them understand the genius of the balance of power between branches of government? How could I communicate the thrill of the Bill of Rights and the protections it provides citizens from abuses of state power? I tried to draw them in with complex, provocative questions, like "Did the American Nazi Party have the right to march in Skokie, Illinois, a town with a high concentration of Holocaust survivors?" Steve, my math teacher buddy, and I had debated this First Amendment issue fiercely. But in my classroom, the same few hands went up while the majority of the class sat by passively, looking rather glazed.

I was determined to change this. One day, I had a brilliant idea about how to bring the Bill of Rights alive. I drafted a student to be part of my plan. Ethan was big and tough and never spoke in class. At least, *Ethan* will be engaged today, I thought, even if my plan fails.

We had been looking at the Fourth Amendment, the right of protection from unreasonable search and seizure. As I was talking about British Redcoats searching the colonists against their will, another teacher (prearranged by me) knocked at the door. I put down my notes on Ethan's desk, excused myself from the class, and stepped outside for about thirty seconds. I removed my watch from my wrist and stuck it in my pocket. When I returned to the classroom, I went to pick up my notes again and stopped.

"Where's my watch?" I asked Ethan.

"I don't know," he shrugged, playing the game well.

"Look, I put my notebook and my watch right here in front of you before I stepped out of the room. Now my watch is gone. Where is it?" I could feel the tension building in the classroom. "Where is it?" I demanded again.

"I don't know," Ethan mumbled. "I didn't do anything with it."

"Don't give me that! I put it down here and now it is gone. And you are telling me you don't know what happened to it?" While I was intensely focused on Ethan's face, I could feel twenty-four pairs of eyes on my back. "Let me see your bag."

"You can't—"

"Give it to me!" I grabbed his backpack. The class was stunned. I could feel it. They leaned forward, on the edge of their seats. *Finally* I had their attention. I was ecstatic. I started to unzip the bag.

Ethan, doing a great acting job, sputtered, "Y-y-you can't do that!"

"You're right!" I exclaimed. "And do you know why?" I crowed triumphantly, "Because of the Fourth Amendment to the Constitution!" On that, like a balloon that has just been punctured by a pin, the tension suddenly deflated. I had lost them again.

I left school that day feeling very frustrated. I had spent hours coming up with a plan that had resulted in about five minutes of student interest. I didn't mind working hard, but it didn't seem right that I was doing *all* the work. What were *they* doing? What were they thinking? I didn't know if they were thinking at all. How could I crack through this wall? The next day, I went to talk to Isabel about it. She said, "Look, Kathy, you don't know that they are *not* thinking. Some kids just don't like to talk in class. Why don't you have them do something? Some kids like to *do*, rather than talk."

I decided to try her advice. But I am not an artsy person and the only project-y thing I could think of was making shoebox dioramas, something I had done in school myself (although it was probably in third or fourth grade, certainly not eighth). So I asked students to bring shoe boxes into school; I wanted to make sure everyone actually worked on the assignment. They had to pick one of the rights guaranteed by the Bill of Rights, create a scene that showed its importance and relevance, and write an explanation of it and why they had chosen that particular right.

I could not believe the transformation in the classroom. The kids were excited. They talked to each other, shared ideas, explored issues around which they would build their dioramas. They were processing their learning and constructing understanding. They were having fun, but most were also accomplishing something. It was clear who was thinking and understanding the issues we'd covered in class—and who was not. I felt like someone had suddenly cut a window into their heads and I could get a glimpse into these students' minds.

Not only did the diorama project reveal way more to me about what was going on in my students' heads, it also challenged me to question my own teaching. Although I had been working at the Graham & Parks Alternative Public School for a couple of years now, the way I had been teaching had been, in fact, quite traditional. While my kids did not sit in rows, they may as well have, given how teacher-centered my instruction was. But my little experiment with the dioramas had opened a door. How could I let students demonstrate what they knew and what they didn't know? Was there only one way, or were there several? How could I help them find the paths to express their thinking? I knew I wanted to move toward doing more projects, but I was not sure how to get there.

A couple of months later, I reconnected with an old friend, Steve Seidel, who happened to be working with Project Zero at Harvard University. Project Zero, at the time led by Howard Gardner and David Perkins, was investigating the development of learning processes in children and adults, particularly in and through the arts. Gardner had recently published his seminal book, *Frames of Mind: The Theory of Multiple Intelligences* (1983). They were interested in project-based learning and authentic forms of assessment. I described my diorama experience to Steve and explained my gut feeling about getting my students more actively engaged in the classroom. "I think we could really help each other," Steve said. "Let me know when you are ready to start."

That fall (1988), I was teaching the Facing History and Ourselves curriculum. Facing History uses the Holocaust as an historical case study of human behavior to examine issues including intolerance, violence, prejudice, identity, and social responsibility. To explore the steps Hitler took to build a totalitarian state, we read *Animal Farm* by George Orwell. There was a wide range of reading ability in the class. Zach and Marie understood the book as political satire, while Ketler and Beth liked reading a story with animals as the main characters.

However, through activities such as regular class discussions, role-plays, and character webs, everyone came to enjoy the book, and all had some understanding of its parallels to the Holocaust.

When we finished the book, I thought, *Well, I guess it's time for the test.* But a test seemed so flat and anticlimactic after all the other work we had done. Furthermore, I knew certain students, like Beth, would not do well on a traditional test. The pencil-and-paper exam would not reveal what Beth had really learned. I could see her freezing up, deciding before she had started, *I can't do this, I don't know anything.* It was important to me that she have an opportunity to show herself, as much as show me, how far she had come in her understanding. She needed a different path. It suddenly occurred to me: *Aha! Projects! This is where I can try doing projects again.*

I'm not sure why I hadn't thought about doing projects sooner. In spite of my diorama success, I had not really incorporated that way of thinking into my teaching practice. I was still stuck in the mode of teach, teach, teach, test. I hadn't yet dug deeply into the philosophy and theory behind project-based learning. I wasn't even that aware of that body of knowledge out there. But, I was lucky to have a highly thoughtful and knowledgeable mentor to turn to. It was time to call Steve Seidel.

"Steve, I think I'm ready to try doing a project with my class, but I don't know where to start."

"What kind of projects do you want to do?" he responded.

"I don't know."

"Well, why do you want to do these projects? What do you want to know about your students' learning?" His questions pushed me to revisit my goals. Or maybe visit my goals in the first place. What did I want my students to understand from having read *Animal Farm*? What was important to remember, to hold on to? Steve and I talked through the goals of the projects, and we talked about the nitty-gritty details. Should the projects be done singly or in groups? Should I form the groups or allow students to choose their own partners? How much class time was I willing to give? What about deadlines?

As I look back at this time, I realize just how critical it was to have support in the process of trying something new in the classroom. I knew I wanted to do something different, but I really wasn't sure what it should look like. It is very hard to create something that you can't envision. Most of us teach the way we were taught. When we begin to question some of the "but-that's-how-we've-always-done-its," we need support and critical feedback. I was lucky to have a friend and mentor to guide me. But, it seems to me, this kind of support should not, and does not need to, rely on luck.

We plunged in. I wanted students to think about major themes from the book, such as power, stereotyping, propaganda. I didn't want to do the shoebox dioramas again, so this time I turned to the kids for ideas. Some students chose the theme of propaganda and started working on a newspaper, the *Animal Farm Gazette*. Another group did a visual art project on the theme of stereotyping and discrimination ("Four legs good, two legs bad"). Others created a comic book in which they explored the theme of power and rewrote the ending of Orwell's book.

The room was often noisy and chaotic. At first this made me very uncomfortable; I felt out of control. Sometimes I would long for the good old days of the lecture-style class. I had felt in charge then. The room had been quiet and orderly. But then I would remember that being in control had actually been an illusion. I did not know what was going on in kids' heads. I did not know who was really listening and who wasn't, who was making sense of the lesson and who was not. Yes, the chaos was messier, but a lot more productive.

Even so, there were moments I was plagued with doubt: Is this a good use of our time? Are students really learning anything? Do the projects really demonstrate understanding? How are we building skills? Yet, through it all, some interesting things happened.

One group of seventh-grade girls decided to build a model of the farm. Maria was a good student but very quiet. She never raised her hand in class and looked pained every time I called on her. Beth missed school a lot and carried a huge chip on her shoulder.

Chavanne's main interest in school was boys. She rarely turned in homework, although she always had convincing excuses. All three girls, however, had gotten hooked on the book. Beth said, "This is the first book I have ever liked." They jumped into their project with enthusiasm. Maria brought in Fisher Price animals from home. Chavanne found a large piece of cardboard for the base, and they used other materials we had in the classroom—paint, clay, tissue paper, markers, etc.

They started coming in every day during recess to work on the model. They enjoyed working together and loved using their hands. I was thrilled to see these three working together and being invested in the project. But as I watched the fences go up and the farm house get constructed, I began to wonder: What does this show about their understanding? They did not have to read, much less understand *Animal Farm* to construct a nice-looking farmyard. Preschoolers did it all the time. What if a parent walked in here? "You build farmyards in the eighth grade?" What would I say? It was great to have them so engaged, but what had they actually learned? Those seeds, or more like boulders, of doubt rolled over me. I started hovering around the girls, listening in on their conversations.

"Let's put Napoleon [the chief pig] in the farmhouse to show how much he is becoming like a human."

"Yeah, let's put him in bed to show how he was breaking one of the Seven Commandments." [*No animal shall sleep in a bed.*]

"And what if we have another one of the smaller pigs bringing a teacup to show how the other animals were serving him and they weren't all equal?" [*All animals are equal, but some are more equal than others.*] I was amazed. Throughout all our class discussions, I had never heard any of the three girls articulate their understanding of the metamorphosis of the pigs.

About a week before the students presented their projects in class, I reported our progress to Steve. With great enthusiasm, I related the story of the girls and their farmyard. I recognized that the girls did not have the same sophisticated understanding of the political satire that the *Animal Farm Gazette* group did, but clearly they had grasped key themes in the book. I was excited about their progress, and mine.

"That's great," Steve responded. "So have you thought about how you are going to assess these projects?"

I was stopped cold. No, I had not thought about that at all. *You mean, the old A, B, C grade thing would not work?* I didn't need to ask that question. I recognized that the complexity of the students' work demanded an equally complex assessment. Just what was an A, anyway? Did the farmyard girls deserve an A, even though I knew they lacked a sophisticated understanding of the book? What about the students who had clearly understood the book but had fooled around in class and pulled their project together at the last minute? What about the boys who had worked hard on their video, but their novice camera skills undermined the quality of their final presentation? What about the group that allowed one student to carry most of the load? Should they all get the same grade? The more I saw of students' thinking, the harder it was to assess their work.

I also started to wonder about grades in general. What is the point of a grade? I thought about how I had felt about grades when I had been a student. I knew I was "good" at certain things because I got As. I was good at reading or writing, but I didn't know why. I knew I was "bad" at math as I had gotten a C in fourth grade. I had accepted these grades as a judgment about my innate abilities. Since I was a "bad" math student, I gave up trying. I barely passed algebra. Grades had defined me, and even the good ones had not given me any useful feedback about my work.

I realized that with the *Animal Farm* projects I actually valued much more than just the final product. There were many different criteria for success: Is there a clear exploration and understanding of theme? Is the work thoughtful and creative? Was the class presentation well-organized? Did you use your time well in class? If you worked in a team, did you contribute your fair share? Did you work well with your peers? Is the final product high-quality work?

This kind of feedback seemed much more useful to me than just a grade. Of course, it would have been way more useful to have developed these criteria *before* students started their projects, so they would have known what was important and how they were going to be assessed. I did realize this. But, in spite of my mistakes, I felt positive about taking the risk to try something different.

The *Animal Farm* projects took three weeks to complete. It was a time of high anxiety for me and for the students. They were not used to making their work public. Knowing they were going to have to present their work to the class raised the stakes. But on the day of the presentations, their excitement was palpable. Len stopped in and admired their work. Beth had invited her mother; I was touched that she wanted to show off her work to her mom. In the five years Beth had been at G&P, her mother had never once visited the school. But that day, she showed up with her new baby on her hip. The whole class gathered around the farmyard as Beth, Maria, and Chavanne explained all the decisions that had gone into the scenes they had created, from where the windmill was placed to the tiny teacup on the night table next to Napoleon. Everyone was very impressed. Beth beamed, and her mother glowed with pride.

There was another interesting outcome from these projects. Students in my other class got jealous. "Why can't we do that?" they complained. I had been teaching two different groups of seventh and eighth graders. One group I had only for English/language arts (ELA). The other group I had for both ELA and social studies. One or two days a week, this class had a double period: back-to-back ELA and social studies. "I have more time with the other kids," I explained. "We just don't have enough time to do this kind of work in one class period a day."

CHAPTER 5

MAKING THEATER, MAKING SENSE
1989–1991

In 1989, I decided to explore another strategy for engaging students—theater. I thought that if students could step into the shoes of a literary character or a historical figure, they would be able to not only develop a deeper understanding of that person or time, but they would also develop empathy. I'd had very little experience in theater myself. I had taken a class or two in college, but my crowning moment on stage was when I had played Long John Silver in our fifth-grade production of *Treasure Island*. I was a shy and insecure girl, so my mother was shocked when I strode out from behind the curtain in my gum boots and an old navy blazer of my dad's, booming, "Ahoy there, maties!" I had two more lines, clearly not a major part. But I never forgot the exhilaration of performing those three lines or my pride in the cardboard waves we had so laboriously painted. In fact, that production had been one of the highlights of my entire school career.

I had a feeling that using drama could be a way of drawing in my students, especially those who were not all that attentive or engaged in class discussions. We had read *The Outsiders* by S. E. Hinton, a popular book at the time about "in" groups and "out" groups, gangs, and identity. We used the outline of the novel to explore some issues that kids were dealing with in their own neighborhoods. Our "play" was about ten minutes long and was not particularly memorable. What was memorable, though, was how many of my students got excited and invested in the process. I had stuck my toe in the water of theater; I was now ready to jump into the deep end of the pool.

That summer, I saw a play about the Bread and Roses Strike of 1912 in Lawrence, Massachusetts. This famous strike had been a critical part of workers' efforts to win the eight-hour workday. Written by Carol Korty, a professor at Emerson College in Boston, *On The Line* captured many of the themes we were going to be exploring that next year: immigration, the Industrial Revolution, the labor and women's movements. The main character was a fourteen-year-old girl, part of a French Canadian family who worked at the textile mills. Marie-Claire defies her father, a first-generation immigrant who does not want his daughter to get caught up in a strike. So, generational tension and adolescent rebellion were also thrown into the fight for workers' rights. I thought it would be perfect for my seventh- and eighth-grade class.

I knew nothing about how to put on a full-scale play. But I knew plenty of people who did. First, I turned again to my friend and mentor from Project Zero, Steve Seidel. I told him my idea about doing *On The Line*. I also told him about my *Treasure Island* experience in fifth grade and how deeply that had affected me.

"What is your goal in doing this?" he asked.

"I want the students to inhabit the characters so they can know what it feels like to be in the shoes of a worker going out on strike, to know their anger, their hopes, their fears," I replied. "I want this period in history to come alive for them. Basically, I want them to have an experience that they will feel so proud of, they will remember it thirty years later."

"That's not too lofty a goal," Steve said, smiling.

Steve had a lot of experience in the theater world. In fact, I had first met him at a workshop that he was leading in playwriting. Before his move to Project Zero (which followed his work at South Boston High School), he had taught drama at an alternative high school in Cambridge. Steve was eager to help—this project dovetailed nicely with our work together on project-based learning and also his research on arts in education. But, even more importantly, Steve had a vested interest. His son Sam would be in my class that year.

I also turned to my official resources. The Cambridge Public Schools had a renowned Arts Department, headed at the time by Judith Contrucci. Every year, the high school's drama team (led by the legendary Gerry Speca) took one of the top prizes at the state-wide High School Drama Festival. I put in a call to Judith's office.

"I want to put on a play," I explained. "I've already chosen the play and have a copy of the script." (Carol Korty had sent it to me).

"But you have to pay royalties to the playwright if you are going to produce the play," Judith said.

Oh. I hadn't thought about that. I wasn't sure how I would come up with the money. I had no budget for this production. *Once again,* I fumed to myself, *administrators are putting up roadblocks.* From my first experience with the Social Studies Department at Medford High refusing to give me textbooks, to the Robert White School where I had to independently raise the money to support an arts initiative, I was used to the lack of support.

"I'll take it out of my budget," Judith said simply. I was shocked. Having someone say, "I will support you; that is why I am here," was, well, mind boggling.

Then she said, "You're going to need a director to work with you." I explained that I had Steve. But we quickly realized that even though he would be very generous with his time, we couldn't count on him to be there every day. After all, he had his own full-time job; he would be able to come once or twice a week, at best. So, Judith arranged for a graduate student in directing, Diana Moller from Emerson College, to come work with us three times a week. Along with Gretchen Peters, my assistant teacher, we had a dream team.

But I wanted the students to be in charge of shaping the play. We started by forming committees. We had a directors group, a set-design team, a costume committee, and musicians (the play had several songs). Everyone would have an acting part. I insisted on this. I knew I would never have volunteered for a part in *Treasure Island*; my teacher had forced me to do it. I was terrified to go on stage. But I had overcome that fear and delivered my three lines successfully, and it had been a huge victory for me. Everyone would have at least one line.

We also discussed the issue of race in the play. Historically, the people involved in the Lawrence strike were white. True, they came from different ethnic groups: French Canadians, Italians, Irish, and other European immigrants. But there were no specifically Black characters. However, our class was very multiracial, including European Americans, African Americans, Haitians, Puerto Ricans, and one Chinese American. *How would we deal with this?* students wanted to know. We all agreed that people see color. Would it be confusing to the audience if the family members were racially diverse? In the end, we decided that audience would adjust and they would ultimately see the character, not their color. (In the future, all our plays were cast without considering race, ethnicity, or skin color, except for one. That one play dealt directly with issues of race and racism; we all agreed that, for that reason, it was critical to cast people with historical accuracy.)

The student directors cast the play. But we didn't hold auditions. We instead asked every student to rank the parts they most wanted to play. So if you most wanted to be Marie-Claire, you would rank it #1, if your second choice was Mama Levesque, you would rank it #2, and so on through the entire list. In this way, we could see which students wanted big parts and who was looking for a minimal role. We explained that no one was guaranteed their first choice, but that we would do our best to give each person a role they would like. We then met as a committee, made a big grid with the names of the characters on one axis and the students' names on the other, and filled in the rankings. I explained to the student directors that two considerations would guide our choices: first, what role a student wanted to play; secondly, who they thought would do the best job playing the part.

Judith was aghast. "You can't cast a play this way!" she exclaimed. While being a staunch supporter of my project, she came from a traditional theater background. "You have to pick the most talented students for the top roles." But my goals were different from a typical play production. I wanted to build ownership; I also wanted to build community. To me, casting the usual way with auditions would encourage too much competition and I wanted to build cooperation and investment. Luckily, Judith just shook her head and let me do it my way.

The first round of decision making was easy, but it quickly got harder as we had to consider roles that multiple students had requested. Marie-Claire, the leading character, was one of these. Three different girls had requested that part, with notes penciled in the side of the form begging for it ("I really, really, really want this part!!!!"). After much discussion, someone proposed a radical solution: Why not cast all three of them? It was a very large part, with many, many lines to learn. We could divide up the scenes and they could rotate through the role.

"Won't that confuse the audience?" someone asked.

"What if they all have the exact same costume, and then take off the hat or a shawl and hand it to the next girl to take over?" someone else suggested.

I was impressed with the problem-solving ability of this crew.

The student directors made another interesting casting decision. I had stepped out of their meeting for a few minutes to check on the rest of the class. When I came back, I saw they had cast Carl in the role of the union organizer from the IWW (International Workers of the World). This character delivers a rousing speech from a soapbox, urging the workers to fight for their rights. It is a page-and-a-half-long monologue, one of the most challenging parts of the script.

"So, why did you guys cast Carl in that part?" I asked cautiously. Carl was a tall, slender eighth grader who was well liked in the class. He also had a serious speech impediment. I had never once heard Carl complete a sentence without struggling.

"We think he just looks the part," said one girl.

"Okay," I responded. "But what about the speech he has to give? It is pretty hard. Do you think he can handle it?"

"Of course!" they all responded. "He just needs help. We will be sure to give him a lot of help."

"Okay," I said. I didn't want to overrule my committee. But I wondered if we were setting Carl up for failure. Later that day, I went to talk to the school's speech therapist, Beth Noe, who had worked with Carl for years.

"Wow! That's fantastic that the kids did that!" she exclaimed. "What a vote of confidence for him."

"But do you think he can do it?" I pressed.

"I don't know," she said. "But I'm certainly going to do everything I can to help him be ready." It was settled; Carl would be the organizer.

The Set Design Team was also hard at work. A friend of Steve's was a set designer at Boston University. We reached out to him, and he invited us to visit him at his theater. He spoke to the kids about the importance of visual images that reinforce the themes of the play. He talked about highly complex sets and minimalist ones. He told them to think about shapes and color schemes.

"Have you ever been to Lawrence?" he asked.

We had been to visit the mills and the boarding houses where the mill girls had originally lived in Lowell, part of what is now the Lowell National Historical Park. But we hadn't been to Lawrence, nor had we gone with the goal of designing a set for a play. Maybe it was time to go back and look again.

We went to Lawrence, armed with sketch pads (no cellphones then), and looked at the massive brick factories and old tenement buildings. We also visited the American Textile History Museum in nearby Andover, where we could see the old power looms up close. One of the docents there was a man in his eighties. He had started working in the mills at the age of five. He was the oil boy, he explained to the kids. Because he was so little, he could run underneath the loom, with the shuttle flying back and forth at breakneck speed, to oil the machinery to keep it running smoothly. The kids were riveted to his story. We explained that we were doing a play about the Bread and Roses strike and he was thrilled. The museum offered to loan us two racks of bobbins for our set. I couldn't believe I was driving home with these historic pieces in my car.

One of the biggest challenges for the Set Design Committee was that Graham & Parks did not have an auditorium with a functional stage. We had a "gymatorium," a half-sized gym with a small stage that was used occasionally for whole-school assemblies. The Phys Ed facilities were already far under par and the P.E. teacher was not about to give up more of her space.

I went to Len to try to get him to pull rank, but he refused. "I don't know what to tell you. I'm not going to take away a teacher's classroom, and that is Pat's classroom. Look around the building for someplace else."

I didn't know what to do. Every inch of our building was being used. I considered looking outside the school, at possible community spaces we could use. Maybe the local library, a church, or the nearby community center. But none of those options was practical. So I went back to the school. I realized there was one space that was big enough and at times available—the school cafeteria. I approached Len again.

"What about lunch and breakfast?" he asked.

"We will work around that," I responded.

"How do Kenny and Buddy [our school custodians] feel about it?" he pushed.

"I will talk with them. I promise we will set up the cafeteria for them exactly as they need it. We will help with clean-up if necessary, and we will always put the tables back the way they are supposed to be."

"Okay," Len concurred. "As long as Kenny and Buddy are okay with it." The custodians were not thrilled with this plan, but they agreed to give it a try.

So now we had a space; we just had to find a way to transform a dark, dingy basement cafeteria into a theater.

Another parent in the class was an artist, and she offered to help us construct the set. Yet another parent volunteered to help with costumes. A colleague of Steve's from Project Zero was a talented musician; she led the minstrel group in learning old labor songs and the famous "Bread and Roses" anthem. Other parents came in to help students memorize lines. Our classroom was buzzing with activity, with young adolescents working, apprenticing, side by side with talented adults. At one point, one student turned to me and said, "This doesn't feel like school; this is like real work."

About two weeks before opening night, deep in the throes of production, Manny raised his hand at the beginning of class. "By the way, are we getting graded on this?" Again, the question of assessment stunned me. I had been so wrapped up in the work of the play, I hadn't thought about individual grades. I suddenly worried that I would lose their energy and commitment to making the play if they weren't going to be graded on it. This proved to be a groundless fear. But it has since made me wonder how much we try to motivate students with grades rather than with purposeful and meaningful work.

Being a teacher, I responded, "Of course you will be graded! This is school!" I wanted to move on so I could ponder this dilemma later, but Manny persisted.

"How?" he asked. "*How* are you going to grade us?"

"Uhhh, I'm not sure yet. But we will figure it out," I said.

I was stumped about how to grade students on a play. In the real world, the audience lets you know whether or not the play was a success. But, I knew I had different goals. Like with the *Animal Farm* projects, I realized that giving a letter grade did not honor the serious complexity of the work we were doing. But also as with the *Animal Farm* projects, I'd never done anything like this before. I wasn't sure what the important criteria were for this production. I decided to ask the kids. I set aside a classroom period for this discussion.

"Last week, Manny asked if I was grading you on the play. I've been thinking about it, and it seems that it is an important question for us to think about. Should we grade individuals' work, and if we do, *how*? How will we know if we have done a good job?" I asked them.

"The audience will clap for us," Gloria said.

"We'll be able to see it in their faces," Sam said.

"Our friends will come up to us afterward and tell us," Leah said.

"So as a group, our audience will let us know if we were successful or not. The audience is like our test. But what about individually? Should individuals be graded?" I was puzzling over this myself. So much of our work on the play had been done as a group. How could we measure individual contributions and growth? On what would we base our evaluations?

"I think so," said Xiamara. "I mean, I've worked really, really hard on this play, and I think I should get credit for that." Other heads nodded in agreement.

"But how can you grade us?" asked Leandro. "Should somebody get a better grade just because they are a better actor?"

"Maybe someone shouldn't be graded on how good they are, but more on how hard they work at it," said Ann. "You know, if they work hard at it, they are going to end up doing their best anyway and that's what's most important."

"How do we know someone is working hard? What do we want them to be working hard at?" I asked. "What does it take to do a good job as an actor, for example?" We started to brainstorm on the blackboard.

"You've got to know your lines."

"You have to know what the lines mean, too."

"You have to speak up so the audience can understand you."

"You can't crack up and 'corpse' your character."

"You should cooperate with the director."

After we generated this list, I then asked students to get into committees and define criteria for evaluation in a similar way for assistant directors, set designers, musicians, publicity agents, and costume designers. Each group considered what was necessary for it to accomplish its task successfully. The assistant directors came up with criteria such as:

- Did you read and understand your scene before rehearsals?
- Did you make good observations and take good notes on what was working and not working in your scene?
- Did you give extra support to actors who were struggling?

The set-design crew focused on other issues:

- Did you participate in the design of the set and offer creative ideas?
- Did you take initiative in solving technical problems?
- Did you help gather materials for the set?

Each committee generated its criteria, and then we met as a whole to share. After carefully reviewing all the suggestions, the class members agreed that we had clear and fair criteria for evaluating individual work in the play. Evaluation did not depend on natural talent or prior experience. We also realized that our list of criteria could serve as a guide for each student. For example, as an actor practiced lines at home, she could ask herself, *Do I really know what my lines mean?* A crew member for the set could think about how much initiative he was taking in solving tech problems. An assistant director could reflect on the way she supported an actor.

At first, I had been frustrated with myself for not having thought about Manny's grading question in advance. I thought I had learned that lesson from the *Animal Farm* experiment: how important it was to have clear goals and criteria before launching into a major project. Maybe because it was such a different kind of project, I didn't think to apply that lesson. But maybe I couldn't have done it, even if I'd thought of trying. Having never produced a play before, I had no idea what it entailed. I didn't even know what a director did. I did not understand all the thinking and work that went into designing a set. I wasn't totally sure how to articulate standards for acting.

Opening night was getting closer and tensions were building. My anxiety level was soaring, and that probably didn't help anything. At an after-school rehearsal the day before the show, emotions erupted. I don't remember what sparked it, but one boy got so angry he punched a girl in the face. She ended up at the hospital; he ended up suspended. We had just lost two of our actors and feelings were roiling. I tried to calm the kids down.

"What are we going to do without Jordan and Katia?" they wailed.

"We need some volunteers, someone to just read their lines," I responded. "We explain to the audience that there had to be last-minute stand-ins, and they go on stage with the script. It will be fine. The show must go on."

That same afternoon after all the kids had left, a big truck showed up and some burly guys carried in stage lights, poles, and hundreds of feet of cables, and dropped it all off in the cafeteria. Judith had promised stage lights would be delivered the day before the show.

"Don't you set them up?" I asked incredulously.

"Nope," they said, and left. I had no clue what to do. So I sat down on the floor and cried. Then I called Steve.

Steve knew what to do. He and I worked until eleven o'clock that night stringing the lights. When we hit the switch and all the lights went on, I was elated. We were actually going to pull this off.

The next night, the show did go on. The backdrop banners of brown paper with black-line drawings of brick buildings with multi-paned windows and mill gears hid the cafeteria's white cinderblock walls, and more brown paper painted like floorboards covered the black-and-white tile floor. The precious bobbin racks were in place, and an old wooden table covered with a red-and-white-checked cloth defined the kitchen of the Levesque home.

The audience filled the cafeteria, sitting on the aluminum folding chairs we had so carefully lined up. Except for one special guest whom we had to sneak in under cover. Carl, the eighth-grade IWW organizer, had worked diligently on his lines with Beth, the speech therapist. She was in the audience, there to encourage him. But he had banned one person from coming to his performance. Carl lived alone with his grandmother. I didn't know what had happened to his parents, I just knew his grandmother was his only family. He was absolutely adamant that she not come to see him. I think he was terrified he would stumble and he did not want to embarrass her. But we weren't about to let her miss this. So, once the cast had gathered "behind stage," i.e., in the hallways outside the cafeteria, we snuck her in where he couldn't see her.

I welcomed everyone to the show, explained how we had been learning about the Industrial Revolution, immigration, and the fight for better working conditions. The play was a culmination of our studies. Then, the lights dimmed for a minute, the actors took their places on the stage, the lights came back up, and, in spite of all the crises and chaos, the show began. There were a few dropped lines, some missed cues, but all was going well. When the lights came up on Scene Five and Carl stepped up to his soapbox, Beth and I moved to the edge of our seats. There were many students, teachers, and parents in the audience who knew Carl and were silently urging him on.

"Stand over here! J-j-j-j-join yyyyour—" he stammered.

Beth whispered, "Start over."

He took a deep breath and started again. "Stand over here! Join your neighbors! Fill the whole common! Stand close together with your working brothers and sisters!" and he took off into the rest of his speech without a hitch. I looked at Beth. Tears were streaming down her face. I saw his grandmother in the back, her face buried in tissues. The whole audience, like an inspired crowd of workers in Lawrence, erupted at the end of his speech. He beamed.

We did two more shows after that, and they went well too. We were all on such a high. Carl's grandmother invited us to her three-room apartment for a cast party. We piled into her living room, sitting all over the furniture and on the floor, ate her Swedish meatballs and homemade brownies, and watched a video of the performance. We laughed and cheered at each scene, and the small room was filled with pride and, can I say it? Love. I had not anticipated that. I had wanted my students to engage in learning history in a different way. But they had learned all sorts of other things too—about the theater and about each other, about hard work and overcoming obstacles, about working together, even when they didn't always like each other. There was such a deep feeling of community, of connection, of accomplishment. We had gotten through the crises, and with blood, sweat, and tears, literally, we had made something beautiful together.

In the days after the play, I asked the kids both to assess their own growth using the criteria we had developed together and to reflect on the whole project. I asked them: "What did you learn about yourself? About your class? About theater? About the life of mill workers?"

I read over each evaluation before writing to students with my own observations of their work. While I also attached a grade to it, the criteria provided concrete focal points as evidence for the grade. But, to me, the students' own reflections about their learning were the most powerful and meaningful part of the assessment. One seventh grader wrote:

> I feel like I know my class much better than I did before we started the play. It's not so much that I've made more friends but that I understand people better. I was also amazed at how well some people did overcoming problems while working on the play. . . . Although I think we could have been taught more information about Lawrence in a shorter time, I feel what we were taught will stick in my mind, because all the time I spent on the play was what I considered hard-working, quality time. I learned a lot of kids in my class had talent in many things and when someone puts their mind to it, they can overcome a lot. . . . I really liked the feeling of always looking forward to school and looking forward to being with my teachers and classmates even when it wasn't school time. I was glad there was something that really wanted to make me sacrifice other things in my life to work on something for school. I think it's going to be hard to go back to a more regular school curriculum.

Some who had worked very hard on the production spoke of the pride they felt in their achievement and the reward they felt for taking risks. One student who had chosen a small acting part lamented that she had not had the courage to go for a bigger role—but she would next time. Another student spoke about how he did not feel totally comfortable taking part in the post-production celebration because he knew he had not contributed as much as he could have.

But my favorite reflection came from Carl. He wrote, "I felt like a knight in shining armor and that I could do anything!"

I was hooked. Play-making would become a hallmark of my classroom for years to come.

Once again, the other class started grumbling. Why did those kids get to do a play and we didn't? Once again, I explained that it was a matter of time. I had one group of students for two subjects, so I had twice as much time with them, and I could bring the ELA and social studies units together. But the more I thought about how powerful the play experience was, the more I wondered about it. Why couldn't we organize our classes so all kids could have a more integrated curriculum? Who was stopping us from doing it?

CHAPTER 6

RECONSTRUCTION
1991–1994

I raised the question with my team. What if we reorganized our junior high program so everyone could have a humanities class?

We'd had seventy-five students divided between three homeroom classes, but now we had a full-time science teacher. If Laura, our science teacher, was willing to take on a homeroom, we could have four homeroom groups and thus create four humanities classes taught by two teachers. However, science at that time was considered a "special" subject—Laura was not obligated to shoulder the duties of a homeroom teacher. But, if she would agree, it would work. It would mean each teacher would have an extra class to teach, but each class would have fewer students, so you could give each child more attention. We all agreed this made more sense, including Laura, who was willing to give it a try.

To be clear, many teachers would not have agreed to this. Homeroom teachers have extra responsibilities: taking attendance, walking their class to and from lunch, having recess duty, coordinating report cards, connecting with parents, and other jobs. It would have been easy, and fully legitimate, for Laura to refuse to take this on. Instead, she said, "Just don't tell anyone in the science department." She was willing to work outside the box, like the rest of the team, to better meet the needs of her students.

"What if the district starts sending more kids?" someone wondered. "They will say we have four homerooms so we should take up to a hundred students."

Someone else argued back, "We don't have any more teachers or resources than any other school, though. We just want to organize things in a different way." We decided to give it a try, and keep it on the down-low.

We also decided that we wanted to design our own schedule. Scheduling is tremendously important in schools and is usually done by principals. It can be highly complex, like piecing together a thousand-piece jigsaw puzzle, and challenging to meet everyone's needs. Administrators steel themselves when making the school schedule. No matter what they do, someone is going to be unhappy. Most teachers want to have their students first thing in the morning, when the kids are relatively fresh. But if your P.E. teacher is available then, somebody has to go to gym; not everyone can teach math or reading at the beginning of the day. Often, principals would fill in their specialists' classes first (art, music, P.E., etc.) and then everyone would work around that. In fact, at least in Cambridge, specialists' schedules drove everyone else's day.

Our team believed, though, that the schedule should be organized by what was best for the learning needs of the students. We knew that, as part of a larger school community, we couldn't have everything we wanted, but what would it look like if we *could* have it all? Which parts were essential to our academic mission and which were we willing to negotiate? We wanted to build our schedule out from the academic core. We wanted each academic discipline to have an hour-long class: math, science, ELA, and social studies. We combined ELA and social studies into a two-hour humanities block, and scheduled math and science classes back-to-back so they could also integrate curriculum more easily. So we needed two two-hour blocks for academics. Specialist classes would also be scheduled in a block so the team could meet together at least twice a week, if not more. We wanted fifteen to twenty minutes for a morning meeting, a common practice in younger grades but less so at the seventh- and eighth-grade level.

We took our draft schedule to Len. He laughed at us. "You want everything your way!" he exclaimed. "What about everybody else?"

"Well, we have to coordinate four different classes in a way that none of the other teachers do. They have self-contained classrooms; they have a lot more flexibility than we do," we argued. "We know we can't get everything we want, but we have identified key priorities."

Eventually, Len and Isabel decided to open up the scheduling process. This could have been a Pandora's box, but they were willing to try something different. They asked each team to identify their priorities for their schedules and to select a representative to attend a day-long planning session to hammer out a plan. The school provided substitutes, as this happened during the school day. A local company offered to sponsor our "retreat" by providing space, audiovisual equipment (an overhead projector), and food (very, very important to teachers).

In the end, we did not get the perfect schedule. But we got a schedule that put academics at the center. We did not get 2-hour blocks, but we got 110-minute ones (so, math and science each had 55 minutes). By integrating ELA and social studies into humanities and having math and science back-to-back and next door to each other, we were able to cut down significantly on transition time between classes, so there was, in fact, more teaching time. We did not get twenty-minute homeroom periods for morning meetings, but we got an extra ten minutes. We lost out to the primary grades on having the kids first thing in the morning, but because we were able to keep our block scheduling, we were okay with that. We also understood why it was important for the younger students to have their literacy blocks early. And, in turn, because of the negotiation process, the other teachers better understood our needs, too.

In reflecting on this process, it strikes me again how important it was that our school leaders both provided meeting time for our team and supported us in trying new things. In addition to organizing the schedule so the team could meet at least twice a week during the school day, our Chapter 188 Drop-out Prevention grant funded the junior high team to meet for three to four days in the summer. Those meetings were enormously important. We set the agenda. Len trusted us to figure out what we needed to discuss. We were not being told to implement some initiative coming from on high. It was not always easy and we did not always get along. None of us had particularly strong facilitation skills (except Isabel, the staff developer, who was not at all the meetings), so we could sometimes go off on tangents or spend an hour talking about something that should have taken ten minutes. But, without the pressures of the school day, we had more space to think together about our practice.

It is important to note that we lost funding for our summer meetings after a few years. When Len told us he had no money to pay the team that summer, we said, "Bummer. But we still have to meet! We will just meet on our own time." And the team continued to meet for two to three days every summer. Furthermore, we found our in-school meetings weren't frequent or long enough to deal with all the business we needed to deal with. So we agreed to meet every morning for fifteen minutes before the students arrived. We would gather around the coffee pot in Laura's science room and talk about any number of things: an upcoming field trip, an incident the day before with a student, coordinating progress reports, a parent complaint, upcoming projects, etc. And if we didn't have any school business to discuss, we talked about movies and books we were reading. But we found these voluntary meetings to be essential to things running smoothly on the third floor of the G&P School.

It was during the in-school (not the fifteen-minute morning check-ins) and summer meetings that the team began to reflect on other parts of our junior high program. We read various kinds of research related to middle schools and young adolescents. One article from the Center for Early Adolescence (CEA) focused on the unique developmental needs of young adolescents.[1] We decided to use the seven different "needs" identified by the researchers to assess our own junior high program. They included the need for physical activity, competence and achievement, self-definition, creative expression, positive social interaction, structure and clear limits, and meaningful participation. We explored each of these needs, discussed if and how we were providing for it, and brainstormed ways to better meet the criteria. For example, regarding the importance of physical activity, the researchers stated:

> Early adolescents need lots of opportunities to exercise their growing bodies and explore their emerging large and small muscle capacities. . . . They need ample quantities of nutritious food to support their physical growth and increased activity levels.

How did the G&P junior high meet young adolescents' need for physical activity? Our students had physical education (P.E.) twice a week. Unlike most junior high programs, they had a fifteen-minute recess. But was that enough? If we were asking them to sit for 55–110 minutes at a time, did we need to give them more of a chance to move around? Were there ways to incorporate more movement into an actual lesson, like making a human graph or physically moving to opposite sides of a classroom in a debate? Was our class-transition time of three minutes really adequate?

What about "ample quantities of nutritious food?" Our students had the latest lunch period of the school; maybe we needed to introduce a snack time?

The "need for competence and achievement" seemed central to any rigorous academic program. According to the Center, "It is common for young adolescents to feel self-conscious and unsure of their abilities during this period of rapid growth. As they encounter more and more opportunities to connect with the real world, they need matching opportunities to demonstrate to themselves and to others that they can do things well. They need opportunities to learn and develop new skills and understandings related to all areas of life."

We were well aware of our students' feeling self-conscious and unsure of themselves. We recognized that the dominant teenage culture was not celebrating academic achievement. In fact, it had seemed that some kids were embarrassed to be seen as competent. No one wanted to be a "nerd." One day, standing in the hallway with Steve, he turned to me and said, "Kathy, how do we make it cool to be smart?" We wanted to change that, but were unsure how.

We considered the need for positive social interaction. Our students moved throughout their day in the same group. Were there ways we could expand their opportunities for social interaction without their losing their sense of a home base? We decided to restructure our classes. We would have two seventh-grade and two eighth-grade homerooms. Each homeroom was split into an A and a B group (just as labels, not reflecting any kind of tracking). We would mix a 7A and an 8A group for humanities. Math and science classes would have two sections of each grade-level homeroom; i.e., my 7B group and the other humanities teacher's 7B group. Students went to specialists by homeroom. This meant that students, while maintaining a core group (e.g., ten fellow classmates in a 7A section), also mixed with at least thirty other students, thus expanding opportunities for social engagement.

We were pretty confident about providing structure and clear limits, and felt that our students had good opportunities for self-definition, not only through our peer-mediation program, student council, and community meetings but in our curriculum as well. The Center emphasized the importance of giving students opportunities "to reflect on their gender, race, culture, religion, and nationality. They need opportunities to reflect on their place in their family, community, and country. They need to participate in experiences that help them discover their interests, talents, and abilities and shape their attitudes, beliefs, values, and character."

The curriculum Facing History and Ourselves was a powerful exploration of identity and social responsibility, but students were also expanding "their interests, talents and abilities" in math and science. In math, for example, a favorite unit was the bridge project. Applying their math skills to real-world problems, students collaborated in teams to see who could design and build the strongest bridge (model-size, of course). We discovered many budding engineers. More importantly, students discovered in themselves an interest they hadn't known they had.

We saw some opportunities for creative expression and meaningful participation. Yes, students had art and music classes once a week, and a concert and an art exhibition once a year—but was that enough? The play had been a big step toward fulfilling both of these criteria, but how else could we infuse our curriculum with opportunities to be creative and participate in real-world events? Steve introduced a "Math and Art" class. There the kids produced beautiful geometric designs. In science, Laura asked students to keep a spring journal, in which they carefully observed and drew the changes happening in the natural world around them.

We didn't have all the answers, but these discussions got us thinking, both as individual teachers in our own classrooms and as a group, about building a strong junior high program that was rooted in meeting our students' developmental needs. We set about doing the easy things on our list (like making time for snack) and set some priorities for what else we wanted to improve on.

Another important influence on the development of our junior high program was the Coalition of Essential Schools (CES). This organization was started in 1984 by Ted Sizer, a leading educational reformer and author of *Horace's Compromise*. The coalition identified nine principles (a tenth was added later) to guide the development of a strong secondary-level education. These included:

- learning to use one's mind well
- less is more; depth over coverage
- goals apply to all students
- personalization
- student-as-worker, teacher-as-coach
- demonstration of mastery
- a tone of decency and trust
- commitment to the entire school
- resources dedicated to teaching and learning
- democracy and equity[2]

The coalition suggested first developing a vision of what a graduate of one's school should look like—before developing the school program. If you know what kind of students you want to send out into the world—what your key values are—you build a program that supports those goals. Again, the team used our planning time to dive into this discussion. We made lists and lists of all the things we expected a graduate of Graham & Parks to be: a good reader, a good writer, competent in math, engaged with the natural world, able to develop a hypothesis and test it out, a critical thinker, kind, compassionate, hardworking, active in one's community, tolerant of differences, active for social justice, a life-long learner, persevering, and so on. But this list was way too long. We knew we had to narrow it down to just four or five criteria. After much debate, synthesizing, and wordsmithing, we finally arrived at these goals for G&P students:

- To have genuine **curiosity**: to ask good questions and always push your own thinking forward;
- To take **ownership** of your knowledge and learning: to pursue your own understanding rather than receive information;
- To do **high-quality work**: to push yourself to the highest possible standard through revision and attention to detail;
- To be a **critical thinker**: to see the complexity of issues, look for multiple perspectives, make connections, and always ask *why*;
- To be a **compassionate and active member of your community** and society: to care about and help others, to treat all people with respect regardless of differences, and to seek ways to contribute and improve our society.

We typed up these goals, made big posters, and hung them up in every classroom.

But we also started talking about our responsibility as teachers in helping students to meet these five goals. If we expected students to be genuinely curious, for example, how would we nurture that in our classrooms? Did it mean we had to conduct our lessons differently? Teachers are used to asking lots of questions, and students are used to giving answers. And not just answers, but correct answers. Was a culture of correctness killing off our students' curiosity? How could we shift that? How could we make it safe for students to ask questions when they didn't understand something? Even more, how could we encourage students to wonder about why the Pythagorean theorem works or how plants turn sun into energy—to think at a different level? We wanted students to go beyond just parroting back information to the teacher; we wanted them to think deeply about their learning.

If we wanted our students to do high-quality work, we needed both to give them time to do it and to teach the skills of revision. I had discovered from my work with the Boston Writing Project how important honest feedback is for a writer. I also discovered that, while adults could easily learn how to give constructive critique, this did not come naturally to young teenagers. I struggled to get my students to give useful, specific, compassionate suggestions to their peers. I started to wonder whether kids were capable of this at all. And then I met Ron Berger.

Ron was a sixth-grade teacher from Shutesbury, Massachusetts. I initially met him when he came to observe my class at the suggestion of Steve Seidel from Project Zero. Ron was pursuing a master's degree at the Harvard Graduate School of Education (HGSE) and had wanted a chance to visit other teachers' classrooms. We later became more acquainted when we were both on a conference panel about project-based learning at HGSE. The day of the conference, I arrived early at the Gutman Library Conference Center and saw a number of extraordinary drawings of architectural design displayed on the walls around the large room. I thought to myself, *Oh, the Harvard Design School must have just had a conference here. These are amazing!*

It turned out that these "dream-house" designs were done by Ron's sixth-grade students. In his presentation at the conference, he shared slides of these spectacular final products.

"You are probably thinking that these are extraordinary students, right?" asked Ron. "Probably a 'gifted and talented' class?"

Everyone nodded. These students' work was nothing like typical sixth graders.

"Well, you are wrong," Ron said. "These are just normal, ten- and eleven-year-olds who live in a rural community in Western Mass. In fact, some of these children have special needs. But I don't think you could pick out which ones."

Then he showed us a student's first draft. Ah, that looks more like a sixth grader's idea of an ideal home. But then Ron showed a second draft. And a third. And a fourth. And then, finally, the fifth and last. We could see a gradual transformation, increasing attention to detail, and a level of craftsmanship that was amazing. How did this happen? Everyone wanted to know.

"I teach them," Ron responded simply. "I show them models of beautiful work. I teach them drafting skills. I teach them what to look for, how to give useful feedback, and how to take feedback. It takes time. But the habits these students learn through this project are invaluable. No, they are not all going to become architects, if any. But they are learning that quality work takes quality time."

I made a beeline for Ron when the panel finished. "I want to visit your school," I said.

"You are welcome anytime," he responded warmly.

We set a date and soon I found myself driving the two hours to Shutesbury Elementary School. The school was a small, one-level building with lovely grounds backing up to woods. Very different from Graham & Parks. But as soon as I entered the building, I could see that our schools shared a common philosophy toward children and learning.[3] Students' work was hanging everywhere. Kids were in the hallways working on all sorts of different projects. Two of Ron's sixth-grade students gave me a tour of the school. My guides described the work at each grade level with knowledge and pride. Then we went into Ron's class.

His room looked more like a designer workspace. Students were spread around the room, some working very intently on their own, others in small groups gathered around various tables, looking at a piece of work together. I went over to listen in. I don't remember the exact conversation, but it went something like this:

"Wow, I really like your idea for . . . ," one student said.

"Yes, that is so cool how you did that!" said another.

"Why did you put this here like that?" asked another.

"I'm thinking about trying to . . . What do you think of that?" asked the student designer.

"You could try . . . ," said another.

"Or you could think of it this way . . ." said another.

"Great ideas! Thanks. I think I'll try . . ."

I thought I was witnessing an adult critique session. Kids gave authentic praise. They also gave each other thoughtful, useful, constructive feedback. I saw another student ask for help from a peer ("Can you show me how you do your lettering? I really like it and I want to do mine better").

I turned to Ron. "How did you get them to do this?" I asked incredulously.

He laughed. "Remember, this is April. They didn't come in in September being able to do this. I spent a lot of time modeling, practicing, doing critique sessions together, critiquing our critiquing! But the kids could see that their work got better when they got good feedback. They bought in."[4]

I was never as successful as Ron in teaching kids how to give and take critique. I'm not sure I had the courage to fully take the time needed for students to really internalize those skills. But I did try. I decided to start the school year in humanities with an art project. Students had to design a cover for their reading-response journal (RRJ) that would show something about them as a reader. I thought it might be easier for kids to understand how to improve something visual, like making a line straighter by using a ruler or erasing stray pencil marks, rather than jumping into something a little more abstract for them, like voice or word choice in a personal narrative. My ultimate goal wasn't to design beautiful RRJ covers (although that was a great byproduct) but to learn how to offer and receive constructive feedback.

Students learned that creating something meaningful took time, critique, and perseverance. Doing multiple drafts of an important project became the norm. Students would proudly announce how many drafts they had done. We saved all drafts so their peers, parents, and others could see the progress they had made over time. Writing in a reflection at the end of eighth grade, one student talked about his picture book on the history of baseball, which took him eight or nine drafts:

> [My favorite project] I did in junior high was my picture book. I liked it so much because I worked so hard on it and in the end I had a great project. I also got the best feeling of accomplishment which you get after working very hard at something for a long time and completing it. This . . . is one of the greatest feelings I have ever had.

I remember one G&P grad coming back to visit and saying indignantly, "Do you know that at the high school they only expect you to do one draft? That's ridiculous! How can you do anything good in just one draft!"

Steve B. was the master of "owning" your work. This seemed particularly important in math. He felt that if a student had simply memorized a formula, s/he did not really "own" it. "Why does that formula work?" he would ask. "If you can't explain it to me, or even more importantly to Kathy, you don't really understand it." (I was the gold standard for math explanations. If I could understand it, anybody could.) He regularly asked students to "Explain It to Me"; and, every Thursday night, students wrote a TW3 in their math journals ("That Was the Week That Was"). In this weekly reflection, students would articulate what they understood and what they didn't.

"I don't really own the quadratic formula yet. Do you start with the X axis or the Y axis?" an eighth grader might write.

This understanding was the essence of owning your work.

Our five G&P goals for our graduating eighth graders had major implications not just for our instruction and pedagogy but for our junior high curriculum as well. If we wanted to encourage students to be curious; to wonder about their world; if we wanted students to be critical thinkers and own their knowledge; if we wanted to commit ourselves to doing high-quality work; if we cared about engaging in our community in authentic ways, both in school and beyond, we had to slow down. We had to "cover" less if we wanted students to learn more. The Coalition explained its guiding principle, "less is more," in this way:

> The school's goals should be simple: that each student master a limited number of essential skills and areas of knowledge. While these skills and areas will, to varying degrees, reflect the traditional academic disciplines, the program's design should be shaped by the intellectual and imaginative powers and competencies that the students need, rather than by "subjects" as conventionally defined. The aphorism "less is more" should dominate: curricular decisions should be guided by the aim of thorough student mastery and achievement rather than by an effort to merely cover content.

As an alternative school, we had considerable autonomy over our curriculum. So we felt we could make decisions about what "less is more" meant to us. This was particularly relevant in science and social studies. Given that no one had ever given me any specific curriculum to teach, I was comfortable with making curriculum choices. What was more challenging was figuring out what was essential to cover in depth and what was less relevant.

I'm not sure how I first learned about "essential questions." It could have been through Steve Seidel, Project Zero, and the Teaching for Understanding project, or it could have been through my own reading of Grant Wiggins and Jay McTighe, the authors of *Understanding by Design*. Or it could have come from somewhere else. But, in the early 1990s, people I knew were talking about "guiding" and "essential" questions. These questions helped to identify what was really important for students to know and understand. It helped teachers to make decisions about where to "go deep" and design curriculum that went beyond just a basic level of knowing information to being able to think critically about a complex issue.

Consider an example from McTighe and Wiggins' book *Essential Questions*:

"What event started World War I?" versus, "Is there ever a 'just' war?"

Which question would trigger students' interest? Which question would lead to an understanding of the complex causes behind World War I? Which question would provoke debate about war in general, not just World War I? Which question would you rather explore?

When I recently looked up "essential questions" on the internet, there were over 3,200,000 results. So, I guess this framework has caught on. One site said, "Need some essential questions? You've come to the right place—here are over 100 essential questions examples by category." I can understand why people would look for a list like this. Essential questions are not easy to develop. It takes a deep understanding of the subject matter as well as a good understanding of the students who will be in front of you to write a good question. The first questions I came up with were not particularly strong. But I think it was important to think through not only what was important to teach my students but also why it mattered, to them or to anybody.

Like with many other new ideas I was trying out, I got excited about this approach. I wrote up my four or five questions on a big poster, pinned it to the wall above the chalkboard (yes, chalkboard: this was the 1990s), and promptly forgot about them. As we were wrapping up the unit, I realized that I had not once referenced any of the questions. I had used them for my own thinking, but I'd forgotten to use them to spark the students' thinking.

I decided, *Better late than never*, and asked the class to write a reflection on the unit using the questions. Their answers were very thoughtful, and I wondered just how much deeper their thinking might have been if these questions had been woven in throughout the lessons. The next year, I had the presence of mind to not only introduce the questions but also to refer to them regularly. The questions came alive and helped us build our understanding of the content. The conversations we had and student engagement in general were significantly improved.

A number of years later, I would work with some other middle schools around designing curriculum, including using essential questions. A group of veteran sixth-grade teachers were trying to develop a more project-based approach to their study of ancient civilizations. It was our first day together, and I asked them a simple and sincere question: "Why do you teach sixth graders about Ancient Egypt?"

They responded, "Oh, the kids love all the mummy stuff."

"But," I persisted, "why do you think it is important for them to learn about that? Why Egypt? Why not other ancient civilizations? Why should they learn about ancient civilizations at all?"

They looked at me somewhat blankly. "Because it is what we're supposed to teach," one of them answered.

"But why?" I pushed. "If we don't know why we teach about this particular history, how will the kids learn what is essential about understanding it? Plus, there is so much to learn about! We could teach a course on Ancient Egypt for a year. How can we make good decisions about what to teach and not to teach?"

"We don't know why Ancient Egypt. It's what we've always done," another teacher said.

"So let's think about why you think this is important," I suggested. "Let's take some time to talk about what you know about Egypt and why American sixth graders should study this in the twenty-first century." We spent the next two hours mapping out what they knew, what they thought was essential, what was relevant to their students and why, and a few essential questions that would guide the curriculum.

"My brain is hurting," said one of the teachers. "But I'm kind of excited to be doing this with the kids this year! It makes so much more sense to me."

The other guiding principle of the Coalition that we particularly embraced was "Student as worker, teacher as coach." When I first heard this, I knew immediately what it meant. I harkened back to my lesson on the Fourth Amendment of the Bill of Rights on search and seizure. I had spent so much time learning about the Fourth Amendment to prepare for that class. I learned about why the Founders cared so much about protection from unreasonable searches and seizures. I studied all sorts of Supreme Court cases related to it. I considered why this was an important issue for teenagers. And I tried to come up with a way to engage them in thinking about the complexities of balancing individual rights and communal safety. I had worked hard. What had my students done? Not much. They sat by passively while I shared a processed version of my own learning. What if I had created an environment where they did the work, with my guidance?

I thought about how I had learned to bake. My mother did not give me a lecture on baking. She invited me to make chocolate chip cookies with her. I really wanted to eat those cookies, so I had an intrinsic motivation to learn. She guided me through measuring the flour, leveling the top carefully with a knife. She showed me how to crack an egg, and then let me crack the next one. She didn't get mad or discouraged if I got a little shell in the egg whites. She just fished it out. She demonstrated how to cream the butter and sugar together and then let me try it. She modeled how to gradually mix in flour and then let me finish the job. She was coaching me and I was becoming a baker, a life-long baker at that. Could a classroom work in a similar way?

The Coalition principles of "student as worker, teacher as coach" and "less is more" actually work in tandem. Having students take a more active role in their own learning also entails slowing down, covering less but going deeper to build real understanding and ownership.

In the mid-1990s, we felt empowered to make these choices about curriculum and instruction. But that was about to change.

CHAPTER 7

REAL ASSESSMENT
1993 – 1997

In 1993, the state legislature passed the Massachusetts Education Reform Act (MERA). After ten years of Proposition 2½, Massachusetts schools, especially in poorer communities with large immigrant populations, were suffering. In the early 1990s, a lawsuit had been brought against the Commonwealth by a coalition of groups which included the National Association for the Advancement of Colored People (NAACP), the Massachusetts Teachers Association (MTA), and Citizens for Public Schools (CPS) for more equitable funding.

In exchange for an overhaul in the way that schools were funded and a significant increase in actual dollars, especially to poorer urban and rural districts, the MERA "required the establishment of high standards that each student would be expected to meet, a statewide assessment system designed to measure progress towards that goal, and an accountability system to hold schools and districts responsible for progress in meeting the new standards."[1] This came to be known as the "Grand Bargain."

There was tremendous debate throughout the state over Ed Reform. While many people welcomed the desperately needed increase in school funding, others worried what the real impact would be of the "accountability" side of the bargain. The Massachusetts Business Alliance for Education (MBAE) and politicians in the state legislature—not educators—had designed these reforms. So people were cautious. Who would design and approve the "high standards?" What would the statewide assessment actually look like? What did it mean to "hold schools and districts accountable?"

My colleagues and I valued the freedom we had in developing our lessons, so we were initially wary about the upcoming changes. We were encouraged, though, when the state's Department of Education (DOE) released its "Common Core of Learning,"[2] identifying broad educational goals, in which:

> [s]tudents graduating from Massachusetts' schools will be confident and capable lifelong learners with well-developed study and work habits, a strong understanding of fundamental concepts and current issues in the essential subject areas, and curious, with a love of learning and pride in a job well done. . . . Upon graduation, all students must be able to:
>
> (1) organize for learning and work; (2) acquire, integrate, and apply essential knowledge; (3) be skillful and responsive communicators; (4) read, write, speak, listen, and observe effectively; (5) appreciate visual arts, music, theater, and movement; (6) communicate in a second language; (7) use technologies and media; (8) be clear and creative thinkers; (9) define complex problems and generate ideas; (10) analyze complex problems and test ideas; (11) solve complex problems and apply ideas; (12) be responsible and active contributors to their communities; (13) understand the rights and responsibilities of citizenship; (14) plan for economic success; and (15) demonstrate personal and social responsibility.

It seemed to us that this reflected a desire to graduate well-rounded, active, and educated citizens who were prepared to participate in their communities. After developing the Common Core of Learning, the DOE convened several groups of educators across the state to develop discipline-based frameworks. Math, science/technology, world languages, the arts, and health were approved by the end of 1995. The English/language arts frameworks, which was a little more controversial, passed in 1997. History and social studies proved to be much more contentious. It, too, was approved initially in 1997, but was revised in 2003.[3]

The Massachusetts Education Reform Act did not just impact curricula. It mandated a range of other reforms, including extending the school day and school year, exploring a commitment to ensuring early childhood education for three- and four-year-olds, and increasing professional development for teachers. Some involved structural and organizational changes, such as moving toward more "site-based" management. Each school would establish a school council that would include the principal, teachers, parents, community members, and, at the high school level, even students. This council would have hiring and firing power, a critical shift in control away from the districts. Another part of the Education Reform Act involved the opening of charter schools.

The biggest, most consequential reform of MERA involved implementing the Massachusetts Comprehensive Assessment System (MCAS). When teachers first heard about MCAS, we took seriously that there would be a *comprehensive* assessment *system*. But it turned out to simply be a high-stakes standardized test. If a student in a public high school did not pass the MCAS by the end of high school, they would not be able to graduate with a diploma. Furthermore, if, based on its students' MCAS scores, a district were found to be "underperforming," the state could take it into receivership.

There was tremendous pushback against the MCAS, even before 1998 when it was first administered to fourth, eighth, and tenth graders. Teachers and parents around the state protested the idea of judging schools and students on one test. People were critical of the amount of time the test took away from teaching. They pointed out how flawed standardized testing has been found to be, especially the ways its cultural bias discriminates against poorer students, English-language learners, and people of color. (The most famous example of this was the year when fourth graders were asked to write a personal narrative about how they would spend a "snow day." There hadn't been any snow days for a couple of years, so a number of immigrant students had never experienced snow. Many of the children were baffled by this writing prompt.) They warned that teachers would be forced to "teach to the test" and forecast a narrowing of the curriculum.

Many parents, students, and teachers from G&P were active in these protests. We had serious discussions about boycotting the test. But, even in light of our many criticisms, we failed to realize at that time just how much these tests would dramatically remake the landscape of schools. Even at the Graham and Parks Alternative Public School. But again, I'm getting ahead of myself.

At the same time that the state was beginning to implement its Education Reform Act, I blissfully continued to work with Steve Seidel from Project Zero around my projects. He didn't come every single week, but he was a regular visitor. It wasn't easy, I discovered, to suddenly change one's teaching practice from a "stand and deliver" model to a "student as worker, teacher as coach" one. I had a vague image in my head of a happy, buzzing, hands-on, engaged classroom where kids supported and helped each other create beautiful products that had an authentic purpose in the world. Yeah, something like Ron Berger's classroom. But change did not come quickly; my first year trying to use essential questions is a good example.

I've come to believe that it is very hard to change one's practice. It takes time and deliberate attention. Even if you can envision your endpoint, most people don't know how to get there. It can be a long, slow process.

Having a mentor, though, makes it easier. Steve S. was patient with me. He would take note of the issues I was struggling with and then ask hard questions that made me think about what I was doing and why. He didn't come in with a handbook on how to "do project-based learning," or with a list of directions, like you get when you ask Google Maps how to get somewhere. Like a good coach, he nudged me along as I was ready. When we would get to an important intersection in learning, he would point it out to me and let me choose the direction I thought made sense.

One day, after we'd been debriefing a class, Steve said, "Kathy, there's something I'd like to ask you to consider."

"What?" I asked.

"I'm wondering if you might start thinking about doing portfolios with your kids," he replied.

"No! No way!" I exclaimed. I started flapping my hands in the air. "I'm just starting to get the hang of this project stuff! No way can I take on something else! I can only do one thing at a time!"

"Okay, okay," Steve tried to soothe me. "I don't want to overwhelm you. But how about this? Could you just agree to keep kids' work? Don't throw it out and don't send it home. Just keep it in a filing cabinet somewhere."

"You're not going to make me do anything with it, are you?"

"Not until you are ready," he answered.

"Promise?"

"Promise."

"Okay then. I will save the kids' work. But I'm not doing portfolios," I said emphatically.

That was probably in January or February. I kept my promise and started saving work. When I remembered, I put the students' work into a big drawer. If kids asked me when they could take something home, I'd put them off, assuring them they'd get it by the end of the year. Then, one day at the beginning of June, Steve came by. He had a bunch of manila file folders with him.

"Are you willing to take a look at what you've collected?" he asked.

"Okay," I relented. I was willing to take an hour to appease Steve; after all, he had given so much time to me.

We started to sort the work out by student. We put names on the folders and spread them out over a few different tables. Then we started filling the folders with whatever work we had from each child. As I was doing this, I was fascinated by looking back at the work the kids had done. I'd forgotten about some of the assignments and was amazed by some of their work. A whole different picture of each student began to emerge.

"This is amazing!" I said. "This tells such a story about each kid's year in this class."

"Yes," Steve responded. "It is really different than looking at a gradebook. Just think if you'd saved things from the beginning of the year."

We talked about how much growth we could see in this collection of student work, and I wondered, if I was this interested in what I saw, how would the kids feel to see the work they'd done over the year? We decided we would use the last day of school to give the kids time to review and reflect on what they saw.

I don't remember if I asked students to write anything this first time looking at their work, but I do know that they were utterly enthralled going through their folders. There was a lot of chatter, laughter, calls of "Look at this!" and "This was the best thing I did all year!" I was hooked. I vowed that we would begin the next year with portfolios.

On the first day of school that September, I asked my new class if they knew what a portfolio was. Someone said that it was a collection of work.

"Who might keep a portfolio?" I asked.

An artist. An architect. A graphic designer. A writer. They offered many different possibilities.

"And why would you want to have a portfolio?" I asked. "Why not just tell someone how good you are?"

"Well," a student explained, "people won't just take your word for it. They want proof of what you can do."

"Exactly," I responded. "A portfolio shows other people what you can do. Rather than take my word, as the teacher, for what you can do, you can show other people, and especially yourself, what you can do. This is a way of really owning your work."

People think of portfolios in different ways. For some people, it is simply a collection of one's work. But I followed these guidelines: collect, select, reflect, project. We would first collect work; that was the easy part. At the end of the term, each student would then review all the work they had saved and select a few pieces that were evidence of their growth: in writing, in reading, in projects. We'd already been saving drafts, so it was easy for a student to show growth from a first to a final draft. I remember having a discussion with a student about a piece he had selected as a writing sample.

"But I loved that other piece you wrote about [whatever it was]. Your final story showed so much growth from the first draft. It is really the best piece I think you've written all year," I argued.

"But I think the one about basketball camp is my best piece," he said. "I want to put that in."

"Really?" I pushed back. "Why?"

"Because I loved going to that camp and I want to share that story. It is where I really show who I am," he responded. "You said we get to select the pieces we want to put in our portfolios. That's the piece I want to include."

He was right. Portfolios were about ownership. I wonder if I'd wanted him to use the other piece because it showed more of *my* work as the teacher. But, in the end, I was glad that he had a story that he was proud of, that he wanted to share with others. He was making choices as a writer, not as a student trying to please someone else.

The next part was hard: reflecting. Just like with critique, most young adolescents did not take naturally to reflection. In my first round of portfolios, I asked broad questions like "How have you grown as a student in humanities?" I got broad answers back. Things like, "I learned a lot" or "I'm a better reader now." Not very insightful. I discovered that I had to 1) give them more questions to help guide their thinking, and 2) share models of good reflections. In my first year, I didn't have any models of good reflections, so I wrote them myself. Over the years, though, I collected thoughtful, articulate, student-written reflections that raised the bar for everyone.

The final step of the portfolio process was to project—that is, to think about what you've learned about your own growth and set some goals for the future. This part was pretty easy for most students. After looking over their own work from the last ten or twelve weeks and reflecting on its strengths and weaknesses, most of them could identify two or three clear goals to work on. It could be something like, "I realize that I tend to leave my assignments to the last minute. I want to start pacing my work better." Or it could be, "I planned to read twenty books this year and I've only read seven. I better get busy if I am going to meet that goal." Or, "I realize that I don't speak up very much in class. I'm going to try to raise my hand at least once every day."

Students shared these reflections and goals in a letter to their parents, and others. They knew their portfolios would be reviewed and that they would have to defend their work. They knew that no one would "take their word for it." The evidence of their work, or sometimes lack thereof, was right there. This was a game-changer in parent conferences. Rather than just telling a parent that their child was "making progress" in writing, I could show them exactly how they were developing as writers. For example, if a student had developed a strong voice or better organization in their writing, I could show that. Conversely, if a student was putting little effort into their work, it showed in the portfolio.

What I hadn't anticipated was how much of *my* work was evident in the portfolio. The first time my students took their portfolios home, I had a panic attack. Anyone could see the kind of assignments I had been giving, they could see the design of the projects we'd worked on, they could see my comments on their papers, they could see everything we had done in a term. When parents opened those folders, they opened the door to my teaching practice too. I suddenly felt very exposed and accountable in a way I hadn't before. What if parents disapproved of what we were doing? What if I wasn't really doing *my* job? But I realized that if I wasn't able to defend my work, that was a problem. If I couldn't explain to a parent what I was doing and why, maybe I needed to change it.

"Accountability" has been a very popular topic among so-called education reformers. "We must hold schools and teachers accountable" has been a constant mantra. But what they have meant by accountability is the use, overuse, and misuse of standardized tests. Over the last twenty-plus years, this kind of "accountability" has driven all sorts of changes in our schools—most of them negative. These tests measure a very narrow slice of student learning, if that.

Contrast a single test score with a portfolio conference in which student, teacher, and parent discuss the evidence in front of them of that child's work. In those discussions, I felt truly accountable to my students, their families, and my community. But it also wasn't on just my shoulders. Indeed, a child's success in school does not rely solely on the teacher. In the parent-teacher-child conferences, we would discuss what the student needed to do to continue to grow and how the parents, too, could better support their child. We became a team with a common goal.

It also was slowly dawning on me why Steve from Project Zero had been encouraging me to start portfolios. When he had first asked me about collecting student work, it felt to me like just one more new thing to try, like it was the "in" thing, the flavor of the month. A lot of school reform feels that way to teachers. A new practice or "initiative" is mandated without any real understanding of why it is being implemented or how it will work. Just like during my School Climate Coordinator days, I could have told people that they needed to start a peer-mediation program or a student government. Without a common, underlying philosophy among teachers and a deep understanding of why those initiatives might be useful, they are bound to fail.

But Steve did not do that. He gave me time to be ready. He let my own understanding unfold. He didn't ask me to do everything all at once; that is, we did not begin with high-stakes portfolio conferences. He let me discover how our project-based approach demanded a more complex and comprehensive form of assessment. Projects and other authentic learning tasks revealed more about students. The more I saw of this kind of student work, the more I needed richer and more diverse ways of evaluating it. Portfolios were a natural outgrowth of our "student-as-worker, teacher-as-coach" approach to learning.

One day, Steve B., the math teacher, said to me, "What's this portfolio thing you're doing, Kathy? The kids are asking me if we're going to do math portfolios. I don't know what they're talking about." I hadn't brought up my work with Project Zero yet in our team meetings. But when Steve B. asked to see what a portfolio looked like, I was excited to show him.

"This is cool," he said. "The kids are really owning their work. I wonder what a math portfolio might look like."

Before long, Laura, the science teacher, was thinking about science portfolios. They both liked how the portfolio could capture so much more about a student's learning. Portfolios became a hallmark of our junior high program.

But we soon would take portfolios one step further. Through Project Zero and my budding friendship with Ron Berger, I saw a video of students from Ron's sixth-grade class presenting their portfolios to a panel of adults as a culminating activity of their year. Each student had half an hour to present their work and answer questions from their former teachers, community members, and their parents about what they had learned. The presence and poise of these eleven-year-olds was remarkable. But what was even more remarkable were the students' thoughtful reflections about their learning.

Just like when I saw Ron's students' architectural drawings in the halls of Gutman Library at Harvard, I couldn't believe these were typical sixth graders, although I knew they were. I thought about myself as a sixth grader—awkward and insecure.

How did he get kids to do this, and to do it so incredibly well? I asked him.

"Practice," he said. "And feedback. And support. And more practice."

It was just like learning anything. If it was worth doing, it was worth doing well. Quality work takes quality time.

I was impressed. I wasn't sure how we could possibly do something like this at Graham & Parks, though. Portfolios still felt new, and we just weren't ready to take on yet another project. Also, we had more than twice as many students as Ron had in each grade level, and to do the presentations meant juggling the schedule with our whole team. The logistics alone were daunting. But I really liked the idea of asking students to present their work, not just to their teachers but also to people in the "real world." I soon saw an opportunity to try it out.

We had just finished a poetry unit and my students had written some beautiful work. While I wasn't up to recruiting a whole panel, I asked half a dozen friends, many of whom were writers and poets, to come to the school. These guests would meet, one on one, with a student for about twenty minutes. I explained to my friends that their job was just to listen. They should give honest feedback but also be sensitive to how vulnerable these budding young poets were.

Students were very nervous about this. Meet with a stranger? Make your work public? I realized I might have a rebellion on my hands. I let the kids sign up for a time slot, giving them some control, but made it clear that everyone would do this. No one would be judging them; our guests were there just to listen to beautiful poems. Most kids were not convinced. But the first round of poets came back glowing.

"She was so nice!" exclaimed one student. "She really liked my poems! I could tell she really did; she wasn't just saying that!"

The energy in the room shifted and everyone eagerly awaited their turn. One young man who had been resistant to writing, and to just about everything else about school, came back transformed. From that day on, he saw himself as a poet. (A few years later, he tragically passed away from an undiagnosed medical condition. The school created an annual poetry award in his memory and honor.)

This experience was striking to me. Students don't expect their work to be public. They produce work for the eyes of the teacher, maybe for parents. Too rarely are their learning and accomplishments held up to the public eye. What a different message to young people to say that adults in the "real world" are interested in and value what you do. It's one thing for a teacher to say, "You did a great job on this, Damon!" It's a very different thing for a student to get that feedback from a more objective observer. I decided to raise the idea of doing portfolio-review panels with my team after all.

Everyone liked the idea. But there was a lot to figure out. We couldn't possibly do them at the end of that year, but we committed to do them the next year. In the meantime, we started asking, and trying to answer, questions. What was the purpose of doing these panels? Was it just to put on a show for parents or did it support our G&P goals and further students' growth in some way? Should we assess these panels; and if so, how? Could a student *not* pass their portfolio review panel; and if so, what did that mean? Would they get a second chance? Were we expecting students to demonstrate mastery of subject matter in this presentation, and what if they didn't? What were our criteria for a high-quality presentation? What should we ask students to present? How could we balance all the different subject areas and also allow students to have some choice? How could we help students to prepare for the panels?

And then there were the logistics. How would we fit fifty portfolio conferences in before the end of school? How could we cover our classes while we ran a panel? Who was going to schedule the panels? How could we recruit so many panelists? Could we find free rooms to do the panels in? And so on.

Lots of questions. But we worked our way through them. We decided that the graduation portfolio-review panels would not be a test of competency but, rather, a time for reflection by the students. It didn't seem fair to wait until the last week of a student's eighth-grade year to tell them they were not up to par in science or writing. Furthermore, we felt it was on us as teachers to prepare them as best we could throughout the year for their transition into high school. This again was the difference between evaluation and assessment. So a student who had struggled all year, or had goofed off all year (we did have a few of those), could successfully present a rather thin portfolio if they demonstrated thoughtful and honest self-assessment. Their panel would be judged on the basis of deep reflection, good preparation of evidence (e.g., showing first through final drafts), and strong presentation skills (e.g., speaking clearly, making eye contact).

We introduced the idea of graduation portfolio-review panels to students on the first day of school that next year. We explained it was something new we were trying and that we would be working all year to help them be successful. We talked about the five G&P goals for our graduates and told them that we would be looking for evidence of their growth. We spoke with confidence, but I think we all secretly wondered if we could pull this off.

We had long had a problem with eighth-grade "senioritis." Our soon-to-be graduates would begin to check out mentally in April, and they were fried by the end of MCAS tests in May. But this year was different. We explained to them that we had recruited the mayor, school committee members, the superintendent of schools, Harvard and MIT professors, high school teachers, and other people from the community to be on their panels. They had better be ready. Our students got very serious. Actually, we were all very nervous. After all, we were putting the whole school on the line, in the spotlight. What if the kids bombed? Just like the vulnerability I felt when I first sent portfolios home to parents, we were laying ourselves open to our biggest stakeholders.

We prepared guidelines for our guest panelists, encouraging them to "push the student's thinking forward." We urged them to ask for specific evidence in students' work. We directed them to challenge students on the language they used (e.g., "What do you mean when you say . . . ?"). We asked them to look for clarity and not settle for vague responses. We wanted them to ask hard questions, while remembering these were twelve and thirteen years old.

In spite of a variety of glitches (panels running over time, parents arriving late, work being misplaced, interruptions by fire drills), the presentations were an enormous success. Jittery students would enter the room tightly clutching their portfolios, and leave not just sighing with relief but beaming with pride, too. I have so many memories of different panel presentations, but the biggest, most enduring one is of people crying. Not just parents, but teachers and sometimes even guest panelists who had just met the kids. They spoke with awe of the young students who had come before them to present and defend their work with poise and confidence. Several people commented that the review panels were like defending a thesis in college.

But it wasn't joyful for everyone. That first year, one (just one) student did not "pass" his review panel. He had clearly not prepared, had little work to show, did not demonstrate any ownership of his learning, and was far from reflective. The panel struggled but, in the end, unanimously agreed that he could not pass. When we told him the verdict, he was stunned. Other kids were, too. They realized that the portfolio review was not just a pro forma act. You had to produce.

The team had agreed that the consequence of failing your panel would be not "walking the stage" with the other graduating eighth graders. You would still get your diploma, but you were not going to participate in the ceremony. However, we made certain that students would get extra support in revising their presentation and would have a chance to do it a second time—even a third, if necessary—to be able to walk. This young man did get to walk the stage with his peers. In fact, while there were usually one or two students each year who did not initially pass their review panels, I can think of only one who failed to eventually rise to the occasion with a second chance.

Graduation-review panels became another hallmark of the Graham & Parks junior high program. It was a rite of passage.

Our gradual move toward portfolios got the team talking about the difference between evaluation and assessment. The traditional report card, with a grade for each subject-matter class, is the classic form of evaluation. You might get an *A-* in English, a *B* in math, and so on. Or, in high school, it can become numerical: a 92 in English, an 85 in math, etc. This gives the student a ranking, which parents can also see. Where do you stand in relation to everybody else? But what else does it tell you? A grade tells you what you are "good at," especially in relation to the other students in your class. With traditional grading and evaluation, it feels like the end of the road. It is static. I got high grades in school in English and social studies. I was "good" at those subjects. I was "less good" at math. To me, it was a given that I was never going to be good at math. Thus, as soon as I could make a choice, I stopped taking math, something I have come to regret.

What if the focus were more on assessing students' learning? What do they understand and what don't they? How can we help them to "own" their learning and growth? Steve B. led the way on this. He started asking students to "analyze" their math tests. There were three categories of error:

1) you don't understand the concept *yet* (I emphasize "yet," because inherent in that one word is the belief that a student can and will understand);
2) you answered a different question (this is easy to do in math word problems), or;
3) you made a silly or sloppy mistake (i.e., you added 2+2 and got 5).

The information Steve got back from these "test analyses" helped guide him in what to teach next. If a group of four or five kids hadn't understood the concept, he could pull them aside and teach it to them. If the majority of the class missed it, he would teach it to everyone. If kids were consistently answering a "different" question, he could teach them how to identify the correct question. If kids were being sloppy, well . . . they started to realize that they needed to take more time and check their work more carefully; they were learning important habits of work.

Another outgrowth of our discussions about assessment vs. evaluation was Steve's test review sessions. If he was giving a test on a Friday, he would hold an after-school study session before it, open to anyone. As an incentive, he offered to add five points to a student's test score, just for coming to the test prep session. Kids were amazed.

"You mean if I just show up for the study session, you are going to add five points to my final test score? Just for showing up?"

"Yup," he would reply.

Bribery, I thought, at first. And it was. But because kids showed up, they had a chance to study and review. And because they had a teacher model *how* to study and review for a test, they did *better* on the test even without the bonus five points. Steve's "bribe" of five test points resulted in students' learning a lot more math.

Keisha was new to our school. She came in the eighth grade. She had been kicked out of her previous school and a few other schools before that. She was a tough character. She didn't care about school, and she let us know that, loud and clear. It was also clear that she struggled with much of the academic work although she was very bright. One day, I was standing in the hallway across from Steve's room when the door suddenly flew open and Keisha came tearing out of the classroom, waving a paper. "I got a 92 on my math test!" she shrieked to the world. Keisha had been going to Steve's after-school study sessions. She had initially snickered about getting five extra points for "doing nothing." But Steve's strategy had worked. He came out and stood next to me as Keisha danced down the hall. "I guess it's getting cool to be smart," he said with a wry grin.

We continued to talk about grades and what message they sent to kids and families. If we wanted to use assessments not just to give feedback to students but to also motivate them, maybe we needed to change our language. We talked about using a scale of 0–4 instead of traditional grades. While the wording changed a bit over the years, we began with:

0=Insufficient evidence
1=Needs work
2=Capable
3=Very proficient
4=Going beyond

We wanted to convey an expectation that you could and would suc-ceed. Rather than an *F*—you *failed*—we would say, "You haven't shown us enough work yet; there isn't enough evidence to assess your progress. Get busy." Giving a "1" rather than a *C* or a *D*, our message was: "You can do better; keep working." A "2" meant you were capable but had room for improvement. "Very proficient" is clear. But what did it mean to get a "4," to "go beyond"? It meant that a student had gone above and beyond what was expected of them. They truly put their heart and soul into their work, a combi-nation of both effort and achievement.

When we presented our new scale to parents, one dad said, "You mean, my son could get 100s on all his math tests and yet not get a 4?"

"That's right," Steve answered. "Math is easy for your son. It comes naturally for him. He doesn't have to work hard at doing well. But we want our students to internalize a drive to go beyond what is easy. It is part of our G&P goals: to have genuine curiosity, to own your work, to commit to high-quality work."

Interestingly enough, kids intuitively understood the concept of "going beyond," and bought into it. It was not unusual to hear a student say, "I really want to get a 4 this time. I feel like I've really 'gone beyond.'" Or a student celebrate, "I got a 4! I got a 4!"

These changes in our assessment practices did not happen overnight, or even in one year. They happened over a period of two, three, and four years, and we were always tweaking and refining what we did. Portfolios, graduation review panels, and our 0–4 scale became institutionalized, but they never became static. For example, in our first graduation review panels, we asked students to select a piece of work from math, science, and humanities. Later, we added a "choice" piece. We wanted to acknowledge that students were learning a lot outside the classroom, too, and that was important to honor along with academic growth.

I will never forget one girl performing her Irish step dancing! She was phenomenal, and I had never even known she took lessons. I realized that I didn't know my students as well as I thought I did, and I resolved to find more ways to bring students' passions into the classroom. A couple of years later, the team decided to shift the focus from needing to show growth in academic subjects to needing to demonstrate evidence of growth based on the five G&P goals.

No one had asked, or told, us to make these changes. There was no state or district mandate to "do portfolios." These practices developed organically from our daily work and reflections on what was working and what wasn't. We did have the critical influence of Project Zero, the Coalition of Essential Schools, and innovative teachers like Ron Berger; we were not working in isolation. But we also had developed a culture of questioning our own practice, of thinking about how we could better support all our students. Equally important, we had a culture of sharing our practice with each other, both our successes and failures. As we tried new things, we accepted that it would take time to do them well. Our mantra was, "If we get 40 percent right the first time around, we count that as success!" We figured it would take three to four years to really get good at a new practice or initiative. This understanding that *change takes time and that failure is an essential element of growth* gave us a kind of freedom that few teachers and schools have in these days of high-stakes testing and "turnaround" schools. We also had the full backing of our principal. Len screened the barrage of demands from the district and state as best he could. Which was very well. Len was a master at protecting his school from the slings and arrows of outrageous requirements.

But, ultimately, the proof was in the pudding. Our kids were doing well. In Cambridge, at the time, there were sixteen public K–8 schools that all fed into one comprehensive public high school. The high school teachers told us that they could always spot a G&P kid: they knew how to write, they understood the scientific method, they could explain math concepts, and they talked about "owning" their work and "going beyond."

"Whatever you guys are doing over there, keep it up! We wish the other schools were preparing kids as well as you are," they told us.

The word was spreading "on the street" too. Good things were happening at the Graham and Parks Alternative Public School.

CHAPTER 8

TEACHING OTHER PEOPLE'S CHILDREN

When I first started teaching at Graham and Parks, there were two small bilingual programs at the school, one for Greek immigrants and one for Haitian-born students.[1] Over time, the Greek program shrank to nothing, but the Haitian bilingual program ballooned. Violence in Haiti in the mid-1980s and 1990s—with the Duvalier regimes and the paramilitary group, the Tonton Macoute—was driving people out of the country in a desperate search for safety and stability. In a matter of a few years, our Haitian student population went from about 5 percent of the school to nearly 25 percent. This was a major demographic shift for which the school was not prepared.

Our Haitian bilingual classes were structured so that bilingual students learned English every day but had instruction in math, science, and social studies in Haitian Creole. So, these students were distinctly separate from students in the "monolingual" classes. This caused tensions between all the staff members and also between Haitian and non-Haitian students.

The Haitian teachers had not signed up to be part of an alternative school rooted in certain progressive principles. The vast majority of schools in Haiti were almost the exact opposite of the model we were trying to create. They were very strict, authoritarian, driven by rote learning, and enforced with corporal punishment. The Haitian teachers were shocked that students addressed adults by their first names, seeing that as a sign of disrespect. They were baffled when students argued with their teachers and when they were told that physically punishing a student was against the law. American teachers were frustrated with Haitian students when they would look at their feet when being spoken to. "Look at me when I'm talking to you!" some teachers would demand. Some teachers grumbled that the Haitian kids were extremely loud and boisterous, even unruly.

At that time, the majority of staff at G&P were white. Few teachers connected with the Haitian bilingual staff. There was an awkwardness around language and race. Some people wondered out loud if the Haitian bilingual program might fit better in a different, more traditional school. "We didn't ask to be taken over by the 'bilingual program,'" a couple of teachers and parents complained. Haitian teachers, feeling like unwanted stepchildren, pushed back, "Would you feel that way if we were white?"

Finally, the school had to address this simmering crisis head-on. With the guidance of the Haitian teachers, we spent a year as a staff learning about Haitian culture, history, and language. The non-Haitian staff learned about the Haitian Revolution against France, the largest and most successful slave rebellion in the Western Hemisphere. We met a Haitian poet and learned about the rich traditions of storytelling (*"Krik? Krak!"*) and music in Haiti. We learned about the Haitian school system, where students had to pay to go to school, so many did not go at all. If they did go, they were taught in French, a language that most children did not know. We learned about bilingual education and the difference between conversational and academic language. We learned about the respect that Haitian families have for teachers and how much they value education. We learned that Haitian students show respect by *not* looking adults in the eye. We learned that while non-Haitian Americans found Haitians loud and boisterous, Haitians found non-Haitians, at least white ones, uptight and presumptuous.

What we were working on is now called "cultural proficiency," and many more school districts are trying to address it. Given the increasing diversity of students in public schools, being aware of and sensitive to cultural differences seems like a no-brainer. But, traditionally, schools expected students from other cultures, both within and outside of the U.S., to conform to the mainstream, dominant (i.e., white, middle-class) culture. In the 1970s and 1980s, many Americans challenged this homogenization. The civil rights and Black Power movements had given voice to millions, including Latinx and Native Americans, who celebrated the beauty and value of their own languages and cultures.

In Cambridge, it is now part of our stated district vision to create schools that are "joyful, rigorous, and culturally proficient." But, in the early 1990s, we at G&P were just beginning to understand how important it was for white staff, and others as well, to be more informed about children from very different cultures than their own. I cringe when I think about our assumptions—about even simple cultural norms, like how a child shows respect to adults. Judging from the number of books being published now about teaching in a culturally responsive way, we still have a long way to go to be truly aware and inclusive.

Relations between the students in the junior high were also strained, particularly between African Americans and Haitians. Students would eye each other in the hallway with suspicion and mistrust.

"They're talking trash about me! I know it!" an American student would complain, seeing a small group of Haitian kids looking at him.

"They say we smell," the Haitian students complained to their teacher, Josiane. They said that some of the American kids held their noses when they walked into a room or refused to sit next to a Haitian student.

Josiane shared her students' complaints with the junior high team. She was angry and protective of them. The rest of us were appalled. We saw ourselves as inclusive, antiracist, and committed to multicultural education. How could this kind of behavior go on at *our* school?

As the faculty advisor to the student council, Josiane invited me to meet with her class. With her translating for me, I listened to a litany of hurts from these young people, struggling to cope with and understand a new and different culture.

"They laugh at us behind our backs," said one girl.

"They won't touch a book or a pencil if I touched it," said another.

"They roll their eyes and squish up their noses when we come in the room."

"They make fun of how we dress."

"They won't let us play football with them. They say we don't know the rules. We don't, but how can we learn if we can't play?" asked one boy.

"It isn't everybody," said another student. "But other kids don't do anything about it."

"Would you be willing to talk about this openly in a community meeting?" Josiane and I asked.

Students were reluctant. No one wanted to be a target. We realized there was only one way to get this to work. We had to get everybody to speak; no one person would be put on the spot. Everyone would share at least one experience (they *all* had had them) in the meeting. Could they agree to take this step together?

Yes, they said. We even practiced what each student would say.

A few mornings later, the whole junior high, about ninety students plus ten adults, piled into the science room for our monthly meeting. Students, legs dangling, sat on lab tables pushed to outer edges of the room. Others brought chairs and squeezed into every possible space. There was the usual jostling, yelling out to friends across the room, and teachers trying to settle everyone down.

Then the teachers gathered in the front of the room.

"We have an issue in our community that we need to address. With everyone. But rather than have the adults talk about it, we want the people involved to speak directly for themselves."

At that, all the Haitian bilingual students stood up and took the teachers' place in the front of the room. The students still seated looked surprised, confused, puzzled; a few looked a little anxious. There was dead silence.

Then Josiane began. "My students need to say some things about how they have been feeling in this school. They will speak in Creole and I will translate so everyone can understand."

She turned to the young man on her left; he took a deep breath and started to share his story. He spoke confidently, the anger and hurt burning just below the surface. He ended by saying, "I don't know why some people don't like me or look down on me. I just want to be able to learn."

He turned to the girl next to him, and she said simply, "I don't like it when people hold their noses when I walk by. That hurts my feelings."

The next student added on, "Sometimes you see us talking in groups and you think we are talking about you, but we aren't talking about you. We might look at you, but that doesn't mean we are talking about you." And they went on down the line, each young person sharing, some more and some less, but all from the heart.

Once everyone from Josiane's class had spoken, she turned to the rest of the students. "Does anyone want to respond?"

The kids were shy at first, but a couple of brave ones raised their hands.

"I'm really sorry you felt that way. I will try to reach out more," said one girl. Others around her nodded in agreement (there was usually a group of kind and compassionate girls we could count on to show moral leadership).

Another girl stood up to speak. "Sometimes it does seem like you are saying bad things about us. How do we know? We can't understand what you're saying."

Others jumped in, "But we don't have to assume that it's something bad."

I wish I could say that everything changed after that community meeting. It didn't. There were still issues between students. But it got better. The ice had been broken. People, both adults and young adolescents, were more aware, and thus a little more sensitive, compassionate, and patient. For the first time, we started having translations in community meetings, so the Haitian students felt more included and engaged. This sometimes felt like a laborious process, to stop and translate everything that was said, but the non-Haitian staff and students realized that if we didn't slow down to do this, we left much of our community behind.

In addition, the longer the Haitian bilingual program was part of the Graham & Parks School, the more integrated students became as they "mainstreamed" into monolingual classes. Soon, the majority of our Black students were Haitian. In my classes, about 35–40 percent of my students had come through the bilingual program. About 40 percent of our students were white and the rest were students of color (mostly African Americans, with a few Latinx and Asians). There was not a lot of overt racism, although students would tell us that we were "just not seeing it." I'm sure the students were right. Teachers miss a lot of things—and white people can miss racist behavior.

We did notice something else, though, that concerned us. Our students of color, both Haitian and non-Haitian, seemed reluctant to talk in class. They would refuse to read a good essay or poem they had written aloud to their peers. When asked for his opinion, it was not uncommon for a student to mutter, "I don't know," and stare at his desk. Or a student would raise her hand, wave it madly in the air in response to a question, and then, when called on, would say, "Oh, forget it." And if pushed to answer, a student might offer a wonderful insight to the class discussion and then finish it off with, "I know that's wrong."

How could we support students of color to feel more empowered in school? How could we create a greater sense of safety? We knew that their engagement in class was crucial to their academic success. Steve suggested creating a new rule. No raising of hands at all. Perhaps it was intimidating to students less sure of themselves when others, particularly a handful of white, middle-class boys, competed with each other to answer first. Their hands would shoot up before a teacher had even finished speaking. If we did not allow hand-raising, maybe that would open up space for other students to share their ideas. People might now call this "cold calling," a common practice in a number of charter schools. The goal of cold calling is to keep everyone on their toes; nobody knows if or when the teacher will put them on the spot so they better be paying attention. Our intention was different. We wanted to slow things down, level the playing field, create more space so certain students did not dominate the air time. Some of us agreed to try this.

After discussing a number of other ideas, Josiane proposed, "How about forming a Black Student Union?" It would be a support group for both African American and Haitian children to talk about their experiences growing up Black in the United States, which might help students feel a greater sense of solidarity and belonging. We all liked the idea and agreed to introduce it the next September.

At one of our first community meetings in that fall, Josiane addressed all the students about the proposal of a support group for Black students in the school. As she talked about the differences in experience between white and Black children and the need for Black students to come together to share their stories with each other, the tension in the room grew thick. She had barely finished speaking when the room erupted. Students were talking all at once, arguing with each other, heads were pumping up and down, hands waved in the air.

"Yeah! We like this idea!"

"You can't do that. It's not fair!"

"It's about time!"

"You can't have a separate group like that. That's discrimination!"

"You're only saying that 'cause you're white!"

"All our lives you've told us we should get along together. Now you're intentionally driving a wedge between us!"

The meeting was heated. Students expressed a wide spectrum of ideas, but nothing was resolved. Some left the room in tears, others in anger, and others were just ready to go to lunch and recess. Passionate discussions continued in classrooms, over lunch, out at the playground. After one or two more community meetings, though, most students, both Black and white, came to accept the idea.

Under the guidance of three Black staff (a kindergarten teacher, a classroom assistant, and Josiane), about fifteen to twenty students met every other week for the rest of the year, including African Americans, Haitians, a few Latinx students, and one white. They talked about a range of issues and eventually produced a play about the importance of knowing your history, which they performed for the junior high, to universal enthusiasm. The next September, at one of our first community meetings, a group of students (rather than a staff person) announced that the Black Student Union would begin meeting in a week. While some discussion and debate took place that was reminiscent of the previous year, the majority of the students were quite accepting.

In addition to supporting students of color socially and emotionally, the junior high team explored ways to ensure all kids experienced academic success. Our biggest discussions focused on how to teach heterogeneous groups of students. We knew the research about tracking. In the 1980s, some educators (and others) started challenging the widely used pedagogy of grouping students by "ability." Jeannie Oakes, in her groundbreaking book, *Keeping Track*, pointed out how this system not only reflected society's class and race inequities, it also helped to perpetuate them. Students of color, immigrants, and poorer whites were consistently and persistently tracked into lower academic levels and vocational programs.

I had witnessed this early on at Graham & Parks, when a guidance counselor from the high school met with each of our graduating eighth graders to design their freshman schedule. This older white woman determined each child's future—depending on whether she signed them up for the "regular" classes or for Advanced Algebra, Honors English, Advanced Placement Biology, and so on. I happened to be in the room when she met with Manny. Manny, a Greek student, was a tall, gangly young man, quiet, and well liked by both students and teachers. Manny was also one of our best math students. We saw him as a future candidate for MIT.

Mrs. S., however, just noticed his Greek surname. "I think you should sign up for the vocational program. People like you do well there."

Manny was too shy and respectful to speak up for himself, but I jumped in. "He needs to be in an honors program," I demanded. "He is one of the strongest students in the whole school."

Mrs. S. was flustered, but I watched to ensure that she signed him up for a top math class. We did not allow Mrs. S. to come back to G&P, and we made sure to have a junior high team member sit in on every student meeting with a high school guidance counselor after that.

Math was the most obvious subject for tracking. Students' sixth grade teachers had recommended certain students for algebra. But Steve noticed that most (maybe all?) of the kids deemed "capable" were white. He also noticed that other kids were listening in when he was teaching his algebra group.

"Do you want to know what we're doing?" he asked them.

Yes, they did. So Steve tried something new.

"I will teach algebra to anyone who wants to take it," he announced. "However, you have to be willing to work really hard and come for extra help if you need it."

The number of kids in his algebra group doubled and was suddenly much more diverse. In order to move on to geometry in high school, students had to pass an Algebra 1 exam. That year, every single one of Steve's students passed the exam. (Read Steve's own account of this process in *The Making of an Extraordinary School.*) Soon after that, he began to teach algebra to all eighth graders.

In humanities, our classes were already heterogeneously mixed. We read whole-group texts a few times a year. For example, everyone read *Animal Farm*. We would work in small groups to summarize our reading, having good discussions about what was essential in each chapter. As I mentioned earlier, students had varying levels of understanding of the book, but everyone understood that is was an allegory about totalitarianism.

We also broke into different-level reading groups. All the books were related by either theme or content, but some were more challenging than others. For example, when we studied the Holocaust, one group read *Night* by Elie Weisel; another read *Friedrich*, the story of a German boy observing the diminishing rights of his Jewish neighbor as the Third Reich took over Germany; and another read *Number the Stars* by Lois Lowry, about people involved in the Danish rescue of Jews. I would give a short "book talk" explaining each book and "how hard" it was. Students would sign up for the book of their choice. Most of the time, students sorted themselves out to the "just right" reading level.

Once in a while, I had students who consistently chose the "easiest" book, even when they could have been more challenged. I felt that all the books we read were high quality, but I did at times nix a student's choice in order to push them into a higher level. If a student chose a book that I thought would be too difficult, I talked with him or her about it. This happened when Jabula wanted to read *Roots* by Alex Haley, when we were studying the African American experience in America.

"Jabula, *Roots* is a really long and challenging book," I warned.

"I know," he replied. "I want to read it."

"I'm concerned that you might get really frustrated with it," I said.

"I am going to read it," he insisted. And he did. He certainly struggled with it and needed extra support, but he was deeply affected by the book and proud of himself for tackling it.

I felt confident in my ability to get any student through any book. With a lot of discussion and scaffolding, students who were not strong readers could access high-level literature. But I started to worry about what would happen to these students, who tended to be Black and brown, when they didn't have someone there to guide them through complex text. How could they become strong *independent* readers? Because of my experience with the Boston Writing Project, I had developed a language around critique and revision in writing that students could learn and "own." They could see what a good "lead" was and how it grabbed the audience's attention. They could see how organization was important, that one idea needed to lead to the next. They were aware of choosing "juicy" words and using a diversity of sentence structures. But reading is a process that goes on in your head. How can students see what I am doing when I am reading? In fact, what *am* I doing when I'm reading? I didn't know how to break down the process of reading in the same way as that of writing.

Then I met Ellin Oliver Keene. Ellin was the coauthor (along with Susan Zimmerman) of *Mosaic of Thought: Teaching Comprehension in a Reader's Workshop* and was the featured speaker at a summer institute I attended. Ellin spoke about the different strategies readers use to make sense of text. Good readers ask questions, activate background knowledge, figure out what's important, make inferences, check for understanding. All these actions are invisible; they take place inside our heads. But if we can "think aloud," we can show learners how to use these strategic actions. Over the next three days, Ellin modeled these actions and engaged us in ways of bringing them to the classroom.

My head was spinning. Finally, someone was giving me the language, showing me a way to help my struggling readers develop the skills they needed to become truly independent learners. I thought, for example, about how much time I would spend developing good questions for my book groups. I would pour over the chapter, thinking about what was important, what big ideas were explored, how the characters were feeling or developing. Once again, I was doing all the heavy lifting. Going back to our Coalition of Essential Schools mantra of "student as worker, teacher as coach," what would happen if I asked the *kids* to come up with the questions?

We were about to read *Dragonwings* by Laurence Yep, a book about a young Chinese boy who joins his father (who had left China before his son's birth) in San Francisco in 1906. "For homework," I announced after our first meeting, "I want you to finish reading the opening chapter and come up with five good questions for us to talk about next time we meet."

"That's it?" the kids said incredulously. "Just write five questions? Do we have to answer them?"

"No," I explained. "We will talk about them together."

"All right! That's the kind of homework we like!" they crowed.

At our next meeting, their story had changed.

"That was really hard," the kids whined.

"I had to go over and over the chapter and really think about it," said one boy.

"That's the idea," I smiled. "So let's hear your questions."

Everybody suddenly got very shy, no one wanted to share.

"Okay," I said. "We will go around the circle and everyone has to contribute just one question." I turned to my left and the boy next to me got very red in the face.

"Do I have to?" he stammered.

"Yes," I responded. "Just one."

"Okay. Here's my question: Do you think you can love someone you have never met before?"

I was stunned. I would never have come up with that question. But what a fabulous question it was!

To be totally transparent, not all questions were as deep or provocative as that. But when someone asked a question like how old was Moon Shadow when he arrived in San Francisco or what year did Moon Shadow come to America, we could talk about what made a good question and how good questions can help us to think more deeply about what we are reading.

I started talking with my team about these comprehension strategies. At first, Steve and Laura pushed back. "We are not reading teachers," they said. But after some discussion, they conceded that students had to read in all subject areas, even math. Everyone agreed to read *Mosaic of Thought* and try out some of the strategies in their own classes.

Laura was introducing a unit on stem cells. Working together, like a Japanese lesson study where teachers craft a lesson plan as a team, we talked about how Laura could use different reading strategies to scaffold the text for her class. She realized that she wanted to be sure that students understood certain critical concepts. She decided to do what would now be called a "close reading" of the text on stem cells. She asked students to identify what they already knew, or thought they knew, about stem cells. She asked them to identify words they didn't know. She asked them to write questions in the margin as they read the article. She charted out students' responses to each of these steps. And that was the first day.

The second day, the class went back to the same article and read it again. Their understanding of this complex text was now much stronger. When Laura shared what she had done with the team, she commented, "I spent two days on something that I usually would have done in one day, or maybe even just given kids to read for homework. I certainly cannot and will not do that with everything we read in science. But I decided that it was important to take the extra time to build a strong foundation in their understanding of stem cells. And that preparation will put us in a better place to do the rest of the unit."

Then it was Steve's turn. As he looked more closely at the reading strategies, he realized that they were very similar to strategies he used in math. For example, before reading a word problem, Steve would always ask his students to first think about what they already know about solving a particular kind of problem—i.e., they would activate their prior knowledge.

Again, we worked as a team to help Steve design his lesson. Here is the problem he was presenting:

Today is Alphonso's birthday. Alphonso's grandfather gave Alphonso some money as a birthday gift. Alphonso says he will put his birthday money in a safe place and add part of his allowance to it each week. His sister Maria asks him how much his grandfather gave him and how much of his allowance he is planning to save each week. As usual, Alphonso does not answer his sister directly. Instead, he gives her some information and lets her puzzle out the answer for herself. Alphonso tells Maria he will save the same amount from his allowance each week. He says that after five weeks he will have a total of $175 and after eight weeks he will have $190. How much money is Alphonso planning to save each week? How much money did Alphonso's grandfather give him for his birthday?

A few days later, Steve reported back to the team on his lesson.

"I first asked the class what they already knew about linear relationships (activating prior knowledge). Then we read the passage and discussed what was important to solve the puzzle. I asked the kids to highlight critical information and cross out what was irrelevant to the math (determining what is important). When we did this, Solomon suddenly perked up. He knew what to do! I think the crossing out of irrelevant information made this easier for a bunch of kids."

Then they discussed the purpose (author's intent) of the problem; that is, what were they actually being asked to do?

"Finally," Steve said, "they worked on the problem and I drank my coffee."

This is now called "disciplinary literacy." Middle and high school teachers are not generally trained to teach reading and writing. We certainly weren't. Most secondary-level teachers have trained in their subject area: history, mathematics, literature, biology, computer science. They assume that their students have already learned how to read. The mantra was "students first learn to read and then read to learn." I don't agree with this. I think students should always be learning to read and reading to learn, in both the early and secondary years. As students encounter more complex and specialized texts, many of them, even the stronger readers, need guidance in how to make sense of it. Reading a history textbook is very different than reading a novel. For instance, by showing students how the text is structured (e.g., chronological, cause and effect), a social studies teacher can pave the road to better understanding.

Understanding the different disciplinary demands of writing is also important. In our humanities classes, we emphasized using the active, not the passive, voice. But one day when I was talking with a science teacher, he said, "I have to keep telling my students to use the passive voice in writing a lab report." What? I hadn't known that. How confusing that must be for students. Unless, that is, we can articulate what kinds of writing require the passive voice and what encourages an active voice.

Deepening our own understanding of literacy across disciplines was one part of teaching heterogeneous groups. We continued to try out various approaches and then debrief together. While we worked as a team, we also individually tried different strategies to support those students who were one, two, and sometimes even more years behind where we wanted them to be.

Steve started a Saturday class. Every other Saturday he would bring a box of Dunkin' Donuts and Swiss Miss hot chocolate mix to school and meet for two hours with the predominantly Haitian bilingual students for math tutoring. Steve would not allow any other kids to come.

"This isn't for you, Megan," he told my older daughter. "You don't need help in math. Your presence will inhibit the other kids."

"But they're my friends!" she protested.

"Hang out with them after class, then. You're not invited."

In this safe space, he could address students' gaps, confusions, and misunderstandings. The kids grew to love this time. There was a lot of laughter and powdered sugar, but there was also a lot of learning going on.

Laura chose a different approach. When it was time for the annual Science Fair, she grouped the more recently arrived Haitian bilingual students together and guided them through a common experiment. This provided more structure and scaffolding than the other students needed, while building solid foundational skills in the scientific method.

In humanities, we looked at our curriculum design. As an integration of literature and history, humanities should be a place where all students both see themselves and learn about others (now referred to as "windows and mirrors"). Did our students of color see themselves in our lessons? Did they have opportunities to talk about important issues in their own lives?

Over the years, we had developed a two-year cycle for our humanities curriculum. One year, we focused on the theme "Justice and Dissent." We used the Facing History and Ourselves curriculum to look at the Holocaust in Europe during World War II as a case study of justice lost. We then looked at the U.S. civil rights movement as an example of the fight to establish justice. We ended the year looking at societies where the issue of justice was more recently being determined, such as South Africa, Israel/Palestine, and Haiti.

The second year of our cycle, we explored the question "What makes America America?" We studied the Industrial Revolution in New England and the impact of Irish immigration in the 1850s. We examined the U.S. South and the experience of Africans in the United States. The third part of the curriculum looked at the expansion west, with a focus on the experience of Chinese immigrants. The year ended with an in-depth study of the U.S. Civil War.

I thought we were doing a pretty good job with our "windows and mirrors." That is, until Enid Lee came to visit my classroom. Enid Lee is an African Canadian educator who focuses on antiracist professional development. The Cambridge Public Schools had hired her as a consultant in the mid-1990s and Len, the principal, made sure she came to Graham & Parks. She did a workshop with the whole staff and then offered to visit and meet with any teachers who were interested in her feedback. I leapt at the chance.

We were doing our unit on the South and the institution of slavery. I was proud of how we had developed our curriculum, and I was sure she would be impressed. She spent the whole morning in my classroom, taking assiduous notes. At the end of the day, when we sat down at the table in the back of the room, she began carefully.

"It's good to see you trying to address these issues. This part of history is often left out of the curriculum."

I smiled, appreciating the acknowledgement.

"But," she said, "I have some real concerns that I'd like to share."

I was taken aback. I had expected the praise to go on.

"First, let's look at language," she said. "Instead of talking about slaves, it is important to refer to them as 'enslaved people.' They were human beings who were stolen from their lives and *en*slaved—enslaved by others."

I hadn't thought about that before. As a feminist, I understood how powerful language is in shaping our consciousness. I could see that by talking about enslaved people, we would constantly be referencing the crime of kidnapping committed against them. *Okay*, I thought, *I can do that.*

But Enid wasn't finished. "I noticed that when you talked about whites or Europeans, you would say 'we' and when you talked about Africans, you said 'them.' When people use the word 'we' or 'us,' it implies that 'we' are the norm; 'they' are the other. Your Black students hear you saying that they are 'other.'" I cringed inside.

Enid went on. "The way you are teaching about African enslavement, it seems like they were just passive victims. When do your students learn about the myriad of ways that Africans resisted their enslavers? It is critical for your students, especially your Black students, to understand this." I was writing down everything she was saying, while trying hard not to feel defensive, to argue back, to point out what a better job I was doing than most white teachers.

She had more. "It is important for students to understand the richness of culture and history that these people brought with them. Enslaved Africans were portrayed as primitive savages. But they came from highly developed civilizations and cultures. You need to challenge those stereotypes. Teach them about Mansa Musa and Sundiata." I didn't know who these people were. I realized that I had a lot to learn, on many levels.

Enid Lee had challenged me with frank, honest, and specific feedback. I could see ways to revise my curriculum that would make it stronger, more racially sensitive, and more accurate. I decided to structure the different units chronologically—who came first? The first Africans to be sold into servitude had arrived on America's shores in 1619, a year before the Mayflower landed in Plymouth, Massachusetts. They were initially traded as indentured servants, but over the first seventy-five years of colonial history, laws were gradually passed that condemned Africans to lifelong slavery based on their "race."

We also framed each case study—Africans, Irish, Chinese—with these questions:

- Why did this group of people leave their homeland?
- What did they leave behind and what did they bring?
- How did they become part of America?

I worked on my language (although I realized how hard it is to change linguistic, or any other, habits). We examined all kinds of resistance by enslaved peoples, from leaping overboard a slave ship to rebellions like Nat Turner's and Denmark Vesey's, to work slow-downs, to just surviving. We learned about slavery in the Northern states and about free African Americans in both the North and the South. And we did find out about Mansa Musa and the great Mali Empire.

What impact did these changes have on our students? Did our students of color speak up more in class? Were they better prepared for high school? Had we closed the "achievement gap"?

We definitely made progress. We did see students engage more. We saw them ask more questions. We saw them developing skills. We saw their pride in doing high-quality work. We saw their confidence as learners grow. But we knew there was more to do to really address the needs of our students of color.

One year, Len had circulated Lisa Delpit's famous article, "The Silenced Dialogue: Power and Pedagogy in Educating Other People's Children" (*Harvard Education Review*, Fall 1988). In it, Delpit challenges "progressive" educators' assumptions that they know best how to teach children from racial and cultural backgrounds different from their own. She gives voice to teachers of color who have felt sidelined and excluded from these discussions about teaching children of color. Using the debate over process- versus skills-oriented writing instruction as a case study, Delpit examines the "culture of power" that dominates and permeates not just schools but also society in general. She argues that while white, middle-class people already know the rules of power because white culture defines those rules, it is essential to teach those rules, those skills, explicitly to children of color if they are ever to have a chance to compete in the dominant culture.

The article was painful to read. I recognized myself among those "progressive" educators who firmly believed that they knew best how to teach other people's children. I hadn't been aware of how rooted I was in that white culture of power. Lisa Delpit introduced me to the insidious and persistent nature of institutional racism and the role it plays in education.

The staff exploded over this article. Some people, particularly Black and Haitian staff, found it validating. Others, particularly white teachers, were insulted by it. They felt under attack. "I don't see color," one teacher announced proudly. "I just see kids."

Len was taken aback.

"Wow," he commented to me. "I thought there were some important ideas in there. I had no idea people would react so strongly." In my view, the angry responses to the article confirmed Delpit's argument that white educators assumed they "knew best."

Recently, I've started wondering about some of our cultural choices at G&P, like addressing teachers and most adults by their first names. As I explained earlier, this was part of the school's philosophy: we saw ourselves in partnership with students, not as authorities ruling over them. In fact, we encouraged our students to question authority. The school, after all, was named after Rosa Parks, who had defied white authority in refusing to give up her seat on that bus in Montgomery. But I'd heard African American and Haitian parents express discomfort with this practice. I even knew of parents who chose to send their children to a different school because they so strongly objected to what they saw as a lack of respect in how students addressed adults.

I had dismissed their objections as people "just being traditional." However, I've started to wonder about this. As our country has had to face its deep-seated and systemic racism after the murders of

Michael Brown, Trayvon Martin, Sandra Bland, Eric Garner, Breonna Taylor, George Floyd, and so many more, I understand the profound differences and dangers for Black Americans to challenge any kind of authority (be it Black boys and girls in many schools or Black men and women dealing with the police). While we at G&P might have wanted to create a more equitable and truly democratic community in our school, our Black and brown students were not going out into a safe, equitable, and truly democratic world. It would have been really valuable to all of us—teachers, parents, and students—to at least have had an open conversation about this. Perhaps the school would have changed its "first name" practice. Perhaps not. But the conversation in itself would have helped us to build a deeper understanding of each other and of our past as a nation.

CHAPTER 9

THE REAL WORLD
CITY SITES AND OTHER THINGS
WE DON'T DO ANYMORE
1994–1999

In the 1970s, the early days of Graham & Parks, the school—believing that it was a developmentally important time for young adolescents—had experimented with eighth-grade "apprenticeships" in the community. In 1994, Len came to the team to ask if we would be interested in bringing this program back. As he said, these young people were "growing out into the world, away from family and school, and we could facilitate this growth." We thought it was a great idea, and he was able to get a small grant to help fund a "coordinator" for the program. This person would do what teachers couldn't—that is, outreach to agencies and organizations to set up worksites.

Initially, we thought of this as a "community service" project, a way our students could learn more about and "give back" to their community. The first year we tried it, eighth graders spent one afternoon a week for two months working in a variety of nonprofit organizations: a local daycare center, a food pantry, an elderly housing project, a homeless shelter, and other agencies.

We had mixed results. Some students had amazing experiences in which they were able to really touch the life of another person. Others worked alone, stocking shelves or sweeping floors, feeling isolated and resentful. They couldn't see how they were helping anybody. Some students were left utterly unsupervised and managed to get into mischief. Some of the agencies gave glowing reports about our eighth graders, how hard they worked and how much they contributed. But others reported that they felt like they were the ones doing community service by hosting these squirrely teenagers.

The teachers also were not satisfied with how our experiment turned out. It was more disruptive to our academic schedules than we'd anticipated, and the seventh graders were mad that they didn't get to go, too. But we were not ready to give up. We believed in the underlying philosophy that young adolescents need to connect to the sphere of adults, be exposed to the world of work, and have a chance to explore their interests beyond school. We could see the positive impact on those students who had had a successful placement, so we went back to the drawing board.

After considerable discussion, the team decided to make some radical shifts. First, both seventh and eighth graders would participate. This meant we had to find job sites for nearly ninety students. Second, we returned to the idea of "apprenticeships" rather than community service. That would give us many more options in finding sites willing to host and supervise our students. Third, rather than going for a couple of hours once a week, the students would have an immersion experience. They would report to their volunteer jobs for one full week instead of coming to school. Fourth, students would keep a work journal, and there would be a project each year linked to their academic classes. We called our new program "City Sites."

Len fully supported our plan. Again, he magically raised the money to hire a coordinator, and we all met with parents about the idea. They had a gazillion questions and concerns. How will children get to and from their work sites? What if something happens on the way to or at the site? What if things go wrong at the work site? Who is responsible? What are the academic implications? Is it worth giving up a week of school for this? Will this be graded? Are teachers just getting a week off? Will kids get to choose their site? How will we find spots for ninety different students? How will Haitian bilingual students be able to participate if they can't speak

English? How do we know if kids show up at work on time? But in spite of these anxieties, parents were excited about the project and we decided to go for it.

We spent hours as a team working with Lisa Dittrich, a former G&P parent whom Len hired to coordinate the job sites. We brainstormed places that might be willing to host our students, talked about how to visit and supervise each student during the week, and discussed how to orient kids to public transportation. We designed a daily journal with writing prompts for each day, we started mapping out interview questions for students to conduct with their "employers," and we considered a variety of final projects we would do when their work week was over.

Once Lisa had recruited local businesses and organizations that were willing to take on our students, we started matching students to placements, thinking carefully about each student's strengths and interests. Ryan, who wanted to be a firefighter, would work at the Cambridge Fire Department. Shavonne, who loved little kids, would be a teacher's assistant at a nearby early childhood center. Jordan loved bikes so he would work at the Broadway Bicycle Shop. We placed students at a local bakery, a ceramic artist's studio, a dance studio, the post office, a coffee shop, an architect's office, a plumbing business, a construction company, the Department of Public Works, the public libraries, an auto repair shop, and many more worksites.

We incorporated more traditional academic work in purposeful ways. For example, each student had to write a letter of introduction to their "employer" explaining who they were, where they came from, what skills they had to offer the worksite, and what their other interests were. We emphasized that this would be the first contact they made with their supervisor, so therefore it had to be good—including spelling and punctuation.

Finding a purposeful project that would pull all these experiences together was challenging. One year, we worked with the city to do a transportation survey. Our students were able to collect detailed data for the Traffic & Parking Department about how people commuted to and from work and the challenges they faced working in Cambridge. Another year, we created an exhibition called *What Makes the City Work?*, showing how interdependent we all are on different services and industries in the city.

My favorite project was a study we did in conjunction with the Cambridge Historical Commission. We had been exploring immigration as part of our humanities curriculum. We decided to bring that study home. We wanted students to get a sense of how much the city had changed in one hundred years, in terms of both what kind of work was being done and who was doing it. Cambridge had been an industrial city in the 1800s, fueled by the labor of Irish, Italian, Portuguese, and other immigrants. Since then, the high tech and biomedical industries have transformed it. We asked students to investigate these questions:

How has work changed over the past hundred years?
How have the people who do the work changed?
How have the workers' neighborhoods changed?
What kind of work do people do now?

The Historical Commission launched the project with a slide-show about the history of Cambridge, and brought historical maps, photographs, and other documents for students to peruse. Each student had to write an essay about their workplace, past and present, based on their research of the site and its neighborhood. We also required them to draw a pen-and-ink illustration of this site; our goal in adding this dimension to the project was to encourage students to look carefully at the space and building in which they were working. A professional illustrator visited each class, sharing his own work and instructing the kids in some of the skills of his craft. These were all compiled in a book we titled *Cambridge at Work: Then and Now*. This felt much more purposeful to us than sending kids out to work at a food pantry once a week. The construct allowed our students to "grow out into the world" while also requiring them to activate their academic skills of research, writing, and drawing to make sense of that learning.

The weeks leading up to the start of the apprenticeships were hectic. As hard as we tried to pick good sites for students, someone was always unhappy. Some were, in fact, bereft. "I have to work with a lady plumber all by myself? Katia gets to work at a cafe with Robbie! That's not fair!" There were job sites that canceled at the last minute, so Lisa had to scramble to find other placements. There were a couple of kids we couldn't trust to be on their own for a week, so we had to find something purposeful for them to do in the school. We worked on how to conduct a good interview as well as how to conduct themselves. We practiced greeting their new employer ("Make eye contact") and how to shake hands ("Be firm, but not too firm"). We taught kids how to read a bus schedule and a subway map. Every student was escorted by an adult on the first day of their jobs, so we also had to recruit escorts and train them.

Even though we had Lisa as a job-site coordinator, City Sites required a tremendous amount of time and work by the teachers to be successful. We naively thought that things would be less intense during the apprenticeship week itself, but they were not. Each day, we visited a few students at their worksites, checking in on both the young folks and their supervisors. Sometimes we had to "have a talk" with one of our students—but sometimes we had to negotiate with the supervisors on behalf of the kids. In the afternoons, the team met to troubleshoot and plan next steps. At night, we read our students' daily journals and responded to them. To be honest, I think we all breathed a sigh of relief when the on-site week was over. Then we had the school-based project to work on.

In humanities, each student worked diligently to write up the profile of their jobsite, then and now. The writing had to be good and the copy had to be perfect. This was going to be published and circulated in the city. So each essay was critiqued and reviewed multiple times.

When I pointed out a few misspellings and missing commas to Chris, he groaned, "No! I've already done three drafts! Why does it have to be perfect?"

"Because we're publishing this for other people to read," I responded. "You don't want to be the one writer whose work isn't perfect, do you?"

He thought for a minute. "Okay. I'll fix it."

When he turned in his final, perfect copy, he smiled. "Kathy, I worked really hard on this, and I did a really good job," he said.

"Yes, you did," I responded. "Doesn't it feel good?"

"Yeah, it does," he replied.

All in all, City Sites took a good three or more weeks out of our normal curriculum, at least in humanities class. Teachers today are incredulous about that, for multiple reasons. First of all, they can't imagine "giving up" that time—taking time out of "academics"—to do this. This is primarily because they would worry that their students would not be prepared for the MCAS (or some other mandated, high-stakes standardized test). Additionally, district leadership would pressure them to stick to a pacing chart and end-of-unit assessments, which are what drive the schedule now. I can also imagine teachers saying, "I teach math [or, science]. It's not my job to run or even participate in a program like this." Furthermore, many liability issues would arise, e.g., seventh and eighth graders traveling on their own, needing to CORI check (Criminal Offender Record Information) every person at a worksite, and more. In short, I'm sure that if a City Sites–type program didn't scare teachers off, principals would refuse to take on the responsibility, or the district would object.

But if we focus on the students—specifically, on the developmental needs of young adolescents—it is clear how important this experience was to our middle schoolers. They needed a chance to spread their wings, with guidance, support, and accountability. It pushed them out of their comfort zones, and it benefited all of them in a variety of ways. For some, they got a chance to explore a career they were interested in (Ryan went on to become a fire-fighter). For others, their confidence grew as their supervisors gave them well-earned praise. Students who might have struggled in math or humanities found success in the work world, supervising toddlers at a daycare center or welcoming guests to a local bed and breakfast. Some students had never ridden the bus or subway by themselves. They came back to school proud that they had inde-pendently navigated their way to a different part of the city. Some of them were relieved to come back to school. They said, "Working is hard! We'd rather be in school!" In addition to applying academic skills (e.g., writing a letter of introduction or an essay about their job experience), they learned critical life skills: how important it was to get to work on time, how to take direction, how to work with people different from them, how to cooperate with others, how to overcome shyness and fears, how to advocate for themselves, how to persevere when things were challenging or hard.

These lessons seem just as important to me as the academic tasks we exclusively focus on now, like writing a persuasive essay or knowing the difference between the X and Y axes. Given all we know about the developmental needs of young adolescents, schools should be designing more programs like City Sites. But, the oppo-site has happened. As standardized testing has increasingly driven the agenda, the curriculum has narrowed to a very limited focus on certain testable academic skills.

Teachers and others talk to students about the "real world" a lot. "If you think this is hard," they say, "just wait until you have to deal with the real world!" But young people don't fear the world beyond school; they are eager to experience it. How different would school be if it were rooted in the real world to begin with? We found, through City Sites and other projects we did at Graham & Parks, that students' motivation increased enormously when a real audi-ence saw their project and when the product had meaning to the students producing it. This seems like a no-brainer, but few schools operate with this as a driving philosophy.

Another critical way that our students experienced this kind of meaningful work was in our annual production of plays. I described in chapter 5 how my class produced *On The Line*, a play about the 1912 Bread and Roses strike. I had been looking for a way for my students to "walk in someone else's shoes," but I inadvertently discovered many other benefits to theater work. Not only did each student develop empathy and compassion for different kinds of people—as represented by the characters that they explored within the world of the plays—but they learned other life skills as well. They learned to articulate and project their voices. They practiced problem solving and creative thinking. They learned planning and pacing (a performance deadline is non-negotiable). They worked together, not in an artificially constructed "cooperative" task but in an authentic way. They counted on each other to know their lines and cues or to put a prop in the correct place on stage. They overcame stage fright and developed confidence. They cultivated patience and perseverance.

Our first play in 1991 had twenty characters. When we restructured the junior high program two years later so that everyone had humanities, I had a new challenge. How could I find a script that had forty-five different parts that was appropriate for middle-school students (remember, my rule was that everyone had to have at least one line) and connect in some ways to our curriculum? I decided we had to start writing our own plays.

We wrote the first one in 1992. The United States was celebrating the Quincentennial—the five-hundred-year anniversary of Columbus's landing in the "New World." The news gave much attention to stories about America as a melting pot and the land of the free, home of the brave. As part of our study of immigration, students researched their own family histories: where their ancestors came from, why they left their homes, and why they came to America.[1] Students brought in family letters, obituaries, newspaper articles, photographs, and other artifacts. We saw a photograph of Amanda's great-grandmother, whose young husband had left her four months' pregnant in Romania to make his way to America; it took three years before they could be reunited. We read an obituary of

Amy's grandfather, who had stowed away on a freighter from Germany when he was fourteen and survived by stealing potatoes. We saw Lizzie's great-grandparents' wedding certificate and wondered how their Irish and Italian families felt about this union, given what we knew about prejudice in Boston at the time. Using these and other students' stories, we improvised scenes, trying to imagine what it had felt like to be in their ancestors' shoes.

But 1992 was a significant year for another reason beside the Quincentennial. This was the year of Rodney King. In Los Angeles, a group of white police officers brutally beat King, a Black man. After an all-white jury acquitted them of any crimes, Los Angeles and other places in the country erupted in protest. We had many discussions about this in class, contrasting the experience of Blacks and whites in America.

We wove these two different threads into our play: the story of European immigrants looking for safety, security, or just a better chance, and the present lives of African Americans, who were still being denied justice after hundreds of years in the country. My two humanities classes each wrote and produced scenes, and then we folded them together like intertwined fingers for our final script. We named our play *Looking for America*. As with *On The Line*, we had student committees for all the work: directors, set designers, costume designers, and stage crew. And everyone had at least one line on stage.

These student-written and student-produced plays became a signature part of my classroom. Each spring, we would use the process of playmaking to revisit the themes and content of our curriculum. We would review all the things we had studied, all the books we had read, all the current events that we had discussed, and reflect on what we had learned. That process deepened students' understanding and helped them make connections to their own lives.

After brainstorming important themes and possible storylines, we would spend two or three weeks using part of our class time to develop the script. Once we had written the script, we would move into full-time production mode. For those next few weeks, an infectious energy would take over the class. Students voluntarily worked during lunch and recess, after school, even on weekends. The number of bathroom and water-fountain requests plummeted. Everyone had a job to do and everyone was focused on a common goal: a fabulous play. Excitement built and nerves frayed. But once the performance began, all the moving parts would slip into place and the magic of theater would take over.

The days after the performances always glowed. Students basked in their success. In reflecting on the play and the process, they clearly felt good about themselves and about each other. As one student wrote,

> I started raising my hand and telling my ideas to my peers for once in my life. This play taught me to open up my inner self and spread my ideas.

Another one said,

> This play brought out the best of everyone. I never thought this was possible, but it is. Now I've learned to believe in everything I do.

And yet another,

> I learned that a community is like lifting up something together. If one person lets go, the whole thing falls on the rest of them. Whenever one of us was not there for a scene, it made a big difference. The whole work fell down the drain. But, in the end, we were really there for each other.

When students reflected on their experiences and important lessons learned at the end of the school year, they often cited the play as a pivotal experience. For example, Nierika wrote,

> The most valuable experience that I have had all year was definitely the play. I had never done anything like it before, so everything was new to me. . . . [M]y favorite part of the whole experience was the feeling I got after one of our performances. I felt proud. I felt more pride than I'd felt for almost anything in my whole life. I was proud of myself . . . but most of all I was proud of the class as a whole. It was amazing to realize what a great thing we could create by working together.

For more detailed descriptions of some of these plays, see "Making Theater, Making Meaning, Making Change," in *Journeys Through*

Our Classrooms and *Why Fly That Way: Linking Community and Academic Achievement.*[2]

Susan, the other humanities teacher, had experimented with doing plays with me when she first joined our team in 1995. She was nervous about putting on a play, so we decided to do one together—with all ninety students! We had just finished studying the U.S. Civil War; all the kids had done an individual research project on some aspect of this time period. One student had studied William Tecumseh Sherman and his March to the Sea. Some explored the role of women as soldiers and spies in the war. A few learned about the renowned Massachusetts 54th Regiment, one of the first African American regiments mustered. Another had researched the Battle of Gettysburg. In groups of four, students presented their research to each other. Then each group chose one topic to focus on to develop a scene for the play.

The final play involved about twenty different scenes that were staged all over the school. Student "scouts" guided the audience, initially all seated in the cafeteria (a.k.a., our stage), on varied tours through the building as the other actors were poised to perform in the library, a hallway, the teachers' room, a stairwell, another stairwell, and so on, until the audience ended up back in the cafeteria for the grand finale.

Plays are no longer done in most middle schools. At least, not in this way of students writing and producing a piece of theater that is based on their own learning from the year. If plays are done at all, they are usually during in an elective period or after school—which is wonderful, but very different from the way we used theater in my class. When teachers hear about our plays—similar to their reactions to our worksite-based projects—they generally respond wistfully, "It would be awesome to do that, but we just don't have time anymore. We could never take six weeks or even three, to create a performance. We have to get our students ready for the MCAS [or fill in the name of any state-required, high stakes, standardized test]."

In recent years, I have talked to numerous teachers and parents about the projects and practices we developed in our junior-high program at Graham & Parks: City Sites and the plays; the bridge-building competition that Steve organized and the murals that Susan's classes painted in the school's hallways (murals became Susan's trademark); our portfolios and graduation review panels; our more ongoing structures of community meetings, student government, and peer mediation. To most people, it sounds like a different century.

And it was.

As we approached the year 2000, things were beginning to change. It started slowly at first, but eventually a tsunami of "education reform" would sweep over public schools throughout the country. The word "tsunami," however, is not an accurate description because tsunamis are a natural disaster. The changes about to be forced on children's education were anything but natural.

CHAPTER 10

ED REFORM CREEPS IN

1998–2001

Our students weren't used to sitting in rows. Some had trouble fitting their names into the tiny little boxes at the top of the test answer sheet. Were you supposed to include a hyphen if you had one in your name? Would you get in trouble if you used your regular name instead of your formal name? None of them had ever "bubbled in" an answer sheet. Some broke their No. 2 pencils within a minute from pressing too hard.

Even though the Test Administrator Manual—whose "script" I was required to read aloud, word for word—encouraged students to do their best, everyone was apprehensive. I'm pretty sure that the people who wrote the manual's instructions had never read them to a group of real children. It took teachers about thirty minutes to read page after page of directions, answer questions, and make sure names, student ID numbers, birthdates, the school name, grade level, etc., were all bubbled in correctly before students could begin taking the test. Anxiety was building. Some students surreptitiously peaked into the booklet. They wanted to get the darn thing over with. Session One of the English/Language Arts (ELA) section of the statewide MCAS was about to begin.

Schools administered the first MCAS (Massachusetts Comprehensive Assessment System) to fourth, eighth, and tenth graders in May 1998. But protests against it had begun long before that. The MCAS had been the lynchpin of the Massachusetts Education Reform Act of 1993: more funding for more "accountability." But people across the state—parent groups, the Massachusetts

Teachers Association and Massachusetts Federation of Teachers, the Massachusetts Association of School Committees, and various other groups—had raised concerns when they realized that "accountability" meant high-stakes standardized exams.

Teachers and parents opposed the use of "one-size-fits-all" tests. They rejected the Massachusetts Department of Education (DOE) ruling that public school students could not receive a high school diploma unless they passed the MCAS (private and religious school students were not, and are not, subject to this requirement). They objected to labeling students and schools based on one test score. They worried that students would be tested on new curriculum frameworks that teachers had not had time to learn themselves, let alone incorporate into their curriculum. They worried about how long the test would take and if it was developmentally appropriate, especially for fourth and eighth graders. They worried that teachers would feel pressure to "teach to the test" and abandon more creative and engaging projects. They worried about how some of the most vulnerable students would meet this challenge. But no one could foresee in 1998 just how far-reaching and destructive this high-stakes standardized testing regime would come to be.

A number of parents boycotted the MCAS that first year, not allowing their children to participate in the test. In retaliation, the DOE said that if a student did not participate in the exam, they would receive a zero as their score. And there was another catch. This zero would be averaged into the scores of all the other students at that school—which could dramatically bring down the school's overall average. This put the school in danger of losing autonomy and might trigger state intervention. This threat successfully thwarted the growing boycott movement. Parents loved their schools; they were fighting for a less rigid and draconian system than the MCAS, but they did not want to harm the very community they were trying to defend.

That first year, we had no idea what to expect from the MCAS and thus no idea how to prepare our students for it. We knew there would be multiple-choice questions and at least one essay in ELA. We had heard about "open response" questions but weren't quite sure what that meant. We believed our students were well prepared in reading, writing, and math. However, they were not experienced in test taking of this kind. So we taught them general test-prep. *Pace yourselves. Don't get stuck on any one question; skip it and move on to the next and then go back later. Be sure to fully bubble-in the circle and stay within the lines. Be sure to bubble-in the correct circle.* (You would be amazed by how many students make this mistake; e.g., they will skip question #4 and go on to question #5, but bubble in answer #4. This throws off all the rest of their answers.) *Eliminate outlying answers and choose between two possible good answers.* I had learned these test-taking strategies in my junior year of high school, when I took the SATs. I couldn't believe that my thirteen-year-olds (and nine-year-old fourth graders) were already having to learn them.

The MCAS, unlike the SAT or most other standardized tests, is untimed. According to The Manual, however, the test was designed so that "most students" would finish each session of the test in about sixty minutes. (ELA and math each had three sessions.) So we were instructed to write the start time and the projected ending time on the blackboard. We should then, halfway through, do a time check, evidently so students could pace themselves. However, when I wrote "Start: 9:20, End: 10:20," a number of them panicked.

"I thought you said the test was untimed," said Leah. She was one of those perfectionists who worked slowly but persistently, checking her work as she went and then again when she finished.

"It *is* untimed," I responded.

"Then why did you write those times on the board?" another student asked. "That makes it feel like it is timed."

"That's just a guideline," I answered.

Another student piped up. "Does that mean if you don't finish by 10:20, you are doing badly?"

"No, not at all." I tried to calm them down. But it didn't make sense to the students to tell them a test was untimed and then make announcements about the time. I agreed with them. "I know it's confusing. I was told I had to write that on the board. But don't worry; you will have all the time you need," I said. "You may begin."

The eighth graders opened their test booklets and began to read the long passages in front of them. I thought I might be able to sit at a desk and correct some papers, but within minutes hands started popping up. I quietly walked around the room to each desk.

"What does 'incendiary' mean?"

"I can't tell you that. Take a guess."

"None of the possible answers makes sense."

"One is the correct answer. Try to eliminate the ones that are most outlandish."

"All of the possible answers make sense."

"Only one is the correct answer. Try to eliminate the ones that seem less likely."

"I have no idea what the right answer is."

"Take a guess."

After the first thirty minutes, I walked up and down the rows, checking to see how far along kids were. I saw that some were still working on the first reading passage (out of three). A couple of others were almost done. A few of my most needy students had closed the test booklets and put their heads down on their desks.

"Have you checked your answers?" I said to Andre.

"Yup," he said with his head still down.

"Check them again," I said, shaking his shoulders.

Grudgingly, he sat up and started flipping through the pages again. "I checked them again," he said, and put his head back down. (By the way, the MCAS rules no longer allow you to ask students to check their answers or review their work once they say they have finished.)

When the "suggested" hour was up, most of the class had still not finished. This presented a new problem for us. The MCAS rules required all eighth graders to take the test at the same time each day (presumably so they couldn't share answers with friends in other classes or schools). But because our humanities classes

were multigraded—that is, they had both seventh and eighth graders—we had had to redo our academic schedule for the MCAS testing days. (Our fourth graders were also in multigraded classes, so
their teachers had to reschedule their students' work as well.) We
had decided that our seventh graders would have extra science and
math while the eighth graders took the MCAS. But we hadn't anticipated how long the testing would take.

By the end of the second hour, at least a third of the students
were still working. Leah was in this group. I knew she would do
well, but she needed to take her time. I was more worried about
Jean-Marc, who had just mainstreamed into an English-speaking
classroom that year from the Haitian bilingual class. I tried to imagine how I would do taking a standardized test in Creole. He was
staring at a passage that started something like this:

> Richard Hollingswood, Jr. sat in his car in his driveway of his Pennsauken,
> New Jersey home, peering hopefully through the drops of water that his
> garden sprinkler rained down on the windshield. [This is a verbatim
> excerpt from a recent practice test.]

Jean-Marc's conversational English was quite good, but I was pretty
sure he did not know the word "peering," nor would he know what
a "garden sprinkler" was. Another Haitian student had gotten stuck
on the word "Pennsauken," trying to sound it out.

"It's a town," I whispered, breaking the rules. She breathed a sigh
of relief and went on.

Some of my students with IEPs (Individualized Educational
Plans for students with special needs) were also plodding along.
They would look at me with pleading eyes, but all I could do was
smile (more of a grimace, actually) and encourage them to do their
best. The students who had finished the test were required to sit
still. They *were* allowed to read a book. (Today, students are not
allowed to read a book until everyone has finished the test.) There
was no talking.

They were all getting antsy.

The teachers made an executive decision. The kids had to take a
break. We gathered up their tests and took the kids outside to the

playground for fifteen minutes (this also is no longer allowed by the MCAS Rules). We then reorganized the groups so those who had finished the test could be in a different room and not disrupt the ones who were still working. By lunchtime, a small group of students still had not finished. They took a break to eat and go outside for twenty minutes, and then, in a smaller room with one teacher supervising, they were back at it. One of them worked up until the end of the school day, when the buses were called. She was proud of herself for persevering. This eighth grader had worked four and a half hours on the test.

The next day, we did it all over again: and the next day, Tuesday, Wednesday, Thursday. The following week, we repeated the same testing schedule, but this time for math. By Friday of each week, the eighth graders were utterly braindead. Their eyes were glazed over and their spirits deflated. It was painful to see our usually bubbly thirteen-year-olds look so gray. Furthermore, we had effectively lost two weeks of classes, for both our seventh and our eighth graders—and for our third and fourth grade students.

Losing that much teaching time was particularly difficult in May, when we were engaged in culminating projects and beginning to prepare for graduation review panels. Furthermore, not only did we lose that critical time, but, exacerbating this problem, our eighth graders decided that school was over for them. To them, the "final" was over—so why did they have to do any more work? Yet, school was still in session for six more weeks. How could we use that time well? We did our best to reel them back in, but we realized that, in the future, we could not go back to business as usual. We would have to complete our curriculum by May. This made the time pressure to cover important material even more acute.

We received our MCAS scores in October of the next academic year. Our eighth graders had already been in high school for two months. I don't remember exactly how our students did—but what did it matter at that point? For one thing, we already knew our students' strengths and weaknesses, far beyond what the MCAS would tell us. And, even if the scores revealed anything useful that we didn't already know, those students weren't in our classes anymore. What could we do with this information now?

The state results, overall, were dismal. Only 20 percent of fourth graders scored as "proficient" or "advanced" in ELA; 34 percent scored proficient or advanced in math. In eighth grade, the numbers were reversed: 55 percent scored proficient or advanced in ELA, but only 31 percent did so in math.[1]

Teachers were not surprised at these results, though many other people were—parents, school committee members, DOE officials, newspaper reporters. After all, Massachusetts students had been scoring at the top of the NAEP (National Assessment for Educational Progress, also known as "the nation's report card") for a number of years in both reading and math. In 2000, Massachusetts eighth-grade students tied for fifth place (out of the fifty states) in math, and yet two thirds of them did not pass the MCAS. In the same year, fourth graders tied for first place on the NAEP, but only 60 percent passed the MCAS. Why did our students do so poorly on MCAS?

"It's hard to see [MCAS] as a positive tool when it translates as so many kids coming home with big F's," said Mary Jo Marion, associate director of the Mauricio Gaston Institute for Latino Community Development and Public Policy at University of Massachusetts Boston, which published an analysis of the first MCAS results.

The champions of MCAS were worried. "We are very fearful of a backlash building," said Abigail Thernstrom, a conservative political scientist and member of the Massachusetts Board of Education. The following year, the Massachusetts Board of Education quietly proposed a lower passing score for the MCAS tests to ensure that failure rates were not overwhelming.

The people in charge did not want to consider that the test itself may have been the problem. Many educational policymakers and pundits considered the MCAS the most challenging state exam in the country. In fact, many of us wondered if the exam's developers had purposely designed it to be so difficult so that public schools would look bad, in spite of contradictory data from other indicators like the NAEP or SATs.

The advocates of "ed reform" instead tried to make a case that our public-school children weren't learning up to their potential, and they waged an all-out campaign to shift public focus onto teachers and the teachers' unions. Clearly, our schools were failing because teachers weren't doing their jobs. Clearly, the unions just wanted to protect lazy "deadwood" teachers and didn't care about children. When teachers and parents pushed back against that storyline, saying that they were protesting MCAS *because* they cared about children so much, MCAS promoters accused us of being "soft" on rigor and excellence, of defending a status quo that was failing the children of our state.

There *were* problems in public schools, especially in urban and rural areas that state and local government had severely underfunded for so many years. There were critical issues around equity for students of color, poorer students, and those with special learning needs. But this was not a secret. As Mary Jo Marion of University of Massachusetts Boston said, "Everywhere in Massachusetts—even in the suburbs—there is a gap between white and minority scores. But we've known about these gaps for a long time. Do we really need a spotlight in a room that is well lit?"[2] Teachers agreed. We didn't need someone to show us the gaps. We needed help finding the solutions to the problems that caused them in the first place.

In spite of the general outcry about the length of the MCAS, the next year the Mass DOE added science and history exams, nearly doubling the testing time. This greatly concerned teachers. In addition to the issue of further disruption to the classroom, they were concerned about what content would be on these tests. The History/Social Studies frameworks had been extremely controversial. Not only were there political disagreements about what these frameworks should include (the early frameworks were heavy on Western civilization and white male history), pedagogical arguments were also raging. The frameworks were basically a long laundry list of facts that the Board of Education decided students should know. For example, the seventh-grade frameworks alone included: Human Origins in Africa up to the Neolithic Age, Mesopotamia,

Ancient Egypt, Phoenicia, Ancient Israel, Ancient Greece, and Ancient Rome. Below, verbatim, is just *one* of the forty-four learning standards listed for this standard:

> Describe the purposes and functions of development of Greek institutions such as the lyceum, the gymnasium, and the Library of Alexandria, and identify the major accomplishments of the ancient Greeks. (H)
>
> A. Thales (science)
> B. Pythagoras and Euclid (mathematics)
> C. Hippocrates (medicine)
> D. Socrates, Plato, and Aristotle (philosophy)
> E. Herodotus, Thucydides, Homer, Aeschylus, Sophocles, Aristophanes, and Euripides (history, poetry, and drama)
> F. the Parthenon, the Acropolis, and the Temple of Apollo (architecture)
> G. the development of the first complete alphabet with symbols for consonants and vowels

Furthermore, students would be tested not just on their current year of social studies—they would also be responsible for the learning standards from fifth through eighth grades as well, which included U.S. and world history, geography, economics, civics, and the kitchen sink.

Over the last ten years, we had developed an engaging and meaningful two-year humanities curriculum cycle. But it was not aligned to state standards because, prior to that time, no state standards existed. During one of the two years, we focused on the theme of justice and dissent, and during the other year we explored the question, "What makes America America?" (See descriptions of each in chapter 4.) While the MCAS might include much of what we studied in our focus on nineteenth-century American history, I knew that it would not touch on knowledge we learned from our study of the Holocaust, using the Facing History and Ourselves curriculum. Nor would it test student on the civil rights movement or struggles in other countries to create a more just society (e.g., Haiti, South Africa, Israel/Palestine), which our students had studied.

One day, after all the kids had left, Len came upstairs to my classroom. I was sorting out papers when he walked in. "I need to talk with you," he said.

"Sure. What's up?"

"Kathy, I know you're not going to like this, but I don't think you can teach Facing History anymore."

"What do you mean?" I put the papers down. I was utterly shocked. Len had been my biggest advocate not only in teaching Facing History but also in helping us to develop our humanities curriculum sequence. I couldn't believe he—of all people!—would want us to abandon something that had had such a deep impact on our students.

He continued. "You know that's not part of the new frameworks. We are going to have to really focus on whatever is on the history MCAS so kids can pass the test."

"Are you kidding?" I demanded, incredulously. "Facing History is the best thing I've ever taught! You know that! Kids come back year after year saying how important a course it was and they will never forget it." To this day, this is still true. When I run into former students, they often reference Facing History and how it helped them think about being an "upstander" rather than a bystander.

"I know, I know," he nodded. "But our kids need to be prepared for the test. I'm worried about how it will affect the school if they do poorly." While Len was confident about how we prepared our students for ELA and math, he knew that we would struggle with a content-heavy test. He feared it bringing negative attention, and possible state intervention, to the school.

"But, Len, the new frameworks are crazy. They cover five thousand years of American and world history. How are we supposed to cover all that? You know that's not how kids learn."

"I know," he said. "I'm sorry. But you've got to give up Facing History."

"No way!" I was getting heated.

Len got heated, too. "Kathy, you are not going to teach Facing History anymore!" This was probably the only time Len had ever ordered me to do anything. "That's it!" he shouted, and started to walk out of the door.

"Then I quit!" I yelled after him. "I thought I worked at a school where people were willing to stand up for something. Do what's right! If we can't do what's right, I can't work here anymore!" I could hear him stomping down the hallway. I was fuming.

The next morning, about an hour before school started, I was in my classroom getting ready for the day when Len walked in. I was still mad. I didn't want to look at him.

"Listen," he said. "I went home last night and really thought about what you said. I decided that I was wrong and you are right. We can't give up something so powerful as the Facing History course. Especially just to prepare for a bad test. If our kids do badly on the test, so be it. We can work with our parents to help them understand our position on this. I'm sure they will support us. I'm sorry."

We hugged each other, and at that moment, I felt incredibly proud of our school.

When it came time for our students to take the History portion of the MCAS (after hours and hours of their taking the tests on the ELA, Math, and Science sections), I gave them a pep talk. "You guys are going to encounter some things on this test that you will know well, and there will be questions about things that you know little to nothing about. Don't worry or panic. Just use your brain to make the best guesses you can. Don't get stuck on one of those questions and don't get down on yourself because you don't know it. This test doesn't show what good historians you all are."

I had looked over the test booklet that morning, before the kids came in. (This is also now illegal according to MCAS rules: teachers may not look at the test booklet in advance, or during the test, or after the test.) I was curious about the kinds of questions my students would be facing. I had been pleased to see that the test included a handful of questions about the American Civil War, which we were studying. *At least they'll be able to answers those*, I thought. My students knew a lot about the deep economic, social, political, and cultural clashes between North and South that had led to America's bloodiest war.

But then, I started to look at the questions being asked. Here is one I never forgot:

> "With malice towards none, with charity for all, with firmness in the right as God gives us to see the right, let us strive on to finish the work we are in, to bind up the nation's wounds, to care for him who shall have borne the battle and for his widow and his orphan, to do all which may achieve and cherish a just and lasting peace among ourselves and with all nations." Which speech of Abraham Lincoln's was this?
>
> a. Gettysburg Address
> b. First Inaugural Address
> c. Second Inaugural Address
> d. Lincoln-Douglas Debate

I've asked many adults to answer this question. Most get it wrong. I knew the answer (c), but we had not gotten to the end of the war yet, and I was pretty sure that few of my students would be able to make an educated guess about it. I thought about how much my students *did* know about the Civil War. They understood how slavery had developed in the South and how cotton became king. They understood why the Industrial Revolution began in New England and how the mills depended on Southern cotton. They understood what the Compromise of 1820 was and the Compromise of 1850. They knew about the abolitionists, like William Lloyd Garrison, Frederick Douglass, and Sojourner Truth. They had visited the African Meeting House on Beacon Hill and stood outside Lewis Hayden's house, where he had threatened to ignite two kegs of gunpowder he allegedly kept under his front porch if "slave catchers" tried to come on his steps. They had read the letters of ordinary soldiers who had fought on both sides of the Mason-Dixon line and learned about the Massachusetts 54th. But they probably wouldn't know which one of Lincoln's speeches stated, "With malice toward none, with charity for all . . ."

Eventually, the History/Social Studies MCAS proved to be such a disaster that the state abandoned it. And a couple of other things changed, too: the DOE decided to require the Science exam only for fifth, eighth, and tenth graders. The Department also separated the ELA and Math testing blocks: students would take the ELA test in late March to early April, and Math in May. While we still had the same total number of hours of exams, at least our students weren't subjected to consecutive weeks of mind-numbing test taking.

When the MCAS was first introduced, some teachers had dismissed it. Teachers were used to initiatives, reforms, and mandates coming and going. Sometimes a local school committee had proposed these changes. More often, they arrived with new superintendents or department heads who wanted to make their mark with their own "innovations." But these changes often did not last. It was not uncommon to have a brand-new math or science or any kind of curriculum rolled out to great fanfare, and with much effort on the part of teachers to learn it—only to have it wither and die out within two or three years. This led to a kind of cynicism, especially among more veteran teachers. "This too shall pass," was a common mantra, especially for something as flawed as MCAS.

How could the DOE continue to push MCAS when, already, so many of the concerns about it had been substantiated within the first years: too much time went into testing rather than teaching; the test revealed more about a student's socioeconomic background than their learning; it was biased against people of color and English-language learners; it was developmentally inappropriate, especially for the younger grades, etc. Surely, the Department of Education would realize this and either seriously modify the MCAS or replace it with something else altogether.

Little did we realize that what we were already experiencing was just the winds heralding the storm. The tsunami was about to hit.

CHAPTER 11

EXIT: GRAHAM & PARKS, ENTER: NO CHILD LEFT BEHIND
2001–2002

The 2001–2002 school year was a big one, for me personally and for everyone else in public schools across the country. First, my story.

It was early 2001 when Len stuck his head in the door in between classes. "Can you stop in to see me after school today? I need to talk with you about something."

"Sure," I responded. I wasn't quite sure what was on his mind, but it was not unusual for him to check in with me about any number of things. We were back on track after our argument over Facing History. Not that we didn't continue to have disagreements. Lively debate was part of life at Graham & Parks.

So I was unprepared when he told me that afternoon that I'd been asked to report to the deputy superintendent at Thorndike Street, the central office of the Cambridge Public Schools (CPS). I was nervous. Was I going to get fired? What had I done wrong? Was it about our MCAS protests? He assured me I wasn't getting fired but he didn't elaborate, either.

"You'll find out," he said cryptically.

Thorndike Street is a huge, gothic, labyrinthian edifice that CPS rented from the Catholic Church at great expense. The building was decrepit, with ceilings peeling, wiring exposed, bathroom doors that didn't fully close, and a tiny, ancient elevator that looked like a deathtrap. There were six floors, but not all stairways led to the next floor; sometimes you had to go down a floor before you could go up. My favorite part of the building was located up a very narrow set of stairs that led to the tippy top of the building, known as the Crow's Nest. It felt a little like the attic where the family's insane uncle was kept out of view. It housed the Early Childhood Program.

Dr. A's office was on the third floor. She welcomed me in, making space at a table that was piled high with stacks of papers and files. We sat down, exchanged a few pleasantries, and then she leaned back in her chair.

"So, Kathy," she started, "are you wondering why I asked you here?"

I nodded.

"Well," she smiled, "I have a proposition for you."

"Oh! Okay," I said, cautiously, "as long as you're not firing me."

She laughed. "No, no, no. We don't want to fire you. We want to offer you a new position in the district. We're wondering if you would be interested in being our middle school coordinator."

"What?" I was utterly surprised.

"We are creating a new position and we thought you would be the perfect person for it," she continued. "You folks at Graham and Parks have created a really strong middle school program. You know that not all our schools have been as successful. In fact, a number of them are really struggling. We want you to share what your team has done with other schools in the city. What do you think?"

"I'm very flattered that you would ask me," I responded. "I do think we've figured out some things that could be useful to other schools."

As she went on, I learned that evidently there was discontent among Cambridge parents—especially white, middle-class parents—about their children's middle school experiences. Enrollment numbers were falling in the sixth and seventh grades as some more affluent parents chose to send their children to one of the many private schools in the area. This was not the case at Graham & Parks, though. We had a large waiting list at all levels, but particularly in our junior high.

"Do I need to answer right now? Can I take a little time to think about it?"

"Of course. Take whatever time you need."

I didn't really want to leave teaching, but I felt passionately about what we were doing at G&P and believed in sharing what we had learned. Harkening back to my days working part time with other Cambridge schools as the "school climate coordinator," I'd found working with adults far more challenging than working with seventh and eighth graders. But maybe it was time to venture out of the nest for a bit. I figured I could try it for a year and go back to my classroom if I wasn't happy. When I let Dr. A know that I would accept the job, my one caveat was that I complete my current year of teaching. I could do some limited work with other schools, but I was committed to my students and families to finish out the year.

Dr. A agreed to this arrangement. Her biggest concern was supporting an upcoming merger between two schools' sixth, seventh, and eighth grades into one middle school program. The reason for this merger was space: the Haggerty School didn't have enough space and the Fitzgerald had too much. Thus, CPS had decided to combine the upper grades into one middle school program. My assignment ("Your mission, should you decide to accept it . . .") was to help facilitate this process. I would continue to teach my classes at G&P but would also use my free periods and after-school time to meet with the principals and staff of the two schools to help them prepare for the merger, set for September 2001, just a few short months away.

From the very beginning, I could see there were going to be problems with this merger. The two schools had widely different philosophies and cultures. The Haggerty School was led by a veteran and visionary educator, Dr. Joe Petner. Joe had transformed the Haggerty from a traditional neighborhood school to one of the first full-inclusion programs in the state (maybe in the country). Haggerty welcomed students with a wide range of special needs, their motto being, "Everyone is different. Everyone belongs." Both staff and students adored their principal and passionately believed in their mission that all children could achieve high levels of learning. They encouraged cooperative learning, alternative forms of assessment, and collaborative leadership.

The Fitzgerald School, just a mere two miles away, was a world apart in terms of culture. Located in Tip O'Neill's Irish Catholic neighborhood of North Cambridge, Fitzy (as it was affectionately called by its community) was very traditional. Many of the teachers had themselves attended the school or the nearby Catholic school, and the pedagogy reflected that. Teachers, staff, and the school community had a fierce chip-on-the-shoulder pride and deep suspicion of outsiders, meaning anyone not from the neighborhood. Tradition was revered; change was suspect.

My first meeting was with the Haggerty teachers. While they were relatively friendly to me, they were in the dark about the impending changes. "No one has asked us our opinion about this," said one particularly vocal teacher. "We don't want to leave Haggerty. We love it here. We love Dr. Petner. We love our families. This is our home." But they knew this change was happening, with or without their approval. They decided they would have to make the best of it. They trusted their principal to protect and support them while making choices that would be good for their students.

The meeting with the Fitzgerald teachers, on the other hand, was a disaster.

"Those people are coming to take over our school," one said.

"They think they are better than us," said another.

"They have all those SPED kids," added another, using the word almost as a curse.

"They have another thing coming if they think they're going to run the show. This is Fitzy. Fitzy is *our* school," a woman declared fiercely.

Heads nodded, arms crossed.

The other challenge at the Fitzgerald was that it had a new principal. After a long-term principal, born and raised in the neighborhood, retired, the district had hired . . . not only an outsider but a Canadian at that! The teachers eyed her with as much suspicion as us other interlopers.

Oh dear, I thought. *This is a train wreck waiting to happen.* I spoke with both principals and with Dr. A about the need to involve the teachers in this merger process and bring them together as soon as possible. To my mind, we needed to invest a significant amount of time in first building trust between the two groups. Then, together, we could try to forge a common vision for their new middle school program.

But it didn't happen. I'm not sure why, but I was never able to get the School Department to free up the time and money (not a lot of either was needed) to bring these two very different groups of teachers together. The administrators seemed to think it was a good idea, but many of my phone calls and emails to set this up went unanswered. Promises of "we'll get back to you on that" were left dangling. Maybe there were too many moving pieces, maybe everyone was just incredibly busy, but time ticked away, and no meeting of the minds took place. For a number of months, I shuttled back and forth between the schools when I could, trying to weave together threads of understanding. But you can't piecemeal together trust.

Schools are all about relationships: between students and students, students and teachers, teachers and administrators, administrators and families, and so on. But the teacher-to-teacher relationship is absolutely critical. In the traditional, egg-carton model of schools, teachers would go into their rooms and close their doors. Their classroom was their kingdom. Just like some people are with a special recipe, some teachers were not willing to share their curriculum or practice with anyone else. "I don't want anyone stealing my good ideas," one might say. "I worked hard on this. I'm not just going to give this lesson away to someone else."

But these attitudes were beginning to change. While it may seem like touchy-feely, kumbaya fluff to some people, research has shown that strong schools are built on positive, trusting relationships and a clear mission that all members of that community understand, can articulate, and practice.[1] This makes sense when you think about it. People cannot have honest and open discussion or debate if they don't feel safe with their colleagues. People will not share their struggles or ask for advice if they are worried that they will be judged or ridiculed. People are much less likely to try something new if they don't trust that others will have their back and support them. If you trust your colleagues and respect them, it is much more likely that ideas and information will flow freely between adults, which can only benefit the students.

I had not read much of the research at that time, but I had lived it at Graham & Parks. We learned, the hard way, that just one person could totally disrupt a team's chemistry. We had had various teachers who either did not or could not commit the time the school expected, or did not want to work collaboratively with the rest of the team, or did not have the right chemistry with the group. It had only been when Susan joined us as the other humanities teacher that our team felt truly solid. It had taken us years to trust one another and build a common philosophy. But, with the impending merger between Haggerty and the Fitz, we didn't have years. We had months. And there were far more possible disruptors, and far less in place to build a successful middle school program.

I was running myself ragged. Springtime was always hectic—City Sites, play production, preparing for graduation and portfolio-review panels, and, oh yeah, the MCAS. But add to that driving across the city to meet with teachers or principals whenever I could, before, during, or after school hours. I'm really not sure how I did it. I both longed for the school year to end so I could breathe, and dreaded it. I had been at G&P for seventeen years. Graham & Parks was my other family—the staff I'd worked with for years, the families I'd known over time, many of whom lived in my neighborhood and became friends, and the kids. Especially the kids. It was hard to think about leaving.

June was bittersweet. After twenty-seven years as principal of the Graham & Parks Alternative Public School, Len Solo was retiring. In addition, our beloved parent coordinator, Ann Bolger, who had also been at the school for decades (the one who had first welcomed me to the school and directed me to the second-floor office), had died of cancer that spring. Len had been the head of the school and Ann had been the heart. The school was grieving. The entire school community found it hard to imagine how G&P could continue to function without Len and Ann.

I couldn't bear the thought of saying goodbye. I explained to people, "I'm not really leaving. I'm sure I'll be back. I just have to get this middle school stuff going. Plus, I'll be visiting all the time as part of my new job."

On the last day of school, after hugging all my students and after all the other teachers had left, I sat on the big gray rug in my classroom and cried. I looked at the posters on the walls: Martin and Malcolm greeting each other; the African proverb, "Until lions have their own historians, tales of hunting will always glorify the hunter"; the Martin Niemoller quote, "First they came for the Socialists, and I did not speak out . . ." I looked at the classroom library, books that I had acquired over the years from multiple yard sales, donations of Harry Potter books as children moved on, new books from the New England Mobile Book Fair or the local bookstore, all organized and displayed on the shelf a parent had built for us. I looked out of the large windows through which I had witnessed so many beautiful sunrises over the City Hall clock tower. I looked up at the shelves above the coat hooks where we stored the boxes of theater materials: costumes, hats, the long muslin backdrops that a volunteer had carefully sewn and that we would hang from window poles to block the cinderblocks in the cafeteria to make our stage. I looked at the filing cabinets, cubbies, and shelving that held curriculum materials, students' work, and games for indoor recess. I looked at my big old wooden desk that I never sat at and mainly used to stack papers that was now cleaned off. I looked at the twenty-four student desks, in groups of four, scrubbed down one last time. I took a deep breath, got up, and walked out, leaving it all behind.

As Cambridge's middle school program developer, my new home was at the Fitzgerald School, so I could be onsite to help with the middle school merger. But when I showed up there in mid-August, no one could tell me where my office would be. Finally, one of the Fitzy teachers, in an uncharacteristically kind gesture, pointed to a small room that had an extra desk with a computer on it.

"Grab it while you can," she said. There was another teacher there, a SPED educator, who was also new to the school, sitting at the other desk.

"Do you know if this is being used by anyone?" I asked.

"I have no idea," she responded. "Feel free to move in!" So I did.

Since my meeting with Dr. A the previous spring, I had received no instructions or direction about my new position. I knew I was supposed to support the Fitz-Haggerty merger, but I wasn't sure what else I was supposed to do. When I tried to reach my boss, she was always too busy to meet or even talk with me. It felt reminiscent of my teacher-training year at Medford High School. It seemed odd to hire someone into a position and then provide no plan, no goals, no guidance, no direction, no budget. I had commandeered my own desk and computer, but had little else. Luckily, I had grown accustomed to figuring things out for myself. I decided I needed to develop a strategic plan for the year.

At that time, there were sixteen K–8 schools in Cambridge, with widely differing sizes, structures, philosophies, and demographics. One school, for example, had a total of ten students in the eighth grade, while another had nearly fifty—though both schools had the same number of teachers. Some schools were semi-departmentalized; others were fully departmentalized. The math teacher never talked to the science teacher, the science teacher never spoke to the social studies teacher, the social studies teacher never spoke to the English teacher. They had no connection with each other, no communication between them, no common vision about what middle school could and should look like. Only two other schools besides G&P had common planning time.

It had taken years of conversation, debate, exploration, and experimentation—with all its failures as well as successes—to develop our successful G&P program. During these same years, a growing body of research and practice was focusing on middle schools and the needs of young adolescents. In 1989, the Carnegie Corporation had issued a report called *Turning Points*, which "concentrated on the considerable risks adolescents face as they reach the 'turning point' between childhood and adulthood." Over the years, Turning Points developed into a national design for middle school change, and an expanding nationwide network of schools, coordinated by the Center for Collaborative Education (CCE) in Boston. Along with a number of CCE-published guides, my bible became *Turning Points 2000: A Blueprint for Middle Grades Education Reform*, an update of Carnegie's original report.

With support from CCE, I developed a strategic plan that focused on three goals for the 2001–2002 school year. My first goal was to build strong middle school teams at each school. Forging a functioning team that met regularly was the foundation on which any successful program would be built. But there were some significant obstacles to this. The first challenge was the schedule. As we had learned at G&P, it takes a clear commitment on the part of the principal (or whoever makes the schedule) to design a fair schedule that puts student learning at its center. Principals had to be on board.

Another obstacle were teachers themselves. I knew that some teachers would not want to give up a "free" period to meet with colleagues. They didn't see the value of meeting with teachers who taught a different discipline.

"Why should I meet with the math/science/English/social studies teachers? I don't have anything in common with them. How are they going to help me?"

Some didn't believe they had any responsibility beyond teaching their own subject matter. They rejected anything that seemed "touchy-feely" to them.

"I'm a teacher, not a social worker. My job is to teach kids, not listen to their problems."

Convincing teachers that meeting with each other was in their own best interest would be a challenge.

My second goal was to develop a Middle School Leadership Team (MSLT). The purpose of this group, made up of a team leader or representative from each of the sixteen schools, was to provide a network and a voice for teachers who had long been isolated from each other. It would enable us, as a district, to develop a common vision of effective middle school programs, act as a clearinghouse for information and resources, and make recommendations on behalf of middle school teachers and students. In addition, we would use our monthly meetings to model and develop leadership skills, such as how to develop an agenda, analyze data, set norms, or use a discussion protocol that teacher-leaders could take back and use with their teams. We would later add three middle school subject-area coaches (math, science, English/language arts; there was no social studies coach) to the MSLT, along with a guidance counselor from the high school.

The third goal was to focus on literacy. One of the biggest complaints I'd heard from middle school teachers was that too many of their students couldn't read. "Why aren't those elementary teachers doing their job?" they'd protest. Most middle school teachers had little to no preparation in teaching literacy skills. Many assumed that if students couldn't read by the time they reached sixth or seventh grade, they must be "learning disabled" and a special educator should help them—it was not the job of the math/science/history teacher to "provide remediation." But our G&P team had discovered that by teaching certain reading strategies across disciplines, our students' ability to make sense of all different kinds of texts significantly improved.

This was another area in which research was exploding. Keene and Zimmerman's *Mosaic of Thought* had been my introduction to reading strategies. Now, a growing body of literature focused specifically on young adolescent readers: *I Read It But I Don't Get It* by Cris Tovani; *Nonfiction Matters*, by Stephanie Harvey; *Teaching Reading to Black Adolescent Males* by Alfred Tatum; and *In the Middle* by Nancy Atwell. If one of our biggest challenges in the middle grades was struggling readers, shouldn't literacy strategies be a priority for developing strong middle school programs?

I finally got a meeting with my supervisor. I presented my three goals and a mapped-out action plan for the year. She seemed to approve of my proposals. Then I begged her for a budget.

"What do you need money for?" she asked.

"I would like to be able to give the Middle School Leadership Team members a stipend," I replied. "They'll be giving up their own time to come to monthly meetings after school and taking on additional responsibilities to plan team meetings. It will be a way to acknowledge the extra work they're putting in. I would like to be able to purchase books for people about adolescent literacy. I would like to send people to workshops and conferences. Teachers need to visit other exemplary middle schools in the area, so we need money for substitutes. I would also like a telephone. Nobody knows how to reach me."

"Well," she responded, "we can certainly get you a telephone. I'll have to speak to the superintendent about the rest. Can you write me up a more detailed budget?"

"Of course," I replied. I'd never written a budget proposal before, but I knew how to get help.

I also asked her to allow me to present my goals and action plan to the principals of all the K–8 schools. It was essential to get their support. Nothing would happen in a school without a principal's buy-in. At the very least, we needed their help to schedule a regular meeting time for their middle school teachers. The principals met monthly. I hoped to meet with them to launch our Middle School

Initiative (this is what I called it) before the 2001–2002 school year began.

I finally got a meeting with the principals in November. I eventually got a small budget, too. It took two years to get a telephone. In the meantime, I turned my energies back to the Fitz-Haggerty merger.

Our first meeting as the newly constituted Fitz-Haggerty middle school staff came just a week before school was to begin. People gathered in the teachers' room. You could cut the air with a knife: resentment, anger, antagonism, animosity, fear.

"Well, here we are, finally!" I said to the group, trying to sound chipper and upbeat. People sat stiffly in their seats, not looking at each other, much less making eye contact with me. "It seems, like with many things in education, we'll have to build the plane while flying it," I said. "We all know that feeling, right?"

I had found a video that showed just that: people trying to build a plane as it hurtled through the air, with their wrenches and pliers in hand as they hung desperately onto the wings or tried to bolt down seats, with passengers already in them, air pouring in through open windows. I thought it might make people laugh and loosen up a little. Acknowledge just how awkward the situation was without actually focusing on it. A few people cracked a smile, but it seemed like most were determined not to give an inch.

"I know it's hard to come together in this way," I continued. "I know people are feeling a certain amount of loss. But we also have an opportunity here to build something together that can be really exciting. Because we don't know each other yet, it's important to at least agree to certain norms. Norms give us guidelines about how we want to work together."

At G&P, we had never actually developed norms, but they had evolved in an unwritten way over time. We didn't have that time now. We had to be more intentional. "So, what kind of commitments do we need from each other to be able to do our best work?"

"End meetings on time," said the science teacher pointedly. I smiled, and wrote it on the newsprint.

"What else?"

People reluctantly started to brainstorm.

"Have a written agenda," said someone.

"Get to meetings on time," another chimed in.

"Not interrupt each other."

"Agree to disagree." And so on.

After some discussion, we whittled the ideas down to a handful of norms and the teachers voted to approve them, unanimously. I felt a sliver of hope. We had managed to cross a great divide and agree on something. Granted, it was fairly basic, not too controversial, but at least we had accomplished that. We went on to talk about a variety of logistical issues and then everyone dispersed back to their own classrooms. I rewrote our new norms neatly onto a clean sheet of posterboard and taped it on the wall of the teachers' room.

The next day, when I went to put my lunch in the refrigerator, the posterboard of norms was gone. Did it fall off the wall and get picked up by the custodian? I checked the trash barrel. Not in there. I looked around but didn't see it anywhere. *I'll just have to redo it*, I sighed.

A couple of hours later, one of the former Haggerty teachers came into my office.

"Uh, Kathy, can I show you something?" She gestured for me to follow her. We went into the teachers' room and she opened the door to a utility closet. "I was coming to borrow a broom," she said, "and I found this." There was the posterboard of norms, crumpled up and stuffed in the corner. "See why I didn't want to come here?" she said. I nodded grimly.

It was a rough start to a new chapter in my career. I missed my classroom every single day. *Why did I leave?* I wondered. Kids were so much easier, and so much more fun, to deal with than adults. I missed my friends and colleagues, my "family" at Graham & Parks. I hadn't realized just how special a community I had had there, and

I had not anticipated how lonely it would be without them all. This was brought home to me even more the second week of school.

It was Tuesday, September 11, 2001, at about 9:15 in the morning when a teacher burst into my office. "Have you heard the news?" she gasped.

"No," I replied. "What news?"

"The Twin Towers! A plane crashed into one of the Twin Towers! And then another plane hit the other one! No one knows what's going on. Turn on the news on your computer."

Stunned, we watched as the news showed a plane flying directly into the second tower of the World Trade Center as the first one belched smoke and flame. The video kept repeating; the plane hit the tower over and over and over again. We watched in disbelief. Then she turned to me, "Hey, don't you have a daughter in New York City?" I nodded, my heart pounding. Yes, my older daughter had started college at New York University just six days earlier. Her dorm was two miles from the Towers.

"Hope she's okay," said the teacher as she headed out the door. I was panicked.

I went down to the main office. The school secretary, Dot, took one look at me and said, "What's wrong, honey? You okay?"

"No," I said. "My daughter is in New York. I need to call her."

"Oh, goodness!" she exclaimed. "Here, give me the number. I will dial it for you." In a daze, I wrote down Megan's phone number. The line was busy. In fact, as it turned out, all the lines were busy. We tried four or five times, but to no avail.

"Listen," Dot said, "I'll keep calling for you. I'll call every twenty minutes until we get her. When I get through to her, I'll send someone up to get you. She's going to be okay. Don't worry, she's going to be okay." She stood up and, even though she didn't even come up to my chin, gave me a big bear hug. It was the nicest thing that anybody had done for me at the school since I'd gotten there. It was the only expression of support or caring I got from anybody that day. I knew that if I'd been at G&P, the whole school would have rallied.

Not that there was much anyone could do (and, as it turned out, my family and I were incredibly fortunate that my daughter was safe). But I knew my community would have held me, and my family, in their arms, both literally and figuratively, the way that Dot did. Like I said, schools are all about relationships.

I rewrote the norms for the Fitz-Haggerty middle school team. I kept them in my office and carried them to wherever we had a meeting, be it the teachers' room, the library, or an individual classroom. We met once a week, which was not really adequate, but it was all we had. I made sure to start and end meetings on time. And to check in on the other norms at the end of each meeting. I tried to support the teachers as best I could and, gradually, I developed some trust with a few of the Fitzy folks. I wanted to focus on big ideas—philosophy and vision—but that was a mistake. At this point, everyone was overwhelmed with logistics and day-to-day crises.

In addition to this work to help strengthen the Fitz-Haggerty middle school merger, I had to start implementing my strategic plan for middle schools throughout the city. Working with all sixteen schools at once was impossible, so I reached out to principals who I thought would be interested in building their middle school programs. Three other schools invited me to work with them. And I continued to meet with my Graham & Parks comrades.

In order to develop the Middle School Leadership Team, I sent out an email to principals, assistant principals, and teachers asking them to identify a school representative to participate in monthly meetings. Even though I didn't have any real power, I tried to make my email look very official and sound like a mandate, even though it wasn't. "As part of the 2001–2002 Middle School Initiative, we are forming a Middle School Leadership Team with representatives from each of the K–8 schools. The MSLT will meet monthly and it is important that every school participate. Please let me know who your team leader will be as soon as possible." I was trying to bluff my way into significance.

Some principals responded; some did not. We generally had 65 to 70 percent of the schools represented at any particular meeting. Of those, a core group of eight or nine schools was always there. Others came and went. I couldn't do too much about that, except to share with the schools what we were doing and encourage them to attend when they could. I could only rely on the power of persuasion.

As for the literacy goal, I started doing workshops on the district early release days. About fifty people attended the first workshop, seven or eight people to a table. Most of the male teachers sat at the back two tables.

"Okay, everybody! Let's start with a little activity." I handed out a short article titled "The House," and instructed, "Please read this passage and underline the parts you think are particularly important with the blue pens at your table."

THE HOUSE

The two boys ran until they came to the driveway. "See, I told you today was good for skipping school," said Mark. "Mom is never home on Thursday," he added. Tall hedges hid the house from the road so the pair strolled across the finely landscaped yard. "I never knew your place was so big," said Pete. "Yeah, but it's nicer now than it used to be since Dad had the new stone siding put on and added the fireplace."

There were front and back doors and a side door that led to the garage, which was empty except for three parked 10-speed bikes. They went in the side door, Mark explaining that it was always open in case his younger sisters got home earlier than their mother. Pete wanted to see the house so Mark started with the living room. It, like the rest of the downstairs, was newly painted. Mark turned on the stereo, the noise of which worried Pete. "Don't worry, the nearest house is a quarter mile away," Mark shouted. Pete felt more comfortable observing that no houses could be seen in any direction beyond the huge yard.[2]

Most everybody set to work reading. Except the back two tables. The men there blatantly refused to even look at the handout. They started talking and laughing with each other. I went over to the tables and said, "Hey, guys. What's up? Are you confused about the directions?" They laughed.

"Naw, Kathy," said one social studies teacher. "We read it already. We're fast readers." They all laughed again.

"Okay," I said, trying to maintain my cool. "But what about the underlining part? I don't see that any of you have marked up the page yet."

"Oh, right," said one guy, who picked up a pen and started randomly underlining things.

Another said, "My pen doesn't work." They all laughed again.

"Come on, guys," I said, laughing along with them. "Just give it a try."

"We will," said a math teacher. "But you're making us nervous, looking over our shoulder like that."

"Fine," I replied and walked away, turning my attention to the other six tables where people were taking the activity seriously.

I asked people to share what they had underlined, and then I gave the next direction. "Now, read the passage again but, this time, think about reading it as if you want to rob this house. Underline what you think is important information now, this time using the red pens at your table." Everyone chuckled and set about rereading the piece, now with a specific intention. A few of the men in the back actually joined in, but most still sat there, refusing to engage, talking loudly among themselves.

After sharing out, we tried one more reading, this time as if someone were interested in buying the house. People could see that, depending on one's purpose or intention, a reader would focus on very different information. "All of us ask our students to read text," I said. "But some middle schoolers, particularly those more struggling readers, tend to randomly underline nearly everything because they don't know what they are looking for. Simply setting a purpose can really help those kids figure out what is important."

As people left the workshop, some of the guys from the back tables walked past me.

"Sorry we gave you a hard time," one said to me, laughing. "It actually wasn't bad, Kathy."

"Yeah," said another. "More useful than I thought." The third one didn't make eye contact.

Not bad, I thought. *Two out of three.* Again, I had to rely on the power of persuasion.

I eventually settled into a rhythm, working with the Fitz-Haggerty teachers, attending the other schools' team meetings each week, preparing for and meeting with the MSLT. I still missed my classroom every day, and I still missed my G&P family. But I could see that the work I was doing was beginning to take hold. Teacher teams were coming together. The MSLT was convening regularly, with a quorum. People were getting interested in adolescent literacy strategies. While it sometimes felt like things were moving incredibly slowly, I understood that change takes time.

Unless it comes in the form of a tsunami.

On January 8, 2002, President George W. Bush, with a fanfare of bipartisan support from Congress, signed into law the most sweeping national education-reform bill in our history. No Child Left Behind (NCLB) struck a bargain similar to that of the Massachusetts Education Reform Act (MERS) of 1993: increased funding for increased accountability. But NCLB went beyond MERA in a number of ways. It required standardized testing in English/language arts and math for *all students in grades 3–8 every year*. It mandated that the results be reported for the whole student population but also broken down into subgroups: racial groups, students with special needs, children from low-income families, English language learners (ELLs), and others. It required ELLs who had been in the country for a year to take the ELA exam. ELLs who had been in the country for *even a day* would have to take the math test.

President Bush declared that 100 percent (that is not a typo) of U.S. students would be proficient in reading and math by 2014. NCLB required states to report Annual Yearly Progress (AYP) showing that each school was consistently working toward that 100 percent goal. If a school could not demonstrate such progress for *every* subgroup, the state would label it as "underperforming" and subject it to increasingly draconian "corrective actions" or "restructuring" measures, including closure.

What was the impact of No Child Left Behind on Massachusetts? Enormous.

We had been organizing against the high-stakes nature of the MCAS for years; increasingly, people were questioning the validity of this kind of assessment. But with the passage of NCLB, it felt like an anvil had dropped on us. The full weight of the federal government was now pressing down on schools, backing one-size-fits-all standardized testing. Furthermore, instead of testing less, we were now testing children every year, in every grade starting from third grade—when children are eight years old—to high school.

In addition, NCLB's "accountability" measures were much more specific and harsh than those in the Mass Ed Reform Act. While the state had found it easy to identify and label "underperforming" schools, fixing them was a whole other ball of wax. The Mass Department of Education mumbled about "fact-finding and panel reviews," but did not offer any help to districts with low scores. As Commissioner Mitchell Chester wrote in his 2014 summary of twenty years of Massachusetts education reform, many districts complained about "the state's outsized capacity to identify low performance relative to its much more limited capacity to offer guidance and assistance."[3]

NCLB didn't offer any answers, either. But it did impose sanctions. If a school missed meeting its AYP (Annual Yearly Progress) goals for two consecutive years, it would be labeled by the state as "In Need of Improvement" which also required it to develop a two-year improvement plan. Students in that school would have the option to transfer to a "better" school in the district. If a school missed its AYP target a third year in a row, the school had to provide tutoring and other supplemental services to students.[4] Missing AYP a fourth consecutive year would lead to "corrective action," which could include firing all staff, extending the school day, or other drastic structural reforms. A fifth year of failure led to total restructuring. This could mean hiring a private company to run the school, turning it into a charter school, or closing it altogether.

The same year that the tidal wave of NCLB crashed over schools, the MCAS became binding. That meant that, beginning in the spring of 2002, students had to pass their tenth-grade tests in order to graduate from high school. (Most states do not do this, nor was this a requirement of NCLB.)

Between the graduation requirement, the increased testing in the elementary and middle schools, and the new focus on AYP, the anxiety levels of children, parents, teachers, principals, and administrators were running high. People were afraid. No school wanted to be labeled as failing, especially with the sword of Damocles hanging over its head. But it wasn't just the sanctions that people worried about; the label itself felt terrible. It felt personal. For teachers, it felt like you as an individual had failed because you did not get 100 percent of your students over the proficiency line. Students worried that if they didn't do well, their school would be closed. Reports of children crying, having stomach aches, and even throwing up before the tests were common. (In fact, the MCAS Administrators Manual began to include directions as to what to do if a student vomits on their test booklet or answer sheet.)

Fear and anxiety were not the only emotions swirling. So was confusion.

What is AYP and how is it determined? Who decides a particular school's AYP? What would the cut-off be for an "underperforming" school? Who would write an improvement plan? Who would approve the improvement plan? What if the improvement plan required funding—where would the money come for that? Were they really serious that if just *one* subgroup did not meet AYP, the whole school would be labeled as failing? What about teachers who didn't teach English/language arts or math? Would they be "held accountable," too?

Principals tried to answer these questions in staff meetings, but often they knew little more than the teachers did.

Confusion, anxiety, fear: as the middle school coordinator, I knew this was not an environment conducive to people taking risks, thinking big thoughts, or pondering educational philosophies. Innovation, experimentation, and growth do not thrive in such an atmosphere. I wondered just how much we could accomplish toward remaking our middle school programs in Cambridge in such a climate. I considered, once again, going back to my classroom. At least there I felt like I could make a difference working with children, and I had some control over my life. But colleagues encouraged me to stick it out another year.

"You're making progress!" they said. "You know it is going to take time. This testing stuff isn't going to last forever, or at least things will settle down with it. Don't give up now."

So I decided to give it one more year.

CHAPTER 12

CONSOLIDATING SCHOOLS AND BEYOND
2002–2003

I figured the 2002–2003 school year would be a time to consolidate the growth of the middle school teams started the year before. We had made enough progress with principals that every school had scheduled at least one common planning time for these teams to meet (not always happily or productively, but the time was in the schedule). We were ready to launch our second year of the citywide Middle School Leadership Team. I had received a small budget that enabled me to stipend team leaders. Small shoots of conversation around middle school literacy were sprouting in various places. I was feeling hopeful.

And then, another blow. This one was not federal or even state. It was at our local level. That September, the Cambridge School Committee announced that it was going to close two to four elementary (K–8) schools due to under-enrollment and budget constraints. They did not know which schools. It might be the Kennedy School or maybe the Fitzgerald or maybe the Harrington or maybe the Fletcher . . .

A new kind of panic set in. A more immediate threat overtook our anxiety about NCLB and the MCAS: Who would get the ax? Rumors flew. Each week, it seemed that a different school was headed for the chopping block. No one felt safe. You know the TV show *Survivor*? This was *Survivor: Cambridge Public Schools*—who was going to get voted off the island? It was unclear how or when the school department would make these decisions. If there had been a culture of fear and apprehension before, it was now amped up to the nth degree. Schools started to turn on each other.

When people far from the classroom talk about moving, consolidating, or closing a school, they tend to view it like shifting chess pieces on a board. But schools are living, breathing organisms. They are rooted in neighborhoods, explicit spaces, personal relationships, and histories. Think about moving your home or changing your job. How long does it takes to "settle in," to find your way around, to develop trusted relationships? With schools, it is no different. In fact, it is far more complex.

How were we going to build school-based teams at a time when teachers didn't know what school they would be in—or if they would even have a job? You can't think about building a meaningful middle school program on shifting sands. I wished that I had just gone back to my classroom, but it was too late. I was committed for the year. I had to figure out a way to move the work forward while acknowledging the difficulty of the environment for all the teachers involved.

I decided to focus on literacy. After all, no matter where you ended up as a teacher, you would still have students in front of you and, most likely, have at least some who were struggling readers and writers. We couldn't change what the School Committee would do, but we could improve our own practice. That was my argument, anyway.

When I had first articulated literacy as a focus for our middle school work, I had asked my supervisor what the district's vision for K–12 literacy was. She'd looked at me blankly. "What do you mean?" she'd asked. I knew Cambridge had been working with Lesley University's Literacy Collaborative, led by Irene Fountas, with attention on K–2 literacy. I'd heard that they were beginning to expand into the intermediate grades, too (3–6). In addition, the high school teachers were just beginning to explore a program called Reading for Understanding, developed by West Ed, a group in California that worked on disciplinary literacy, that is, literacy in different subjects or disciplines. It seemed to me that Cambridge should have a consistent philosophy and practice around literacy from kindergarten to twelfth grade. I didn't want to develop a Middle School Literacy Initiative that was not in line with what was happening pre–and post–middle school. But nobody seemed to be in charge of overseeing a district plan.

To figure out how to develop such a plan, I met with elementary teachers and literacy coaches, who helped me understand the Lesley Literacy Collaborative model. I also met with Joan Soble, the newly appointed high school English coach, who was leading the work with Reading for Understanding. Joan had been my daughter's beloved English teacher. I knew, trusted, and admired her. She helped me to develop my middle school plan so that it built a bridge between elementary and high school. We would work closely together for a number of years.

In spite of my many criticisms of the new state and federal regulations, one worked in my favor for the literacy initiative. This was the requirement that educators renew their license every five years, proving (through documentation) that they had earned a certain number of PDPs (Professional Development Points). When the state Ed Reform Act had first introduced license renewal and PDPs, I had thought it was ridiculous. To my mind, good teachers were always learning, always expanding their skills and knowledge base. Did we need to be told and policed to do this? At Graham & Parks, developing our professional practice was baked into the school culture. We read different articles and books, talked about various pedagogical approaches, attended conferences and workshops, reflected on our work, and learned from each other. We had worked with Project Zero, the Coalition of Essential Schools, Expeditionary Learning, the Center for Collaborative Education. That's what teachers did—we learned, and learned, in order to teach well.

The "professional development" (PD) we had received from the district, on the other hand, had been a joke. It felt like it was being done *to* you rather than *with* you. It never felt relevant to your teaching life. It didn't address the real issues you were facing each day in the classroom. These sessions were usually run by "experts" or "consultants" who always seemed to be far from the classroom. They lectured as we teachers sat there passively, exhausted at the end of a long day. I have rarely heard teachers say anything good about PD. That's why the attitude of the men at my literacy workshop did not surprise me. In their defense, they had sat through many useless PD sessions. They had no reason to think that mine would be all that different.

However, there was one exception for me: the Cambridge Middle School Drama Collaborative. This initiative was started by Judith Contrucci, the head of the Arts Department for the Cambridge Public Schools, and the person who had fully and unquestioningly supported my playmaking and theater work. It had been Judith who had found Diana Moller, the theater director from Emerson College, to guide me in our first plays. It was Judith who had paid for the trees of lights every year when we had to transform the cafeteria into a performance space. It was Judith who had told me I was crazy in all sorts of instances (casting by committee, having student directors, choosing to perform *The Caucasian Chalk Circle* with middle school students) but had supported me anyway. She was committed to bringing the arts, especially theater, to middle school kids.

What made the Cambridge Middle School Drama Collaborative so unique compared to other professional development organizations or lecturers? First of all, attending its sessions was voluntary. Judith *invited* teachers to try something new. The people who signed up for it wanted to be there. Secondly, it was immersive. There were six full days of workshops (not on a Saturday but during the school week, interspersed throughout the year), during which time we worked with two talented professionals from the Wheelock Family Theater in learning drama games, scriptwriting, acting techniques, and more.

The collective provided ongoing support. We met once a month after school, where we were able to try out new activities and deepen our experience in drama. At one of these after-school workshops in a school library, our drama trainers told us to "create a rainforest." After an awkward pause, the dozen of us started transforming into different animals, one being a monkey swinging from "tree to tree," another a sloth hanging upside down, someone else a cougar sliding stealthily between the legs of the library tables. My friend Nancy, who was very shy, became a tree. I turned into a toucan and leapt up on the table, crouching and cawing, when a surprised teacher walked in. She stopped in her tracks, we all froze, and then everyone burst out laughing. We were learning to go outside our "comfort zone" and take risks. It was like my Boston Writing Project experience when I learned just how nerve-wracking it can be to share a piece of writing with others. I knew exactly how hard that was, how vulnerable it felt. Doing these exercises gave us all an insight into what it felt like for our students to try these crazy things, too.

We were also able to share out what we were trying in our classes—whether they worked or not. We had a nonjudgmental community of colleagues with whom we could disclose successes and failures. We learned from each other, we were inspired by each other, we supported each other.

In addition, we had two full days of consulting time with our Wheelock experts. They were willing to do anything we needed to support our work. They would come and do workshops with our classes; they would meet with us to plan a class or activities; they would watch us in our class and give feedback. Each teacher decided what would be most beneficial for themselves, and the experts came to us when we needed them.

All these components of the Middle School Drama Collaborative honored teachers. The structure acknowledged the importance of immersion in new learning, the value of doing what you are about to ask students to do, the diversity of each participant's needs (some were brand new to using drama in the classroom), the opportunity to make mistakes, the importance of feedback without judgment or punishment. There were no requirements about producing a play or anything like that. There was simply an invitation to try something new, with a lot of support.

I wanted to keep these lessons in mind as I developed my plan around literacy. Although teachers had to earn PDPs for their license, I wanted the work to be an invitation, not a mandate. I did encourage whole teams to sign up for the course so we would be building team capacity as well as individual skills, but they didn't have to. I would come to their school so they didn't have to travel anywhere, and I could support them in their classrooms if they wished. It would be hands-on, and, like we had done at G&P years earlier, together we would develop lesson plans that teachers could use the next day.

I was ready to launch my Middle School Literacy Initiative. I shared the overview of the plan with the Middle School Leadership Team and invited schools to sign up for a ten-hour onsite course. Once again, I tried to make it sound official, as if it had the full weight of the district behind it. A couple of schools expressed interest. And then I panicked.

How could I lead a ten-hour course on literacy? I was not a literacy expert. I was a humanities teacher who had read a bunch of books, been to a few workshops and institutes, and struggled through trying out strategies in my classroom. I didn't really have the district's support; they were distracted with school closures. I didn't have a budget to hire a real expert. But then I remembered how during much of my teaching career my colleagues and I would have to figure things out ourselves. How at G&P we tried new things, knowing we would struggle, but that that was part of the learning process. I realized that I didn't need to, nor should I, enter into these literacy courses as an expert but, rather, as a fellow learner. After all, that "expert" dynamic was what I was trying to change. I was hoping to support teams of teachers who could experiment and learn together. If they could do it around literacy strategies, they would learn to do it around other challenges they experienced in school, too. My lack of expertise was, in fact, an opportunity to counter the usual model of professional development.

I want to be clear here, though: I am not saying that we don't need experts. We do. In the Drama Collaborative, it was key that teachers were able to work with professionals from the theater world. Ideally, Cambridge would have systematically developed a K–12 literacy initiative based in current research and practice, and would have provided the kind of professional development and ongoing support that Judith Contrucci had offered us in drama. Having that kind of expert teaching, advice, and support is not, however, in conflict with teachers tackling problems in collaboration, learning together, learning from each other. In a vibrant teacher team, people share the challenges of their everyday world and support each other in solving them.

The literacy courses went well. While we didn't expect middle school teachers to become reading teachers, they started to understand the obstacles that adolescent readers face. For example, they became more aware of the challenges of middle school texts. Many elementary teachers know the Five Finger Rule, an easy way to see if a text is too hard for a student—but I didn't know one middle school teacher who knew it. Ask the student to read a page of text aloud. If they falter over more than five words on the page, the text is beyond their reading level. As have most middle school teachers, I'd had students in my class who struggled over more than five words in a *paragraph*. I hadn't realized just how impossible it was for the child to understand the content of anything s/he was reading if the text was that difficult for them.

We talked about how many struggling readers don't know that they can reread a passage if they don't understand it the first time. I was astounded when I first asked students about this.

"You mean that isn't cheating?" one student asked.

"You mean it doesn't mean I'm stupid if I don't get it the first time?" Just the opposite: good readers reread when they are confused.

Struggling readers don't always know which words in a text are critical to meaning and which are not. Here is an example: "The man was wearing a Tyrolean hat." Most twelve-year-olds don't know the word "Tyrolean." While a good reader will know enough to not get too hung up on that word, it could stop a struggling reader dead in their tracks. On the other hand, consider the sentence: "That was antithetical to their beliefs." If you skip over the word "antithetical," you will not get the point of the statement.

We also encouraged teachers to think about reading within their specific discipline. For example, science can be vocabulary-heavy. If teachers think ahead about key vocabulary words or help students to identify words they don't know, they are giving them strategies that will boost their understanding. One science teacher realized how many words had Latin or Greek prefixes and roots that students didn't seem to know. So she made a chart that she put up in her room with twenty of the most common of each. When a student didn't know the meaning of the word "biodiversity," she would point to her chart. In math, teachers know that solving a word problem depends on knowing what is important in the text and what isn't. Showing students how to look for information relevant to the math opened a door for some struggling math learners.

And the literacy courses were instrumental for deepening bonds between the teachers. To give just one instance: the upheaval around school closings, which was causing general citywide anxiety, had particularly rattled the Fitz-Haggerty middle school merger. Our team of Fitz-Haggerty teachers had just been upended the year before and were now facing another year of ambiguity and anxiety. Luckily, a number of them liked the idea of the ten-hour literacy course. Not everyone participated, but enough did from each "side," and that gave us a focus to begin to build trust and respect across that team.

In addition to the literacy work, the MSLT continued to meet once a month. In spite of the chaos in the district around school consolidations, we were able to accomplish some things that year. In support of the literacy work, we developed a districtwide summer reading plan. The Cambridge School Department had had no summer reading expectations for any grade—even though, according to the research, kids reading in the summer is an important way to prevent "summer slide." We drafted a policy statement, designed a template for a summer reading contract, and set up book exchanges to ensure that all students, regardless of their income, could take home books of their choice.

Scheduling was the other big challenge the MSLT took on. As I've discussed, everything begins with scheduling. Teachers need time to meet. Students need time to work—i.e., longer periods than the typical forty-three minutes. Students need time to meet with teachers—i.e., a homeroom or advisory group. At our monthly meetings, people shared strategies that had worked for their own schools while we also advocated for the district to enact more timely and equitable scheduling decisions.

Another focus of the MSLT was building stronger ties to the high school. As mentioned before, Cambridge had sixteen (soon to be twelve) elementary schools feeding into one comprehensive high school. Most middle school teachers had little connection to the high school. Few of them knew any of the high school teachers, even within their own departments. In my many years at Graham & Parks, we had never once had a high school teacher come visit our classes, nor had we visited theirs.

The MSLT decided it was time to bridge this great divide. So we arranged for middle school teachers to shadow former students at the high school for a half day. This gave them a chance to get a firsthand look at what teachers expected of incoming students. As we debriefed each visit, we began to understand why some of our students were falling through the cracks when they passed from the eighth to the ninth grade. We pushed the different department heads to hold meetings that included both middle and high school teachers so they could look at how their work was aligned, or wasn't. Finally, we invited a representative from the high school Guidance Department to permanently join the MSLT.

Then, thanks to the Collaborative Design Team (CDT), our team found significant curriculum support, even during this tumultuous period. The CDT was the brainchild of two visionary curriculum leaders: Joan Stern, the head of Library Services, and Joanne Krepelka, the head of Educational Technology. Their goal was to bring teachers together to develop more project-based curriculum that integrated research and computer skills. That academic year, 2002–2003, they reached out to me to see if I could help them connect with more middle school teachers.

I realized that I had participated in one of these grants myself, at G&P. We had been studying the Civil War and wanted students to research a topic of their own interest—naval battles, women as spies, General William Tecumseh Sherman, the role of music, and so on. Susan (my humanities partner) and I realized, though, that it was difficult to find information that students could access, at least for some of the more unusual topics. We wanted students to do their own research, but we had learned from experience that they needed an "assist." If we could provide them with a couple of "starter" articles or documents, they would have a more solid base to then branch out on their own research.

When we met with our librarian, Jean, she told us about the Collaborative Design Team's grants.

"It's not too late to apply for one," she said.

"What would we use the money for?" we asked.

Jean suggested, "Let's meet with Joan and Joanne and ask them. They might have some ideas about how to help us."

So we did. They offered to give us a stipend to research and collect the articles, photocopy them, and organize them into folders. This would take hours of work, though, that neither Susan nor I felt we had.

"Pay one of your student teachers to do it," Joan suggested.

We could do that?

"Yes!" she said. "The purpose of this project is to support teachers! If that's what would be most helpful to you, then that's how you should use the money."

Because of this small injection of funding, our Civil War research projects were much more successful and of much higher quality than in previous years. We were also able to better support our more struggling readers. We kept the "starter packets" and were able to use them multiple times, so it was an investment that carried far beyond that class. Over time, we started new packets and added to others. This project continued long after I left G&P.

I was thrilled to work with Joan and Joanne again, and was even happier when Joan Soble, the high school English coach, joined our team, along with a few other curriculum folks. Joan brought a strong connection to two initiatives from Harvard's Project Zero: Teaching for Understanding (TfU) and Making Thinking Visible (MTV). TfU is an approach to curriculum design that has four components: choosing a generative topic, identifying big understanding goals, designing performances of understanding, and ongoing assessment. MTV is an approach to developing deeper thinking with students. As the Collaborative Design Team worked with an expanding number of teacher teams across grade levels, teachers began to incorporate these new approaches into their curriculum planning and instructional strategies.

Over a few years, hundreds of teachers participated in Collaborative Design teams. Each year, we had mini-conferences where people were able to showcase and share their work with their Cambridge colleagues. This was teachers helping teachers (not the current website, Teachers Pay Teachers, where teachers try to make a few extra bucks sharing lesson plans). There was true cross-pollination, as one teacher-team's project inspired another. And the cost of it all was a tiny fraction of what the district spent on any outside PD.

So, there were bright spots in the work with middle school teams. But, as we approached spring, and the CPS budget deadline, things were heating up. *Which schools will close?* was the question on everyone's mind. Finally, in the spring of 2003, there came an announcement:

- The King Open School would move and take over the Harrington.
- The Fletcher would merge with the Maynard.
- The Cambridgeport would move out of Cambridgeport and into the old Fletcher building.
- The Peabody would take over the Fitzgerald (including the Fitz-Haggerty merged middle school).
- The Graham & Parks would move to the old Peabody building.
- The Longfellow would merge with the Kennedy.
- The Amigos would share a building with the Dr. Martin Luther King Jr. School.

Four out of Cambridge's sixteen schools escaped unscathed.

It seemed like the School Committee's approach to avoiding making some people upset was to make everybody upset. I was upset, too. And I was done. I decided to resign from my position and go back to my classroom. In spite of the good work we had managed to accomplish that 2002–2003 year, I didn't see any possibility of making headway with middle school reforms under those impending changes. Everyone's bandwidth would be taken up with moving, merging, or closing.

Our superintendent at the time was also done. She had lost the confidence of the School Committee and the community in general. The city launched a search in the early spring and by May 2003 a new superintendent had been hired. JMG was coming from the Midwest, from a much larger district, and seemed to have the unanimous support of the School Committee. The word on the street was that he was tough but fair. After months of confusion and chaos, Cambridge was looking for a strong leader, someone who could take charge, be decisive, get things done. He seemed to be the man for the job.

The morning after I decided to go back to my classroom, I went to our monthly meeting of curriculum coordinators. We had a surprise visitor—our new superintendent. He wouldn't officially be starting until August, but he wanted to begin to meet and connect with people. He seemed relaxed and confident, if not overly warm or friendly.

"You have a problem here in Cambridge," JMG began. Everyone sat up a little straighter. "You have a serious achievement gap here between wealthy and working class, white and Black children. What are you doing about it?"

He looked around the large conference table, as people squirmed a little uncomfortably in their seats. A few offered information, but he did not seem impressed.

"There are no excuses. This has to change. As far as I'm concerned," he continued, "teachers do the hard work. Your job is to support them."

I was dumbfounded. I had never heard an administrator speak this way. He put teachers, the people on the frontline, at the forefront? According to our new superintendent, everything administrators did should be in the service of helping teachers do their job well. He spoke about the imperative of closing the achievement gap, and equity and excellence for all children. He didn't mince words. I felt a glimmer of hope. This guy was no-nonsense. Maybe with a strong leader who had a clear vision, we could actually build strong middle school programs after all. I decided to give it one more year.

CHAPTER 13

JMG

2003–2005

In mid-August, I pulled together some documents for the new superintendent that outlined our middle school strategic plan and initiatives (described in chapter 11). These included support for teachers' practice and professionalism, development of the city-wide Middle School Leadership Team, and continuation of our literacy work. The documents reflected our other work, too, like building bridges between the high school and the middle schools; streamlining scheduling; Collaborative Design Team projects; and regular meetings of the district's middle school teachers, across disciplines. I felt proud of the things we'd accomplished in the past two years, in spite of the lack of institutional support from the district.

I brought a packet of these documents over to Thorndike Street (CPS's central office), where the superintendent worked. As I started up the building's big stone steps, I realized JMG was right in front of me. I called out to him and bounded up the stairs to catch up to him. "Hi, Dr. ___," I said. "I'm Kathy Greeley, and I am the middle school program developer for the district. I'm excited that you are joining CPS!" He stopped and looked at me.

"I was just dropping off some materials for you about what we've been working on in the middle schools for the last couple of years. But I'd be happy to quickly walk you through what's in the packet. Do you have a minute?"

He stretched his arm out to look at his watch, and said, "No. I don't."

As I wrote in the last chapter, JMG was no-nonsense. Even so, I was a bit taken aback. I stammered, "Um, well, okay. Here is the packet. If you have any questions about it, I'd be happy to talk with you." He took the packet and turned to go into the building.

Then he stopped and turned around. "How long have you had this job?" he asked.

"Um, two years," I answered.

"Are the middle schools better now than they were two years ago?" he demanded. He was not smiling.

"Uh, well, that's a complicated question."

"No, it isn't. Are they better now than they were two years ago? What have *you* done in two years to make them better?"

"I think we're on the right track," I managed to say.

"I asked what have *you* done to make them better," he snapped.

Brain freeze. "Uh, I tried to outline that in the report I brought you."

"So you've had two years and you can't tell me what you've done to make the middle schools better." He turned on his heel and strode away.

I stood on the steps, shaking. Not a very auspicious beginning.

Even though we were facing a tumultuous year of consolidating, closing, and moving schools, I thought all this transition offered a critical opportunity to develop quality middle school programs across the district. I hoped that, in spite of my initial encounter with him, I might get some support from the new superintendent. But I quickly discovered how out of touch I was with the ground game. Teachers were absorbed with just getting their classrooms set up; finding out where the cafeteria and gym were (not to mention the bathrooms); meeting and adjusting to new colleagues, administrators, and families. It would be quite a while before we could talk about a middle school vision.

Then a new crisis emerged in the Cambridge Public Schools. It turned out that the high school—Cambridge Rindge and Latin School

(CRLS)—was in danger of losing its accreditation. It became clear that the superintendent's focus, and that of district administrators, was going to be on getting CRLS through this process successfully.

So, realizing—again—that I could not expect support from Thorndike Street, I went to the schools where they wanted me. I continued to chip away at my plan—supporting teacher teams, working with the Middle School Leadership Team, running professional development on literacy strategies, working to bridge the eighth to ninth grade transition. Basically, I put my head down and plowed on. But, yet again, I found myself wishing I had followed my instincts the previous spring and gone back to my classroom.

As the year went on, however, I felt good about the work that we were doing. While there weren't revolutionary changes, I could see progress. Teachers were developing into team leaders at their schools. Teacher teams were talking together more about building a developmentally responsive middle school program within a K–8 building. People were trying out the literacy strategies. The Collaborative Design Team was growing rapidly, with many people interested in doing integrated, project-based work—some of whom had never done so before. A few of our proposals to the high school had taken root. Middle school teachers were meeting in discipline-based groups across the city for the first time.

By the end of the year though, despite all of this progress, without more of a commitment from the district to focus on middle school reform, the frustration I felt outweighed our accomplishments. It felt like déjà vu all over again. I was ready to quit.

I shared this sentiment one day with one of the principals I had come to work closely with and trust. He was highly respected by his staff, beloved even, and he had always encouraged his teachers to experiment and speak up. He had managed one of the trickiest consolidations that year—of a progressive school (that had grown out of the Graham & Parks model, years earlier) with a very traditional one—and, although a bit battered and bruised by the process, he was still standing.

"I think I'm done, Tim," I said. "I think I'm going to go back to teaching."

I wasn't sure how I would do that because G&P now had two young, amazing middle school humanities teachers. They had taken up the mantle of the G&P program and had also started some other wonderful projects. They were doing a great job. No employment opportunities there. But I was open to, excited even, about working at a different school. Also, I was tired of my consultant role. I wanted to be a member of a community again, rather than moving from school to school. And going back to the classroom would give me a kind of control over my own environment that I hadn't felt in years.

"But, Kathy! The whole focus for next year is going to be on the middle schools—finally!" Tim explained that the superintendent had announced this plan to the principals. "You've been waiting for this for so long! Don't give up now!"

I hadn't realized that that was the agenda for the 2004–2005 year. No one had said anything to me about it. But other principals and administrators I spoke with confirmed Tim's message.

My supervisor had once told me that I was like a dog with a bone. I don't think she meant it to be complimentary, although she said it with a laugh. It was true that I don't like to give up on things. I don't like to admit defeat. Our hard work had led to progress in the middle schools. Certain structures were in place. We were poised to make a significant difference with our middle school programs in our K–8 schools. *The district was finally going to focus on this work?* I dared to believe this. *Maybe Tim was right. Why leave when you are just on the brink of a breakthrough?*

I decided to give it one more year.

But that breakthrough did not happen. In late August, the superintendent announced that the district needed to spend another year on the high school. Things were in a precarious state there and CRLS needed more support. The district would push back the middle school agenda another year. By this time, it was far too late to find a teaching position in the schools. I couldn't believe I was stuck yet again. A déjà vu of déjà vu.

I felt I had no choice but to persist. After all, although I didn't have a lot of support from the people above me, I did have a strong network of teachers, teacher leaders, some principals, and curriculum coordinators around me on whom I relied for inspiration, feedback, encouragement, collaboration, and guidance. Our Middle School Leadership Team continued to develop and deepen trust among the school representatives, in spite of the fact that we never had full participation from all of the (now twelve) K–8 schools. I loved working with the Collaborative Design Team, which came to involve a number of elementary and middle school teachers. I continued to attend team meetings in various schools, encouraging teachers to think both how to build a more developmentally appropriate middle school program, much of which we based on the principles of the National Turning Points Network.

But another change was afoot. While the superintendent kept his attention on the high school, he also launched new district-wide assessments in math and English/language arts that teachers were to administer three times per year.

This took people by surprise. Teachers were already greatly concerned with how much school time the MCAS took up in the spring. Why would we add more standardized testing? It felt like students would be taking tests all the time!

JMG explained that Cambridge teachers would design the district assessments for Cambridge teachers; they would not be for anything related to the MCAS or the state. These would be "formative" assessments, meaning that schools would use them to measure how well students were doing and what adjustments teachers might need to make to support them.

"But we already know that," a number of teachers objected.

"You think you do," JMG responded, "but it's not uniform across the district. This will give us important data."

Several teachers volunteered to help design the assessments. Yet, the final version of the tests looked remarkably like a mini-version of the MCAS. People wondered if the real purpose of these district assessments was to give students practice for the Big Kahuna.

One day that fall (2004), I joined a team meeting at the Peabody School. Under the city's school-consolidation plan, the Peabody had just taken over the Fitzgerald, which—just two years earlier— had merged its sixth, seventh, and eighth grades with the Haggerty School's. The Fitz-Haggerty teachers resented the takeover by the Peabody. This school community had, yet again, to deal with a new mix of teachers, feelings of resentment (on all sides), and a different principal. I had been working with the team to negotiate this difficult transition.

In today's team meeting, the teachers and the principal were talking about students' disruptive behavior. They had established a fairly strict detention policy—for tardiness, for "disrespecting" a teacher, for not having your homework done, and for many other offenses.

The math teacher raised her hand and said, "You know, I really wonder about this detention policy."

"What do you mean?" another teacher asked sharply.

"Well, do you notice who the kids are on the list? First of all, they are mostly Black. And secondly, they are the same kids, day after day after day." All the adults at this meeting were white, except for the math teacher, Maria, who was Puerto Rican.

"They're the ones who are disruptive!" exclaimed another teacher. "I can't help it that they don't do what they're told."

The principal sat back and watched as the teachers argued.

"But what are we really accomplishing by having the same kids in detention? Clearly, they aren't learning to change their behavior," Maria argued. "Maybe we should try a different approach."

"You mean just pander to them?" snapped the science teacher.

"These are problem kids and they need to learn to get their act together," the history teacher said emphatically.

"But that's my point," Maria insisted. "They aren't learning. They're just learning to see themselves as bad." This teacher was challenging not only her own thinking but everyone else's, too. She was looking at a school policy and pointing to the evidence that it was not working to meet the stated goal. This kind of dialogue among teachers could be very productive. This was an example of colleagues coming together to solve a problem. I was excited.

After a few more minutes of debate, the principal spoke up for the first time. "We will not be changing the detention policy," she said flatly. "What's next on the agenda?"

Maria looked stung, like someone had just slapped her across the face. The history and science teachers who had been particularly vocal about punishing kids looked smug. Other teachers, the ones who had remained silent, looked down at their laps.

I was furious. I couldn't believe that the principal had squashed this important discussion. Isn't that the definition of crazy—doing the same thing over and over, hoping for a different outcome? But maybe the outcome didn't matter to her. Maybe she wasn't interested in supporting these struggling students, mostly boys of color. Maybe she wanted them to get that message, that they were "bad" kids. Maybe she didn't want her teachers to be problem solvers. Maybe she didn't want her staff to have agency. Maybe she didn't want change.

It was in that moment that I decided to make a change. I could see the power a principal had to create a strong school environment. She could support her staff or discourage them. She could encourage thoughtful debate or shut it down. She could empower her teachers to be creative thinkers or simply insist on conformity. She could invite different perspectives or impose her own authority. I thought of the ways that Len, our principal at Graham & Parks, had nurtured an environment that was based on trust in teachers. Maybe it was time for me to step out of my role of friendly persuader and more firmly into a role of leadership. Maybe it was time to become a principal.

The Boston area is home to many good principal programs, but one in particular appealed to me: the Principal's Residency Network (PRN), affiliated with the Center for Collaborative Education and Northeastern University. I personally knew the two people who ran PRN and had deep regard for them as educational leaders. Larry Myatt was a founder of Fenway High School, one of the most successful non-exam high schools in Boston. Meg Anderson had been a school leader at CRLS in Cambridge, and I knew how much her teachers trusted and respected her. Larry and Meg led PRN, and the principals of all the schools that were part of the network served as its faculty.

But what I most liked about PRN was its year-long, full-time paid internship to work alongside a principal in a school. I knew I was a hands-on, experiential kind of learner, so this program was more attractive to me than being in classes all day and working with an administrator for a couple of months. Through PRN, I could once again be part of a school community while learning what it took to be a principal, starting in August and going all the way through June.

The one challenge with PRN was finding a principal who would be willing to commit to the PRN meetings and requirements. It definitely took a huge commitment from someone who was already insanely busy. The leading principal would need to attend regular network meetings and events, as well as supervise me. I needed to find a principal who not only was willing to put in that extra time but was also someone whom I respected and from whom I wanted to learn. I considered going back to Graham & Parks, but I decided it was important to be in a different kind of school.

One day, as I was visiting a middle school team at the Dr. Martin Luther King, Jr. school (MLK), one of the more challenging schools in the district, the principal of the school stopped me. "I hear you're looking to do a principal's internship," she said. "I would love to do it with you."

I was surprised and pleased, but a bit hesitant. Not only was Carole a new principal and new to Cambridge, she was very young, just twenty-nine years old. I was old enough to be her mother. I had been working in schools nearly as long as she'd been alive. *Shouldn't I look for someone with more experience?* I wondered. But I didn't want to be ageist. In fact, I felt that I learned a lot from people younger and less experienced than I. They had fresh perspectives, a different energy, new ideas—and I remember how frustrated I had felt in my twenties not to be taken seriously by older people.

Nowadays, many principals are in their twenties and early thirties, but this was not typical in 2005. Most principals at that time, especially the ones whom I had admired, had spent a number of years in the classroom. They were seasoned veterans and had a good understanding of pedagogy, politics, and people—all important for a principal to be successful. I do believe there are certain "naturals," people who somehow have the right instincts very early in their career, who are the exception to the rule. But I am dismayed by the trend to hire younger and younger people to be school leaders—not just principals but superintendents as well. Often, these folks have been trained in a corporate management style (one school leader I knew revered Jack Welch, the former CEO of GE, and the book *Good to Great*) and buy into the data-driven demands of the corporate reform movement. They are usually steeped in the model of "no-excuses" charter schools (even when they are working in public schools), regard teachers who speak up as problematic or even insubordinate, and have been taught how to evaluate and judge teachers rather than nurture and support them. Many have never known a time, even as students, when standardized testing wasn't the driving force in education. They know little of progressive, democratic models of schooling and can't even envision them.

But Carole struck me as one of the exceptions. She had come into a very traditional school that had been known for its resistance to change and had managed to win over much of the staff's trust in a short time. Although the previous principal had been there for over twenty years and had been much loved by his community, the teachers I spoke with were positive, even enthusiastic, about this new blood.

I had one other hesitation, though. MLK was located in a historically Black neighborhood of Cambridge. The students and families at this school were primarily Black. Most of the teachers were white. MD, the assistant principal, was one of the few Black staff at the school. He had also applied for the principal's job, and CPS had hired this younger white woman from outside of Cambridge over him. How would it feel to him, as well as to the community at large, to have another white woman join the leadership team? Carole urged me to speak with him directly.

MD and I sat down together in his office. He was a bit wary at first. But when I explained the reason for our meeting, he relaxed slightly.

I told him, "I'm excited about the possibility of working at MLK, but I cannot accept Carole's offer without first running it by you. It is important to me that you feel comfortable with this. If not, I'll keep looking for a school to do my internship."

"Why do you feel that way?" he asked.

"Because I understand the role of racism in our society and in our schools. I believe children need to see people who look like them in positions of authority and power. I know that, even with the best of intentions, as a white woman, I don't see or experience the things that people of color do," I responded. We talked more, sharing a bit of our own backgrounds and histories. We also talked about issues of race and racism, in the Cambridge Public Schools and beyond. I tried to make it clear that I was committed to working on those issues if I came to MLK.

"If that's truly how you feel, then I would welcome working with you here. I think you, Carole, and I can make a really good team!" he said, reaching his hand across the desk. We shook on it, and a new chapter in my life was about to open.

I don't remember much of the rest of that year. The district was not hiring anyone to take my place as the middle school program developer, so I knew that the work with the Middle School Leadership Team would most likely languish.

But we had instituted a number of changes that would continue without me:

—Teacher teams were meeting on a regular basis now in all twelve K–8 schools.

—Academic departments were meeting with sixth-, seventh-, and eighth-grade teachers on a regular basis.

—Some schools had embedded disciplinary literacy practices.

—The Collaborative Design Team would continue to work with integrated teams of teachers to develop strong thematic, project-based curricula.

—Teachers had broken out of their isolation in their own schools and had more of a network to connect with others.

—Communication continued between the high school and middle school teachers, who had implemented new protocols to help students transition into the ninth grade.

It frustrated me that we had never had the full force of the district leadership behind us; I could only imagine the progress we could have made if we had had their support. But I did recognize that we had implemented and institutionalized many improvements that helped both teachers and students. It was time for me to move on.

CHAPTER 14

IS THIS WHAT A PRINCIPAL DOES?
2005–2006

I spent the first day of my principal internship at the Dr. Martin Luther King, Jr. School looking for chairs. Actually, some chairs had been delivered that morning, but they were not the right chairs. We were trying to set up a reading lab for middle school students; the chairs we had received were for kindergarteners. I spent hours that day walking around the building, peering into boxes, looking through purchase-order forms, calling people at Central Office (who were all on vacation), and trying to reach vendors. *Is this what a principal does?* I wondered. Yes, I found out—this is what a principal does. And a thousand other things as well.

In the beginning of the year, I followed Carole around much of each day. She included me in all her meetings—with teachers, students, parents, district administrators, and all the other people who demanded her time. After school, we would sit in her office to reflect on and process all that had happened that day. She would always ask me first for my thoughts but was open and honest with hers.

Along with shadowing her, Carole suggested that I spearhead a couple of projects for the school. The first seemed like a natural fit: supporting the middle school teachers in developing a humanities model. The humanities curriculum at Graham & Parks had been the first in the city, but since the mid-1990s other schools in the district had adopted the model. Carole was concerned about rigor in her upper grades. She thought an interdisciplinary and project-based approach would engage students more. She had spoken with her teachers about it, and they seemed enthusiastic.

The second initiative focused on identifying a "social competency" program to introduce to the school. In a survey conducted the year before, MLK teachers and parents had indicated the need for a common and consistent way to handle student behavior. My role was to lead the K–8 faculty through this search and selection process and to develop an implementation plan that would begin with staff training the following summer. I was less enthusiastic about this project as I was skeptical of social competency programs, but Carole urged me to keep an open mind.

After four years of working at the district level, it felt good to be part of a school community again, even if it was a new one for me. It was wonderful to be around students again; I especially enjoyed the sixth-, seventh-, and eighth-graders. I even looked forward to my daily duty of supervising the cafeteria in the morning and occasionally covering recess. Most teachers were friendly or at least polite. One group eyed me more skeptically, though—the unofficial "Welcoming Committee." Five or six older Black women, most of them grandmothers of students in the school, sat in the front lobby every morning presiding over court. They not only knew nearly every child in the school, they knew their families. They not only knew their families, they knew generations of those families. They chided a seventh-grader for being tardy too many times, reminded another to get their homework done. These women were the school elders. They were powerful and not easily won over. I had approached them early on, knowing that their approval was key to my acceptance at the school. I persisted in being friendly, but I was pretty sure they saw me as one more white person trying to mess with their school.

One day in September, maybe the second or third week into school, I was standing just outside the school office talking with a teacher when three eighth-grade girls came tearing past us, laughing loudly. "Excuse me," I sighed to the teacher. "I think I have to deal with this." I called to the students, but they ignored me. I managed to catch up with them just as they were about to run up the stairs. I put out my arm to block them. "Come on, ladies," I said. "You know you're not supposed to run through the halls like that."

"Sorry, Ms. Greeley," one of them giggled.

"Okay. Look, please walk back to the office door and try again, this time the right way." They shrugged their shoulders and did as asked. I watched as they retraced their steps and then headed up the stairs. I could hear them snicker just as they got out of sight.

"Good for you for making them stop," said the teacher who had witnessed the incident.

"I think I'm being tested," I said to her. She nodded in agreement.

The next morning, I was surprised to see S, one of the girls from the hallway incident the day before, sitting in the school office with a woman whom I presumed was her mother. I greeted them, but neither would make eye contact with me. I went to drop off my coat and backpack when Carole asked me to step into her office.

"But I need to supervise in the cafeteria," I said. "No one is there."

"I've asked someone to cover for you," she responded. "Please come in and sit down." I was puzzled, but I took a seat at the round table she had in front of her desk. She sat down across from me and sighed. "It seems that a student is claiming that you assaulted her yesterday."

I was stunned. "What?"

Carole took a deep breath. "S—'s mother has made a formal complaint against you. She said you grabbed S by the arm and twisted it so hard that she has bruises. I have to ask you: Did you grab her?"

"Are you kidding? No! I would never do something like that. You know me better than that."

"Kathy, I know this is upsetting, but I'm responsible for investigating this matter. I have to follow the protocol. We're waiting for the district lawyer to show up and a police officer. We need to get all the details from your perspective. We'll then interview S and her friends who were with her at the time, and then any other possible witnesses. I'm supposed to send you home until all this is cleared up, but I'm just going to ask you to stay in my office for the day."

I felt humiliated. Here I was in the principal's office, not as a school leader but as an accused criminal. I was new to this school. No one really knew me. Three fourteen-year-olds held my future in their hands. Were S's two best friends going to turn on her? Could I really count on them to tell the truth? I had little confidence that things would go my way, even though I had done nothing wrong. Luckily, that teacher had been there in the hallway with me at the time, but she couldn't see around the corner to actually witness my stopping the girls on the stairs.

We waited in the office for the district's lawyer to arrive, along with a Cambridge police officer. Everyone who walked by the office wondered what was going on. After hearing my side of the story, they called in my accuser and her mother. Carole asked to see the girl's bruise, but they couldn't find anything. The mother insisted, though, that I had grabbed her daughter and brutally wrenched her arm. The girl just nodded and shrugged her answers to Carole's probing, her eyes cast down at the table.

Carole then called in the two other girls who had been involved with the incident. "Did you see Ms. Greeley grab and twist S's arm?" she asked.

They laughed. "What? Naw, Ms. Greeley didn't touch her. Or any of us. She was just telling us to behave. We were being a little crazy."

I was surprised, and relieved. Carole then called in the teacher who had also been a witness. She, too, corroborated my story.

I thought that would be the end of it. Clearly, the girl, or the mother, had fabricated the story. For what reason, I wasn't sure, but I was ready to get on with my work. But that was not the protocol. I had to remain in the office the rest of the day as administrators reviewed and filed paperwork. As the day went on, news spread of the accusation. Some teachers came by the office to express sympathy or support. Some avoided any eye contact. Students, particularly the older ones, looked warily at me. I knew that they knew what had happened. I didn't know if they would ever trust me again, regardless of the truth. After all, the students and family involved were Black; I was white. It wouldn't be the first time a white person's word had prevailed over a Black person's claim of injustice.

It turned out that the mother who had leveled the accusation (and it was the mother, not the daughter) did have a vendetta against the school. The previous spring, the school had filed a 51-A, a legal charge against a parent or guardian that automatically involves the Department of Social Services (DSS). School personnel are "mandated reporters," meaning they are required by law to report even suspicion of a parent or guardian's neglect or any kind of abuse, or be subject to criminal charges themselves. In my experience at Graham & Parks, this call was not made lightly. People worried about negative repercussions, and, too often, the involvement with DSS produced few positive outcomes. I didn't know the circumstances that had led Carole to call DSS the previous spring, but I did better understand why this mother acted the way she did. I was a pawn in a bigger game that involved race, class, and power.

It was hard to walk into the school the next day. Carole had instructed me not to discuss this incident with anyone—staff, students, or parents. "But," I'd objected, "everyone has heard that I supposedly assaulted a student! I want to be able to clear my name."

"I know it's frustrating," Carole responded. "As a leader, you will learn that you can't explain everything to everybody. You just have to live with it. For legal and other reasons, it's the best thing to do."

I reluctantly conceded. But I dreaded facing people.

Of course, the first group I encountered was the Welcoming Committee. While they had previously eyed me with mistrust, this morning arrows of condemnation pierced my body. Their suspicions had been confirmed and they had passed judgment. *Guilty, guilty, guilty.* I smiled at them weakly, but they just stared back with reproach. The truth is, these women were living the statistics that I only knew on paper. Children and families of color are routinely overrepresented in every form of discrimination and institutional interaction, be it the referral of Black boys to special education programs, the suspension and expulsion rates of Black students, involving Black families with the DSS, and/or the involvement of the police department and the court system in school-based disciplinary issues. They had no reason to trust me; they had a whole lot of reason *not* to trust the system.

I went up to the third floor, where the middle school was. I was hoping that the kids would feel some sympathy for me. After all, S's friends had negated her accusation. But that was not the case. As kids walked down the hall, some avoided eye contact. Others looked directly at me and then burst out laughing once they had passed. Small clusters of chatting students would fall silent, giving sidelong glances as I walked by. I felt like a wounded animal among predators: they could sense a weakness. Because even though I knew (and they knew) I had done nothing wrong, I knew (and they knew) I was going to be just a bit more wary in my interactions with them. My natural inclination was to talk to the kids, especially the girls involved in the incident, to share my feelings and listen to theirs. But, with my gag order, that was not an option.

A few days later, Carole again called me into the office. "Did you see the *Cambridge Chronicle* today?" she asked. This was our weekly local paper.

"No," I responded warily.

"Well, it's not a big deal, but there's a little article in it about the incident with S."

"What?!" I couldn't believe it. She pulled out a copy of the newspaper and pointed to a short paragraph in the crime section. That was pretty much the only section of the paper I ever read. It listed all the crimes that had happened in the city that week and it was useful to know what was going on in different neighborhoods.

The article couldn't have been more than six or eight lines. It stated that "a principal intern" working at the M. L. King School had been accused of assaulting an eighth-grade girl. It said that the incident was "under investigation." It did not say that the accusation had been proven to be utterly groundless. It did not say that the parent who had made the complaint had a grudge against the school. While it did not mention any names, it didn't need to. There was only one principal intern at MLK and everyone knew who it was. I was absolutely devastated.

"But they dismissed the case!" I objected.

"I know," Carole responded. "Just ignore it."

It is difficult to describe how much this rocked me. I had worked (and lived) in Cambridge for over twenty years and had a reputation in the community. Would people read the *Chronicle* and judge, or even wonder? Was this incident going to end my career? It was a false accusation. I did not want to "just ignore it." I wanted to tell people the truth. But I had been told to keep my mouth shut. I felt powerless in the court of public opinion. I knew I had to find other ways to rebuild trust, especially in the school. I did not realize just how long this would actually take.

I decided to focus my energy on my projects, beginning with humanities. I had loved teaching humanities and had worked with a number of different teachers in adopting the model. I thought it would be good for me to work on something in which I had confidence. When I'd started PRN (Principal Residency Network) in August, Larry and Meg had asked us about the "high-wire act." What did we anticipate would push us, ask us to dig deep, confront our assumptions, require the courage to step out on a limb (or a wire)? *Well*, I'd thought to myself, *introducing humanities to the Martin Luther King School won't be it*. But I was wrong.

Like many middle schools, MLK had been departmentalized so that sixth-, seventh-, and eighth-grade students had separate classes (and teachers) for reading, language arts, and social studies. Carole wanted more integration of skills and content, more opportunities for project-based learning, and less time wasted in transitions. She was concerned that students weren't being challenged enough, that the work, especially in language arts and social studies, was rote and uninspiring, and that some of the teachers' expectations were too low.

In the spring before my internship, Carole and I had met with the three teachers who would constitute the humanities team and presented the idea. Jack, a young part-time reading teacher who had just been hired for his first full-time teaching position, was enthusiastic. Joan, a talented veteran of thirty years at MLK, was moving from the fourth grade to the middle school. While less enthusiastic than Jack, she was open to the idea of trying something new. She felt that the interdisciplinary model of humanities was not all that different from what she had been doing in her fourth-grade classroom. Sharon, another veteran teacher, a close friend of Joan's and one of the few Black staff at the school, was more hesitant. She explained that she'd heard about humanities for years, thought it was a good idea, but was worried about whether she could make the shift.

Carole had concerns about Sharon's teaching. Although Sharon had attended numerous courses and workshops over the years, her practice never changed. Students copied work from the board and filled in worksheets, showing little understanding of the material. She used the same lesson plans year after year. She even taught the same vocabulary and spelling words, not checking if her students already knew the words or not. Carole proposed that Joan and Sharon co-teach the sixth-grade class, and I would meet with them three times a week for planning. With this kind of support, Sharon agreed to give it a try.

At one of our first planning meetings, when Carole was not present, Sharon confessed that she really didn't want to do "this humanities thing" after all. She was "comfortable" with her teaching. Joan and I suggested taking the small steps of integrating some of the content of the humanities class (on ancient civilizations) as a source for vocabulary, spelling, and writing mechanics, but Sharon was resistant. She expressed fear of "letting go" of a structure to which she was accustomed. She felt that she had identified the key words, grammar, etc., that her students needed to know to pass the standardized tests and that, if she deviated from that, she would be undermining their ability to succeed.

I brought articles from leading journals like *Educational Leadership*, *Reading Teacher*, and *Phi Delta Kappan* to share with the teachers so we could discuss current research and good practices. Each time we planned to discuss an article, though, Sharon "hadn't had a chance to get to it." I offered to teach some model lessons for

Sharon's class, and she welcomed this idea. She found the lessons "very interesting" and, with support, started trying some of her own. She felt positive about how the lessons went, and students were responsive, but without my encouragement she tended to fall back on her worksheets and textbooks.

Whenever I suggested looking at students' work together or asked what Sharon was seeing in their writing, Sharon said either that she didn't have the papers or hadn't had time to read their drafts. When students eventually did get their papers back, Sharon had focused on spelling and punctuation, with little attention to the students' ideas, organization, voice, or other elements of good writing. I tried to draw in Joan, who was embracing the humanities model, to reassure and inspire Sharon, but she did not want to antagonize her friend and colleague. "I don't want to seem like I know it all," she said privately.

With Jack, a different issue arose. While he had paid lip service to a humanities model and collaborative planning, he turned out to be a lone wolf. He would sit in our humanities meetings with Joan and Sharon and not say a word. He too had "not gotten around to" reading the articles I was sharing. When he was invited to speak, he declined. He was not interested in brainstorming together or receiving any kind of suggestions, much less any feedback. He was, in fact, the most resistant member of the team. His disdain for me was palpable. He did not show up for planning meetings and resisted writing lesson plans, so I often didn't know beforehand what he was going to do in class. While he had a good rapport with students, his class felt like a freewheeling chat. He did not have clear criteria or expectations for his assignments, gave little feedback to students, and took forever to return their work.

At first, I tried to ignore his passive hostility. Since he didn't make time to meet with me, I reached out through emails, saying things like, "What are you thinking about for the next step for book groups?" or "I had a thought about . . . What do you think?" or "Let's work on scoring the kids' [projects] on Monday (if you agree with my suggestions).” But, over time, my communication with him became increasingly strained.

Carole met with him and explained that she wanted him to do these plans, using either a model from Joan or from a humanities teacher at another school. She also laid out other expectations she had of him. It all seemed very clear, but the next week, when I asked him about the plans, he told me they weren’t required.

“Actually, Jack, they *are* required,” I said.

“Is this a district expectation for all teachers or what?” he demanded.

“Carole is asking for this level of documentation from the whole King humanities team,” I explained. “It gives us a written record to refer back to, it helps Carole know what is going, and it gives me a chance to look at ways to support you all.”

“I want to see it *in writing*, then. From Carole,” he retorted.

“I’m sure she would be happy to do that for you,” I responded, tight-lipped.

By December, Carole’s frustration with Jack was growing, too. She gave him a critical evaluation and put him on a Corrective Action Plan. CAPs are intended to help teachers target specific areas for improvement. A good CAP outlines explicit practices and doable goals—along with the supports that the school will provide to the teacher—that the evaluator would then assess within a certain time limit. The CAP is also a warning. Teachers need to show some progress toward those goals or they face another negative evaluation and possible dismissal (especially if they have “provisional” status).

But are CAPs successful in nurturing strong teaching? I’m not so sure. If a process is fair, the steps outlined in a CAP should come as no surprise to the teacher. Specific practices or skills that a teacher needs to work on should have been addressed long before the need for a formal intervention. But what does it say if a teacher continually resists feedback?

In Jack’s case, he had received specific feedback (and offers of help) for several months. He did make some progress, but he dragged his feet at every step. "If this is what the district seems to want me to do, I guess I have to do it," he said more than once. If a teacher is only going to grow and improve his/her practice in response to prodding from an administrator, do you really want that person on staff? At what point do you decide to give up on a teacher? How much time, support, guidance, and resources do you invest in someone before deciding that they are not right for the job?

With a veteran teacher like Sharon, helping her to develop her practice was more complicated. As one of the few Black teachers in the school, she was a critical part of the community. She had a lot of strengths in dealing with students and families. Her class was always organized and orderly. Students did not mess around in her class (the rules were always very clear). They did well enough on the standardized tests, even if Carole and I felt she was not particularly rigorous, much less inspirational. She did try to make some changes to her curriculum, but it was clear that without continual pushing she would fall back into her comfort zone.

Having strong teachers is the most important part of a good school. But how to make this happen is one of the most difficult challenges that principals face. Carole was committed to supporting teachers to grow and develop in their classrooms. But these two were not the only staffing concerns Carole faced. There were a handful of other staff on her radar. In the spring, she decided to meet with the director of Human Resources and the district lawyer to discuss her dilemmas. She invited me, as usual, to go along.

In the first case she presented (neither of the teachers I was working with), Carole had brought every memo, email, attendance sheet, documentation of meetings, etc., that she might need. She had informed the employee of her concerns, had given feedback (both positive and critical), had set up a corrective action plan, and was still having problems.

The lawyer (MM) described the progression of discipline—verbal warning, written warning, written reprimand, suspension. She talked about the difference between written warnings and a written reprimand (the reprimand is harsher). If things don't change after the reprimand, Carole could make a recommendation for a suspension. This would then lead to a hearing. It would take a long time before the employee could be dismissed.

MM also encouraged Carole to reiterate the history of complaints in a letter. This has the effect of showing the seriousness over time, providing the employee with a clear picture of the issues, and supplying a context while documenting what has been done for outsiders (e.g., an arbitrator). She stressed the importance of documentation and of tone. She said the tone of written memos should not be chatty or friendly but rather formal.

The Human Resources director (BA) took a very different stance. She recommended "lightening up." She said the employee had had a good record over time and had been respected for her work. She pointed out the importance of maintaining a good working relationship with someone and that people do go through hard times in their lives.

As I sat listening, I was struck again by how complicated this work of building strong schools is. It takes a tremendous amount of time and energy. When there's a problem, the time that goes into both supervising and then documenting it takes time away from other very important work. It was interesting to hear the lawyer on the one hand and the HR director on the other. While one was concerned with legality, evidence, and fairness of process, the other seemed to think more about human relations. I could see that they really needed to work together.

I also realized that building a strong staff is a long-term process, one that takes time and deliberate process. At the end of the school year, Carole had to make a cut in staff. She cut Jack. And when the assistant principal position opened up (MD had taken a principal position in another school), she hired Sharon, where she could put her strong organizational and disciplinary skills to good use.

I spent a lot of time that year thinking about how school leaders can help teachers grow and improve their practice. What had helped me develop as a teacher? It had taken years to change my classroom from a stand-and-deliver model to one that was more student-centered. And I had had a supportive principal, a team committed to growth, wonderful mentors, and a school culture that felt safe and encouraged experimentation. But I was also actively *trying* to change! Maybe the key is exactly that: I *wanted* to change. I knew something wasn't working right and I wanted to do better. But where had that self-reflection come from? I could have blamed my students, or the district, or society. But somehow I felt inside of me that *I* could do better.

I had assumed that all teachers felt that way. That's how my colleagues at Graham & Parks had operated. When students were struggling, we wondered why and what we could do to change that. *Why does Sean act out in my class and not yours? Why are the girls so quiet in class discussions? How do we teach to a widely heterogeneous classroom so that we challenge the more advanced learners without leaving the struggling ones behind? How can we better integrate our Haitian bilingual students into an English-speaking classroom without making them feel even more "other"? What should we do when we have seventh-graders who can't read the text in front of them?*

At MLK, and maybe many other schools, it was different. The teachers seemed to consider sharing their struggles or raising questions about their practice as admitting weakness, rather than strengthening their teaching. What does make people change? I know that few, if any, people change because they are told to. In fact, if a teacher doesn't see the need for change herself, it's almost impossible to make progress. How do we encourage teachers to be reflective about their own practice? Is it something innate or can it be learned?

I believe it can be learned, and that it is, in fact, an essential part of training strong teachers. Pasi Sahlberg, the leading authority on the successful transformation of Finland's schools, explains how reflective practice is built into teacher training in his book *Finnish Lessons*. In Finland's model of teacher education, interns are taught to be researchers as well as teachers. They are asked to constantly assess their own work—what is working with their students and what is not. According to one professor from the University of Helsinki,

> Teachers must adopt a research-oriented attitude toward their work. This means learning to take an analytical and open-minded approach to their work, drawing conclusions for the development of education based on different sources of evidence coming from the recent research as well as their own critical and professional observations and experiences.[1]

But this is not just on teachers. It is critical for school leaders to create a culture that is safe enough for teachers to be self-reflective—safe to ask questions, safe to share struggles, safe to try something new and fail. When Sharon first revealed in September that she was not really open to "this humanities thing," I couldn't understand why she hadn't voiced her real feelings earlier. Why had she (and others) publicly agreed but privately resisted? Carole had approached them sincerely about their interest and willingness to try the humanities model. I doubt we would have proceeded with this project if the teachers had indicated they weren't open to it. Had they seen it as a tweak as opposed to a significant shift? Or did it have more to do with the traditional relationship between teachers and principals? Were they unaccustomed to being asked for their input and their endorsement? Did they not feel safe to express their real opinions? In a truly democratic school, healthy and honest debates would take place among teachers and administrators. Teachers would trust that their voices would be heard. Teachers would feel empowered as decision makers. Teachers would feel respected as professionals. Carole was trying to create that kind of environment at MLK, but perhaps she hadn't been there long enough for her staff to truly trust that.

By the end of the year, while we had made some progress, I did not feel particularly successful at my task of implementing a humanities curriculum at MLK. Although Carole assured me we did make some significant progress, it was hard for me to see. But I had learned a lot. I learned that change takes time. Any real, significant lasting change does not happen overnight. I knew this as a teacher, but it was different to live it as a school leader. Most people do not understand this about schools, which are intricate, complex, deeply relational workplaces. I also learned, or relearned, that in order for any kind of positive change to take place, there must exist a foundation of trust and respect that enables the various stakeholders in a school to speak openly and honestly. Creating this kind of culture takes an explicit commitment to team building, deliberate planning, and, yes, time. Something corporate reformers don't seem to understand.

My other major project that year reinforced these lessons. My charge was twofold: to help the staff select a social competency program that would resonate with the school's culture and mission and to develop a plan for implementing that program for the following year.

At first, I was very skeptical of this project. Not because I don't believe in the importance of the social curriculum. Far from it. I firmly believe that the academic curriculum and social curriculum must go hand-in-hand. They enhance each other. In fact, I would even say that academic development that is inclusive of all children *depends* on a strong foundation of a safe and respectful community. You cannot separate social and academic learning. (This is the focus of my book *Why Fly That Way? Linking Community and Academic Achievement.*) But I doubted the efficacy of many of the programs I'd seen that allotted a class period once or twice a week to teaching values like "respect" or "compassion." To me, those values had to be infused throughout every part of school, lived and breathed every day by all in the community.

I had another concern about this project. I wondered if it is was just too much for the staff. When Carole had come to the school the year before, she had initiated a number of significant changes, including a major new literacy initiative in grades 1–5. In October, I wrote to her:

I am concerned that people are already overwhelmed with the number of new initiatives in the building. There are SO many things going on. They are all good, but I see people struggling to keep up and do well with the things they have already taken on . . . I worry that if we ask them to take on another piece that we will either tip people over the edge or we will just get surface level work.

Carole understood my concerns, but she wanted all the basic building blocks for developing the school in place first. *You can't construct a building without first having laid a foundation*, she argued. I could see her point, but schools weren't construction sites, either. They involved people, not bricks, and people could only do so much at one time. I referred to another guideline of the Coalition of Essential Schools: *Less is more*. Let's take on less, but do it well, develop real ownership of the practice. We jokingly talked about being the yin and the yang of change—a healthy tension between moving forward and deepening the work. This tension wasn't just between Carole and me; it is a constant tension in improving schools. This can be a beneficial thing, especially if people have a voice in the process and the leaders have a long-term plan.

But with the pressures of the so-called Education Reform movement, principals and superintendents seem to have lost the yin side of the equation. They layer on more and more new initiatives, not realizing that the staff just can't absorb it all, much less "own" these changes, even when people plead, object, or even break down crying. I have seen dedicated teachers labeled as "resistant" or "negative" because they have tried to voice how overwhelmed they and their colleagues are feeling. People far away from the classroom do not understand how complex it is to adopt a new curriculum or to shift one's pedagogy in a significant way. Yes, administrators and other district leaders have the big picture; they can see issues that people working in the trenches cannot see. But teachers have the hands-on experience that no one else has; they can see up close what may and may not work at a given time. That is why it is so critical that school departments (and others) hear and respect teachers' voices in all kinds of decision making.

When Graham & Parks was first founded, the school governance structure had institutionalized this philosophy. Teachers and parents had equal representation on the Steering Committee. The principal was a nonvoting member. Unlike many school councils today that tend to just rubber-stamp district decisions, the G&P Steering Committee had real power over school policies. Parents and teachers didn't always see eye-to-eye, and that was expected; they brought different perspectives and different needs to the table. But there was a commitment to working toward a consensus that built both understanding and buy-in. Yes, thorny issues sometimes left some people dissatisfied, but we did not have teacher burnout from a cascade of external mandates and new initiatives.

After researching a variety of social competency programs, Carole and I met with each teacher team to present three different options: Responsive Classroom, Open Circle, or developing our own plan. Responsive Classroom took a holistic approach to developing social-emotional competencies through a set of practices and teaching strategies that teachers can draw on throughout the school day. Open Circle provided a curriculum complete with scripted lesson plans that focused on social-emotional awareness in a separate class period once or twice a week. The home-grown approach, that I favored, would involve teachers in a more reflective process about the needs of their own school and a review of the growing literature about social-emotional learning.

I had wanted teachers to visit classrooms using these programs, but the staff was impatient. "We don't want to visit anywhere. Let's just vote." Someone suggested holding a staff breakfast during which people could have some informal discussion with a broader range of teachers, and then vote using ballots. So that's what we did.

The staff overwhelmingly chose Responsive Classroom. But, interestingly enough, a significant number of votes (nine out of forty-three) selected no program. On their ballots, they explained that they did not choose a program because they felt so overwhelmed by all the other initiatives. Carole managed to figure out that all of these votes had come from the K–2 team. We were shocked! They had been the biggest supporters of Responsive Classroom. When we spoke to the team about it, they explained that they just had too much on their plate and this was a way to register their concerns.

Again, just like with the humanities decision, I wondered why these teachers hadn't voiced their fears earlier. Carole certainly had provided a forum to do so. Perhaps this staff was unaccustomed to honestly sharing their opinion. Perhaps they didn't want to disappoint this new and energetic leader. Or maybe they didn't think their opinion would actually matter. But it did matter. Carole and I agreed that we had to acknowledge these concerns publicly. We sent out a memo to share the results of the vote and to directly address teachers' fears of overload. We pledged to roll out this new program very gradually and to integrate it with the academic curriculum they were already working on. In the end, the staff voted unanimously to return to school one day early in September to launch Responsive Classroom training. We had made an important step, and remembered to keep it small.

The original interest in adopting a social competency program came from a concern about student behaviors. Too many students were being sent to the office. Teachers had complained that students lacked the social skills they needed to be successful in school and in life. Responsive Classroom would give teachers a common language, structures, and tools to help develop these skills in an ongoing way. But I was also excited about another approach to disciplinary issues.

I had first learned about restorative justice practices from a close friend and neighbor, Carolyn Boyes-Watson, who had written extensively on the subject and established the Center for Restorative Justice at Suffolk University in Boston. Carolyn and I frequently shared a glass of wine on Friday afternoons. Sitting on her porch sipping pinot grigio, she explained to me that restorative justice offered an alternative approach to our criminal justice and school disciplinary systems. Unlike traditional systems of punishment, restorative justice practices sought to repair harm, empowering the person or people harmed while holding the wrongdoer accountable in a way that was healing to all, including the community.

In schools, I knew that detention, suspension, and expulsion were pretty ineffective deterrents and did little to resolve some of the issues that may have caused a student's negative or disruptive behavior in the first place. I was drawn to the idea of *restoring* something that had been lost or taken away. It reminded me a bit of our G&P peer-mediation program in the 1980s. I liked the idea of empowering victims while challenging wrongdoers to be accountable for their actions, including the whole community, which is also impacted.

Carolyn invited me to a weekend circle training in Chelsea, a nearby city with a large immigrant population, a high poverty rate, and significant problems with gangs. Roca, a social service agency started in 1988 with a mission to "disrupt incarceration, poverty, and racism," was hosting a series of trainings on "peacemaking" or "talking" circles. I decided to go, even though I hated to give up my precious weekend.

There were thirty-two people gathered in one large circle in a rather nondescript conference room. We were a motley crew. About half the people in the circle were under the age of twenty-five, including a number of teenagers. A slight majority were people of color, mostly Black and brown. It was split fairly evenly between men and women. Many of the youth seemed to know each other; but, like me, some others knew no one.

The circle process is actually quite simple. There are just a few "rules." First of all, it is essential that all people sit in a circle so that everyone can see everyone else. Secondly, a "talking piece"—which could be a rock, a feather, some kind of meaningful object—is introduced by the circle "keeper." The keeper sets the intention or focus for the meeting and then passes the talking piece to her left. Once the next person receives the piece, s/he can speak for as long or as little as s/he wants. S/he then passes it to the next person on the left. If you want to speak in response to that person, you have to wait until the talking piece comes to you; you cannot jump out of turn.

Thirty-two people is a very large circle, not an optimal size. It took a long time to go around the whole circle, giving each participant the chance to speak. But as people shared their stories about what brought them to the training, I was mesmerized. In the circle, time slowed down and space opened up. No one looked at their watches or wondered when there would be a break. It felt like the constant static and buzz of everyday life was cleared away and we could really see and hear each other.

The circle is a profoundly democratic process. Big talkers who tend to dominate space find themselves listening. They can talk as long as they wish, but only when the talking piece comes to them. This means people actually have time to process what someone is saying, rather than just react in the moment. The circle has the opposite effect on people who are shy or reluctant to speak. These folks suddenly find there is a safe, receptive space for them to share their thoughts and feelings. They know that no one is going to jump in and interrupt them or cut them off. They have the power to stay silent if they choose, as no one is required to speak in the circle. But I don't think I have ever seen this happen. It may take a while, but eventually people trust the process enough to open up.

There are many different reasons to hold a circle. It can be used to address an issue in the community. It can be a way to solve a problem. It can be a way to resolve a conflict. Circles can be held to hold someone accountable for breaking a rule or even a law. Some circles are for people to come together to support someone in crisis.

By the end of the weekend, I was charged up. I could see a variety of ways to use the circle in school—with students, with staff, with families. Carole was open to giving it a try. The question was how and when. We didn't have to wait long for an opportunity to arise.

Jalen was a tall, lanky eighth-grader who was quite popular in the school. While he wasn't a star student, he was kind and funny and liked to make people laugh. That's what he was doing at the school dance that Friday night—trying to make people laugh. He decided to do a cartwheel on the dance floor and, as his long legs extended up to the sky, a knife fell out of his pocket. Kids were shocked and reported it to the staff chaperone. By Monday morning, the school was abuzz.

Cambridge had a "zero tolerance" policy around weapons: automatic expulsion. Everyone was upset. Jalen was an important part of the community; everyone knew he was a "good kid." Carole didn't want to expel him. But that was the district rule. It turned out, however, that a loophole existed. If a student had a special education plan, the school could choose to readmit him after a forty-five day outplacement. Jalen had a special ed plan.

However, when Carole started talking about Jalen's eventually returning to the school, Sharon rebelled.

"He broke our trust," she said. "He put us and the students in danger," she argued. "He knew the rule and he chose to break it. He needs to learn about consequences."

Clearly, Jalen had made some bad choices that impacted his community. Maybe this was a good time to try out a talking circle, I suggested. It would give people in the school an opportunity to share their anger and fears with him, and it could give him a chance to make some kind of amends, whether he eventually returned to the school or not.

With Carolyn's help, we carefully planned for the circle. We explained the process to the teachers who had objected to Jalen's possible return, as well as to Jalen and his parents. The circle is utterly voluntary. No one should feel pressured to participate. If all parties did not agree to it, the circle would not happen. The goal was not to decide Jalen's ultimate placement but, rather, to repair the harm he had done to his community. He could ask a couple of friends to join the circle, or even a community person like a pastor or a sports coach. His parents were welcome to join. He knew that teachers and a couple of students who were not at all happy with him would be there, as well. Everyone agreed to give it a try. Carolyn agreed to be the circle keeper. Even though circles are a very simple process, they are not always easy. It takes some skill and experience to guide a circle in a positive way. Given our first foray into a restorative practice, we all felt better having her expertise.

About twelve people joined the circle. Interestingly, some of the staff had trouble with the process. Some seemed uncomfortable with being on an equal footing with students. One staff member in particular, who had missed some of the orientation to the circle that Carolyn had started with, repeatedly spoke out of turn and seemed to think this was a way for the community to chide Jalen. Carolyn gently tried to reshape the process. Eventually, each person had their turn to talk about the knife incident and how it had made them feel. Throughout, Jalen sat between his parents with his eyes cast down on the floor. When it was his turn to speak, he apologized to people, and tried to explain.

"I had the knife because I was afraid of some people in my neighborhood. I thought it would protect me. I didn't mean to bring it to school; I feel safe here."

His father spoke next and thanked the school for the opportunity to speak in the circle. "Jalen isn't a bad kid. I know he did something wrong and he knows how upset we are with him. But I hope you can see he isn't a bad kid."

Was the circle a success? What would constitute success, given that Jalen's placement was not even under consideration? We were hoping for understanding. We hoped that Jalen might have a different awareness of the consequences of his actions on other people— which he did. We hoped he would understand that he was part of a community who cared about him—which he did. We hoped his parents could see the school as an ally rather than an enemy—which they did. We hoped that the teachers who felt so angry and betrayed by a thirteen-year-old boy could have compassion—which some did. We hoped we could offer a different, healthier model of responding to harm—which we were beginning to do.

We continued to try circles in a variety of ways. We formed one circle for another eighth-grade boy who was struggling with depression.

Pedro was not showing up for class and the school psychologist was worried he was having suicidal thoughts. We pulled together a "circle of compassion" for him, made up of a teacher (of his choice), his church pastor (also his choice), a friend from school, and his whole family. Our goal was to come up with an action plan, with steps for Pedro and other circle participants, to help him get back on track. People pledged to come together once a month to support him, for as long as it took. But it turned out that we didn't need to meet more than that once. As the talking piece moved around the circle, people were able to tell Pedro just how much they loved and cared about him. Then it was Pedro's older brother's turn. He looked at his brother and apologized for not being there more for him. He told Pedro that he loved him with all his heart and that he would always love him. As he spoke, he got more and more choked up. I watched as tears streamed down Pedro's face. When Luis was done speaking, he got up and hugged his little brother, as the rest of us watched in silent affirmation.

It sounds like magic, but Pedro started coming to school. He started doing his work. I don't remember if he started counseling or not, but his family felt they'd met their goal.

Not all circles end as successfully as this. Some of the other circles we tried that year certainly didn't. Often this was because we did not always have the time it takes to run a circle properly. Sometimes we had not prepared properly. But I could see the power in the circle, not just as a problem-solving mechanism but also as a way of practicing being in a democratic community and giving people, both students and staff, agency.

The one other circle experience worth mentioning was our fifth-grade girls group. MLK had only one fifth-grade class, with eight or so girls in the group. They had been together since kindergarten, and some negative feelings and attitudes had developed over time. The girls were constantly bickering in class and taking turns ganging up on each other. Joan knew these girls well, as they had all been in her class the year before. "What if we tried a talking circle with them?" she suggested one day.

"Great idea!" Carole responded. "Can you run it for us, Kathy?"

I was willing to try, but I knew I could not do it alone. I was an older white woman; all the girls were Black. I needed to find a "co-keeper" to whom the girls would be more able to relate. Just by chance, I ran into a former student, a young Black woman who had grown up in the neighborhood who was currently working for a Cambridge social service agency. Would she be able to help run the circle? I asked. She checked with her boss and enthusiastically joined our little project.

We met for ten consecutive weeks. It took a while to build trust, but the girls came to look forward to the circle. They started interacting with each other differently, building a whole new kind of bond. Their teacher reported much-improved classroom behaviors.

Then one day the third-grade teacher came to me. "I don't mind you taking the third-grade girls, but can we find a better time for it?" she asked.

"What?" I replied, puzzled. "I'm not taking your girls."

"Really? Then I wonder where they're going!" she exclaimed. "Shoshona has been coming to get them once a week. She said they are doing a girls' group circle."

Sure enough, the fifth-grade girls had decided that the talking circle was so successful they wanted to help some of the third-graders with their conflicts. They had started a circle all on their own! And it was going well. I was thrilled to see them take this on. But other people were not as happy with these fifth-graders going rogue and put a stop to it.

Talking circles and other restorative justice practices are not silver bullets. They can't and don't solve every single conflict or problem. One challenge in using these practices in a school setting is that they take time. Time is a scarce commodity in schools. There is never enough time. And now, with the pressures of standardized testing, time is even more precious. While newer teachers may not be as aware of it, as a veteran I can see the insidious speed-up, like on an assembly line, in schools; teachers are asked to do more and more, with less and less time to do it. Given the high-stakes nature of mandated tests, teachers are reluctant to give up "instructional" time for something like a talking circle.

Teachers are under increasing pressure to focus on reading, writing, and math skills to the exclusion of other kinds of learning. This is why "social competency" programs that are not deeply integrated into the practices and culture of a school end up failing. "We don't have time for that" is a common refrain. Taking an hour or so for a talking circle feels like a huge compromise to teachers.

But I would argue that the lessons students learn in a circle are critical to a democratic society: how to articulate one's thoughts and feelings, how to listen closely, building compassion and patience, developing problem-solving skills and self-control. Aren't these just as important life-long skills as how to identify the topic sentence or to write a five-paragraph essay?

Maybe even more important?

It all comes back to our vision of what we want our schools to do. What do we value in our society that we need schools to inculcate in our children? When parents are asked this question, they often say they want their children to learn to read and write. They want them to be good in math. But they quickly move on to other skills and qualities they want their children to have. They want them to think critically and creatively, to problem-solve, to be kind, to understand people different from them, to get along well with others, to make friends, to be able to work with a group, to be able to work independently, to be persistent, to work hard, to hold themselves to high standards, to take care of their environment, to practice tolerance, to be confident in themselves. When schools take the time to truly integrate the academic and social curricula, our students can learn these skills, habits, and attitudes that help them be productive members of a democratic society.

Responsive Classroom and our talking circles were good tools for the MLK teachers. But, I wondered if the school culture also reflected a deeper issue. While the school had 85 to 90 percent students of color, nearly all the teachers were white. How much did race and racism impact the social dynamic in the school? How could we even begin to address that? Carole, MD, and I decided that one way was to simply begin to talk about it among ourselves—two white women and a Black man. That may not have seemed like much of a solution to a very big problem, but we felt it was a start. How often do we talk explicitly about race in our professional lives, or even in our private lives? How often do we talk about race to people who are of a different race?

We agreed to set aside a full hour to begin this conversation. We sat in MD's office and Carole asked staff that we not be disturbed unless there was an emergency. Creating this kind of space in a busy school day is rare, but it's essential to create a safe space to allow for honest conversation. MD kicked off the discussion with a question: "Where do you even begin?" The issue of race and racism is huge and permeates most everything in our society. How do you turn that around?

We brainstormed a number of possible approaches for the MLK School. First, we talked about staffing. How do we recruit, hire, and retain a more diverse teaching staff? We knew this issue was much more widespread than just in our school. It is a national issue. But some districts around Cambridge had been more successful than we had in hiring teachers of color. Boston, for example, under court order, had increased its staff of color to 35 percent. Cambridge had about 17 percent. I agreed to do some research into that.

But changing the diversity of your teaching staff takes time; it's a long-term project. What can we do in the short term? How can white people become more aware of being white? I shared my experience of working with Enid Lee, the antiracism trainer, and how she had helped me realize the subtle (and not-so-subtle) ways I was perpetuating negative images of Black people, even when I thought I was actively trying to face prejudice, stereotypes, and racism. I had learned then that, as a white teacher, I had a responsibility to all my students to explore and understand my privilege of whiteness. Perhaps we could introduce some articles, films, speakers to open up this conversation?

Another area we could address was the curriculum. The school put on a marvelous Dr. Martin Luther King Jr. birthday celebration every January, and in February (Black History Month), portraits of African American activists and achievers would appear on bulletin boards. But, in general, the curriculum was traditional and white. What would it take to change that? How would we revamp a curriculum if the people involved in working on it were not also highly educated around race and racism in America? Would we have to work through the district curriculum coordinators or could we make changes on our own?

Finally, we discussed working with parents and families to build a dialogue about the racial tensions that lay under the surface. How to do that was not at all clear. With so many other initiatives going on, we knew we couldn't launch something new that year. Teachers were already overwhelmed. Furthermore, tackling the tough issue of race would require focus, planning, and expert guidance.

We all agreed that our first "roundtable" talk about racism was productive. Unfortunately, it was also our last. We scheduled another session, but it had to be canceled at the last minute. We tried again, and the same thing happened. There was always some kind of immediate demand that had to take precedence—an incident with a student, a parent meeting, a rescheduling of a special education meeting. Daily school life is not conducive to reflection on deep systemic issues.

Ten years earlier, in the 1990s, I had been part of a group called the Cambridge Rainbow Education Task Force. We helped to elect a slate of three Black candidates to the Cambridge School Committee, which had never before had more than one Black representative. Working with these new School Committee members, we were able to mandate an annual "Student Data Report" that disaggregated key academic data by race, gender, and socioeconomic status. We looked at grades, the demographics of honors and Advanced Placement classes, course failure rates, retention rates, and other data. We also looked at disciplinary data like suspensions and expulsions, as well as special-education referral rates.

This data clearly demonstrated deep divisions in our liberal city, based on race and class. We pushed for hiring more educators of color and we challenged practices of tracking. We argued for increased funding for early childhood education and for structuring schools so all children would be known well by at least one adult. In 1996, we sponsored a study on successful African American boys. Rather than looking at why Black males were failing, we chose to focus on why some were succeeding and made recommendations for changes in the School Department based on that information. These included a focus on K–12 literacy, creating a challenging multicultural curriculum with a focus on diverse perspectives and voices, and providing professional development on the impact of expectations, instruction, and grouping practices for students of color.

I wonder what our schools would be like today if we had succeeded in implementing *and sustaining* these practices. What would our schools look like if we had committed ourselves to "equity and excellence," a popular slogan in Cambridge and beyond. What if we had made that a real priority? An *urgent* priority. Interestingly enough, proponents of standardized testing argue that we need data to tell us how our students are doing. They say that these tests have revealed the so-called achievement gap that had been "hidden." But these inequities were not hidden at all. They were in plain sight. What the Rainbow Education Task Force did was to quantify these inequalities in a much more detailed and comprehensive way. What if the millions and millions of dollars that would be poured into standardized testing over the *next quarter of a century* had been used to focus on helping schools to truly leave no child behind?

My year at the Dr. Martin Luther King Jr. School was nearly over. A lot had happened since that first day looking for chairs. I had learned that, as a principal, you have to think about students, teachers, families, district leaders, community leaders, the media, the state education department, even national politics—*and* chairs. You have to know your people: students and their families, staff members and their families. You have to know when someone is going through a hard time at home—a sick child, an elderly parent, a pending divorce. There are constant tasks and unending demands. You have to have a strong voice and yet be a good listener. You have to make sure everything is working and that teachers have the resources they need to do their jobs. (I had loved that Len loaded G&P's copier with paper every morning so teachers didn't have to do that.) You have to be able to inspire your community and still deal with a leaking roof.

I also learned that you have to have a long view of change. Like Rome, a complex institution like a school is not built in a day. Meaningful change takes time. There is no silver bullet, contrary to what the corporate reformers want the public to think. Real school improvement is complex, but we already know how to do it. We know a lot about how children learn, and what makes schools work, for all children. We have hundreds of models of successful schools to look to and learn from. To me, real growth is predicated on building a collaborative culture in which there is trust and mutual respect. This is far from the current climate of fear and punishment that currently dominate our schools.

By the end of my internship, I didn't know if I really wanted to be a principal. The job seemed overwhelming. I wasn't sure I could do it. I wasn't sure I *wanted* to do it. I half-heartedly applied to some assistant principal positions. Twice, I was a finalist but ended up losing the job to a person of color. I honestly felt the schools had made the right choice. I strongly believed, and still believe, that when teachers reflect our communities, this strengthens our schools and our society. Finally, schools were starting to hire more teachers of color. I considered going back to teaching, but somehow that didn't feel right, either.

My job as the middle school program coordinator was still open. Maybe things had changed in the district and I could use my new-found wisdom from my PRN internship at that level. I decided rather dejectedly that, at least for now, I would return to my coordinator job.

CHAPTER 15

SILVER BULLETS
2006–2008

It was August 2006. I walked up the steep front steps of the Thorndike Street Central Office. The building hadn't changed. It was still in a dilapidated state, bunches of colored wires hanging from the ceiling like masses of spaghetti, paint peeling in large chunks on the hallway walls, floor tiles cracked or missing. It was depressing.

The deputy superintendent's office looked the same, too, as it had a year ago. Papers were piled in high stacks on almost every surface. Dr. A stood up from behind her large desk, and beckoned me towards a round table. We sat down and she crossed her arms.

"Don't go thinking that you can just do whatever you want, like you did before," she said. "You're lucky you even still have a job."

I was stunned. Where did this hostility come from? It was true that I had created my own agenda previously. But that was because she had not given me any direction whatsoever.

"From now on," she continued, "you are reporting to me and you are doing what we tell you to do."

"Okay," I responded. "What do you want me to do?"

"You are going to coordinate the AVID program," she said.

I groaned inside. I had first heard about the program a couple of years earlier. Cambridge had been groping around for a way to address racial inequities in the high school. People had talked about it as if it was the best thing since sliced bread, so I was skeptical. I never trusted packaged programs that promised the moon. I was, and still am, a firm believer in change from within—from the hard work of hammering out a common vision, of building a safe and

respectful environment, of encouraging and empowering teachers to be self-reflective and critical practitioners. I couldn't believe
that I was now going to become the official promoter of the latest
so-called silver bullet for inequity. But I had learned from Carole
and our work at MLK that sometimes external packaged programs
could provide the spark and structure to help a school grow. I would
at least give it a chance. Plus, I didn't have much choice.

AVID stands for Advancement Via Individual Determination and
was started by a high school English teacher in the San Diego area in
the 1980s. The goal was to take students from traditionally underperforming groups (such as low-income Black and Latinx communities) who were in the academic "middle" and provide extra,
explicit support to them so they could get into college.

The AVID program had been operating at CRLS, Cambridge's
public high school, for a couple of years, and the School Department had recently hired a CRLS-based coordinator for it. In addition, AVID was expanding its program into middle schools, adapting
the curriculum for younger students. The district had selected
four middle school programs (Cambridge had K–8 schools at that
time) to participate. As the district coordinator, I would oversee
the development of these new programs and support the one at the
high school.

AVID articulated certain essential requirements for a school
to participate in its program. Selecting the right students was the
first criteria. Students were supposed to have a 2.0–3.5 grade point
average and good test scores, "college potential with support," and
"drive and determination." In addition, they had to be from at least
one of the following categories: low income, first to attend college
in their family, or historically underserved. Participation in the
program, for both students and teachers, was voluntary; no one
could be assigned or coerced. Students attended a daily AVID class,
preferably starting in ninth grade and continuing throughout their
senior year. They learned reading, writing, critical thinking, speaking, researching, and organizational and study skills.

AVID's methods were not particularly revolutionary. They were simply good practice. For example, in AVID classes, students learned how to annotate text and build vocabulary. They studied Bloom's and Marzano's taxonomies around higher-order thinking, and learned how to ask and answer more complex questions. Students were taught how to organize a notebook and take Cornell notes, a system that encourages them to process and reflect on their reading. It organized students into collaborative working groups supervised by college tutors trained in AVID's methods, teaching them to learn to work productively together, while encouraging independence.

AVID also sought to introduce these skills to teachers beyond the AVID classes. In fact, their stated goal was to "restructure the teaching methods of the entire school." The AVID teacher was charged with planning workshops and trainings for other teachers in the school on how to use these methods, as well as others, like running Socratic seminars or designing lessons that incorporated WICR: writing, inquiry, collaboration, and reading.

According to AVID's national trainers, selecting the right teacher to lead the program in a school was key. The AVID school coordinator should have strong teaching and organizational skills. They should be someone other teachers respect and even look up to, with a track record of helping "disadvantaged" students be academically successful. The ideal AVID school coordinator/teacher held her students to high expectations while providing the scaffolding and explicit instruction in the "hidden curriculum" that some students, particularly those of color, may have had trouble accessing.

As I learned more about AVID, I felt I could, in good faith, promote and support the program. I attended my own AVID training and was impressed with the people I met from around the country. They seemed like highly skilled teachers committed to equity and excellence. But when I went back to Cambridge to begin my work as the AVID district coordinator, I discovered a very different scene.

A physical education teacher was coordinating the AVID program at the high school. She was a lovely person, a good P.E. teacher, a great basketball coach, and had worked hard to help get her players scholarships and college placements. But she didn't have any training, or even strengths, in academics. Much of the AVID curriculum was confusing to her (Socratic seminars? Cornell notes? Marzano?), and she felt she was in over her head. She was also one of the most disorganized people I'd ever met. Not a good trait for someone who was supposed to be teaching students executive functioning.

I wasn't at all sure why she had been invited to be the AVID program coordinator at CRLS.

"They asked for volunteers," she explained. "I thought it would be fun and something different from coaching." This was the first red flag.

Luckily, Linda and I were able to develop a strong working relationship. She was transparent about the ways the job overwhelmed her. I was willing to support her in any way possible. We started by recruiting our college tutors. Linda had good connections to Harvard's sports programs and was able to identify a number of enthusiastic college undergrads to run our twice-weekly study groups, and I trained them in AVID's methods. In addition, I helped Linda plan her AVID class every week, mapping out each lesson together. The program offered a plethora of resources, but she hadn't understood how to use them. I also helped her plan the weekly team meetings with the three other AVID teachers in the high school. They, along with Linda, each taught an AVID class to a group of twelve to sixteen students.

As part of my district coordinator responsibility, I was supposed to observe the AVID teachers and give feedback (as a coach, not an evaluator). In one of my first visits, I observed a teacher who was working on a vocabulary lesson with a "concept" map. A concept map has a large oval in its center and four boxes in each quadrant of the "map." Students are supposed to write a vocabulary word in the oval; then in one box write a synonym of the word, in another box write an antonym, in the third box write a sentence using the word, and in the fourth box draw a picture that illustrates the word's meaning.

The teacher had written the word "AVID" on the board. She explained that this was the name of the class and asked if anyone knew what "avid" meant. *Good way to start,* I thought. She asked them to get out their pocket dictionaries and look up the word.

One student raised his hand and said, "Avid means greedy." Other kids nodded in agreement.

Really? I thought. *Greedy?*

I tapped a student on the shoulder and asked him if I could look at his dictionary. Yup, that was indeed the definition offered, but certainly not the one I would be teaching in an AVID class. I expected the teacher to explain that words can have multiple meanings and that we need to look at all of them and choose one that made sense in the particular context. But she did not do that.

"Okay," said the teacher. "So let's put 'greedy' in this first quadrant as a synonym." She went on. "So what is an antonym for 'greedy'?"

Another student responded, "Generous?"

"Yes, that's great!" she said. "Now, how about a sentence?"

"I am avid for more candy," offered a girl.

"Great. Now, draw something in the last box that reminds you of the word," she finished. I watched as students drew stick figures with slanted eyebrows grabbing things from other stick figures.

I didn't know what to do. This was the first time I was observing this teacher. I certainly didn't want to contradict her in front of her students. I also didn't want to criticize her, knowing that would not be the best way to build a positive, trusting relationship. I had learned from my PRN internship that sometimes you had to sacrifice short-term goals to reach longer-term ones. But I also didn't want students leaving the class thinking that avid meant greedy.

As I wrestled in my mind about what to do, the teacher asked one more question: "So why do you think this class is called 'AVID'?"

A boy raised his hand and said, "Maybe because we are greedy to"—I was waiting to see what he might possibly come up with—"learn?" he finished.

"Great!" she exclaimed. "Good work!"

The class ended.

This was not an example of the high quality, rigorous instruction that AVID classes were supposed to embody. Maybe it was just an anomaly, though. I decided to reserve judgment and give it some time. But this was a second red flag.

The next time I visited this teacher's class, she was not there. It was first period and school started at 8:00 a.m. The students were there, though. Some had pulled their chairs together to chat, while others were slumped in their seats with their hoodies up and headphones in.

"Where's Ms.—?" I asked. "Is she out sick today?"

"Naw," one of the kids responded. "She's always late."

Really? I thought. *Shouldn't the AVID teacher model good work habits, like getting to school on time?* I tried to ask the kids how they felt about the class, but they were not too interested in sharing. Maybe they weren't awake yet. At 8:10 or so, the teacher bustled into the room, hung up her coat, rifled around at her desk for another five minutes, and finally asked the kids to get out their notebooks. *What about an apology for being late?* I wondered. *Or an explanation even?* But there was none. Another flag.

Once again, I wondered how this teacher had been selected for the program. The two other teachers in the program were doing somewhat better, but I did not get a vibe of high expectations or rigor from any of the classes. Nor did there seem to be a sense of community. Part of the AVID appeal that students from other high schools around the country had described was the feeling of belonging to something special. They described a sense of camaraderie and commitment to each other. And pride. The kids at CRLS seemed to feel more that they had been targeted rather than selected. "I don't want anyone to know I'm in the AVID class," one student told me. "Kids think AVID is for losers."

I was concerned. If you are going to buy into a program, there has to be fidelity to the implementation process. This did not seem to be the case in Cambridge. One of the most important criteria for creating an AVID program—identifying strong teachers—was missing. I raised concerns with my boss. She told me to talk to the high school principal.

CS had been the head of the English Department before becoming the principal of CRLS. He had been a wonderful support to me when I was teaching, and I had a lot of respect for him. He would have been the perfect AVID teacher. He was a strong educator, deeply committed to his students, and highly respected by his colleagues. But he was now overseeing a large school broken into four different "houses," and with an enormous number of demands on his time. He knew of the AVID program but had not been involved with setting it up. He certainly did not understand AVID's expectation of a schoolwide buy-in to its methods. Nor did he know much about the actual structure of the AVID class and curriculum.

When I shared my observations about how CRLS was implementing AVID, he sighed and shook his head. This was going to be complicated. Schedules were already in place, materials already purchased, staffing already assigned, training already given, students already selected, classes already meeting. This wasn't a matter of just tweaking a few things here or there; it was about fundamentally fixing something that had been implemented incorrectly—i.e., a case of not just building the airplane while flying it, but *re*building it in the air. Wasn't it Frederick Douglass who said, "It is easier to build strong children than to repair broken men"? The same is true with programs. CS encouraged me to provide as much support and guidance to the AVID teachers as I could. He offered to give them more release time for training. Beyond that, nothing could really be done at the time.

Things at the middle schools weren't much better. In one school, the AVID teacher was a burnt-out veteran on the verge of retirement; she had one foot out the door. In another school, the AVID teacher was not even a teacher; she was the school counselor. Like Linda, she was a lovely person who cared deeply about students but

254 CHAPTER 15

had no teaching skills at all. The two other schools had selected academic teachers, but it was unclear why the schools had chosen them to lead the program. It seemed that the schools' leadership, like the high school's, did not really understand AVID's essential elements. Why did these principals even want AVID in their schools?

Here's my analysis. Administrators are always on the lookout for more resources. It is a rare school that has everything it needs to do its job well, or sometimes even do its job at all. This is particularly true in urban and rural districts. So when a new program appears on their radar, they often leap at the chance to "get something" for their school. Rather than look at their needs and develop a plan to meet those needs, they look at where the money and resources are and then squeeze into the guidelines. It reminds me a bit of my mom, who announced she had bought a double cemetery plot for herself hundreds of miles away from where she lived. When I asked her why, she said, "It was such a good deal, I couldn't turn it down!" Perhaps some Cambridge principals were feeling the same thing. Being offered funds, training, and materials for a national program that seemed to have an amazing track record was just too good a deal to turn down. But I'm not at all sure how much they or their teachers understood what they were signing on to.

You have to understand the essence of any program or reform in order for it to have any chance at success, and you must have a long-term commitment to implementing it. This was clearly missing in our AVID schools in Cambridge. But it's not just Cambridge that makes this mistake. This is a common practice. Take the idea of "advisory groups." Research has shown that middle and high school students tend to be more successful when they have a strong personal connection to at least one adult in their building. By forming groups of ten to twelve students with a staff advisor who meets with their advisees anywhere from once a week to every day, this personal relationship becomes institutionalized. If schools review that research with their staff, provide training and resources, and nurture the "buy-in" of the adults, these programs do have an impact. But without those steps, when administrators simply tell teachers that they are now going to lead an advisory group, they tend to just go through the motions and, eventually, the groups fail—"proving" to the resistant educators that they were a waste of time in the first place.

Principals may have wanted AVID in their schools for another reason, as well. After five or six years of "ed reform" and No Child Left Behind, schools were scrambling to find anything that would help them raise test scores, particularly for students in chronically underperforming groups. AVID was especially tempting because it promised to help a population that was performing just under the threshold of proficiency. Educators had started practicing a form of triage. Triage is a system that medical personnel on the battlefield developed to deal with emergencies when resources were critically short. Who could be saved? Who was hopeless? Who might be able to hang on a bit if they didn't receive immediate attention? With increasing pressure to improve MCAS scores and decreasing funding for schools—leading to cuts in staff and other resources—schools were forced into making similar decisions. Should they should target students who needed just a few more points to raise their test scores into the proficiency column? Or should they invest in the lowest-performing students, hoping to move them out of the failure or "warning" pool?

For the next two years, I worked with our AVID programs, trying to support, encourage, educate, and push for stricter adherence to AVID's expectations. We made some progress, but, in the end, the four middle schools dropped out of the program. The high school did continue with it for a number of years, with new staff. I'm not sure how effective it was. I do know that the district spent at least $150,000 on AVID in the two years that I was the district coordinator—which does not include my or other teachers' salaries. We hardly got the bang for our buck.

Teachers go crazy when they hear about this kind of district spending. It is in stark contrast to the power of funding given, for example, to the Collaborative Curriculum Design Team (CCDT) initiative, which was a homegrown, educator-led initiative that impacted scores of teachers and hundreds of students (see chapter 12). The CCDT budget was used exclusively to support teams of teachers in developing project-based curriculum that integrated research and technology resources, be it for a stipend, printing expenses, buying books, or purchasing cameras for film projects. Many of these initial purchases had an impact far beyond the first year of funding. Once a teacher had a video camera, she could use it for years to come. Or a set of books could be read by multiple classes. Most importantly, once a team had developed a curriculum, it could be used again, including by other people. The CCDT created a network of participating teachers, encouraging them to share with each other across grades and schools. They hosted exhibitions in the high school library so teachers from around the city could see the work the Design Teams were doing. It was slow, grassroots work that had a profound effect.

This raises perhaps another reason why both administrators and "reformers" jump onboard particular bandwagons: they are seeking the quick fix, the silver bullet, the one reform that will make everything else that is wrong in schools right. "Silver-bullet thinking" dominates corporate "ed reform." When ed-reform philanthropists and foundations throw the clout of their money into the pot without understanding a particular program or change, failure is imminent.

One example—among many—of this phenomenon is the "small schools movement" promoted by the Gates Foundation in the early 2000s. The concept behind small schools is not new, but, looking for the next quick fix, Bill Gates and other reformers latched onto the idea. They did not understand that breaking large, anonymous high schools into smaller learning communities is just the beginning of a significant reform, not the end. They did not understand that a small-school structure is a piece of a larger complex puzzle. They did not understand, as Deborah Meier, the godmother of small schools, said, "Small schools are not the answer; but without them, none of the proposed answers stand[s] a chance." Lacking this understanding, the Gates Foundation and others spent over one billion dollars breaking large high schools into smaller ones but did little else to support other critical reforms. A few years later, this "paradigm shift" was declared a failure.[1] How many other so-called reforms have ended up in the graveyard of failed policy shifts?

Sadly, this tends to promote the perception that schools cannot or will not change. Unfortunately, people outside of schools are not aware of the stress these never-ending "quick fixes" impose on teachers and their students. Even the community loses as they foot the bill. While people like Bill Gates and Mark Zuckerberg move on to the next "big idea," it is the people who work in schools who are left to pick up the pieces. Again.

When I returned to my job as the middle school program developer and AVID district coordinator in September 2006, my office had been relocated from one of the K–8 schools to the CPS central office at Thorndike Street. Initially, I was unhappy about this move. I liked being in a community, surrounded by kids and the bustle of school life. Now I felt more isolated than ever. To get to my office, one had to go up three flights of stairs, along a hallway, down half a dozen more stairs, around a dark corner, and up another flight of stairs to a landing where there were three small offices in a row. I had a window that looked out at the granite blocks of the building. There was room for a desk and chair, a bookshelf, and one file cabinet. It felt like a tomb.

But I soon discovered certain advantages to my hideaway office. First, two other women were also in exile there. We became a little support group for each other. Cathy worked there part time as a data analyst, and Candyce was the grant writer for the district. Cathy was hugely helpful in teaching me how to read the data reports she was constantly being asked to churn out. Whenever I couldn't remember what some acronym stood for or how a data-set was formulated, she would carefully explain it to me. Candyce, the grant writer, was a comrade. She shared a similar vision of what schools could and should be like. She agreed that too often administrators chased money without being thoughtful or strategic about how to use it. She was proactive about her job, researching many different grant options and helping schools find funding that really served their needs.

Another advantage, it turned out, was being closer to district leadership. Even though my office was squirreled away, I was frequently in other parts of the building for various reasons. Because I was physically more visible, I was included in more meetings, discussions—and gossip. I had a front-row seat to the inner workings of this level of administration.

I could see people coming and going. I could see who had frequent meetings with JMG, the superintendent. I noticed who had open-door policies, and who didn't. I noticed who volunteered to take on work, and who didn't. I noticed who was asked to take on work, and who wasn't. I noticed how people prepared for meetings, or didn't. I noticed who left early, and who stayed late.

I also started noticing a lot of people crying. I watched principals for whom I had a lot of respect leave the superintendent's office in tears. I saw people retreat from a meeting with him into their own office and then abruptly close the door. I saw people stiffen when he walked into their office and then breathe a sigh of relief when he left. I heard him berate people and cut them down with sarcasm. You could feel the tension permeate the building. There was little laughter, little water-cooler chat. A climate of fear pervaded Thorndike Street, and indeed the whole district.

JMG had never been an easy man to deal with, but I remembered my first impression of him when he'd addressed the curriculum coordinators. He'd seemed to have a real commitment to supporting teachers and improving schools, and he was determined to close the "achievement gap." He didn't care about being popular and was willing to make tough decisions to achieve his vision. In his first years in Cambridge, he brought some sense of order and accountability to what had been a rather chaotic district. He'd told me once that Cambridge had a "culture of heroes."

"Isn't that a good thing?" I'd asked. "Don't we want heroes?"

"No," he'd replied. "One person jumps in to save the day. Then another, and another. Then you just have a bunch of individuals putting out fires. There needs to be a system, and a chain of command. There needs to be order."

I hadn't been sure I agreed with him, but I'd been willing to give his method a try. Maybe we needed some tough love. However, from my new perch in the heart of the beast of Central Office, it seemed that there was a lot of tough and not much love.

One day, a School Committee member approached me. The superintendent's two-year contract was up for renewal. This was JMG's fourth year.

"Kathy, in the last contract rounds, your testimony in favor of the superintendent convinced me to vote for him again," the member said.

It was true that I'd testified in favor of JMG at a public hearing. Even though he had rubbed some people the wrong way, I'd felt he was doing a decent job and needed more time to carry out his plan. After the hearing, the superintendent's contract had been renewed by a four to three vote.

The School Committee member continued, "I was planning to vote against him, but you changed my mind. Now, I'm asking you again. I'm hearing a lot of disturbing things about morale in the district," he said. "People seem to feel very discouraged. I trust your opinion. What do you think? Should we give him another two years?"

I hesitated. Was it wise to talk to a School Committee member about this? Probably not. But it was true that morale in the district was at an all-time low. It was heartbreaking to see so many dedicated, smart, hardworking people discouraged, upset, beaten down by this man. I was worried. Cambridge was my city, where I lived and worked and raised my children. Yes, we needed strong leadership. But a leader can be strong without being denigrating. A leader can be firm without humiliating people. I decided to tell the truth.

The superintendent lost his contract. I can't remember the actual vote, but I do remember the quiet sigh of relief throughout the district.

A month or two later, JMG called me into his office. His secretary had only told me that he wanted to speak with me about a certain proposal. I was baffled, but curious. When I entered his spacious office, he gestured for me to take a seat across from him. "I've been thinking about you," he opened. *Really?* I was surprised. "You know the principal internship program that we have in the district?"

I was familiar with it. In order to nurture more homegrown leadership, Cambridge had started its own administrative certification program. An intern would work full time with a Cambridge school principal, like the Principals Residency Network, while receiving both a full salary and a $5,000 stipend. Two positions were open each year.

"I think you would make an ideal candidate for this program," he said.

I was confused. "But I've already done that," I replied. "I did that at the Martin Luther King School through the Principal Residency Network."

"Yes, I know," JMG said. "But I know you would really like to take on a leadership position in Cambridge, and MLK is a very small and somewhat unique school. I think it would be great for you to work at another, larger school."

"I'm not so sure I would fit in very well at that school," I said. I knew the school he was talking about; it was one of the least receptive schools I'd been working with on the middle school program.

"You'll get a very different perspective working there. It will make you much more qualified for a lead position in the future," he countered.

"I don't know," I stammered. "I'm really not sure that's what I want to do anymore,"

"Really? We need people like you in leadership," he urged. "I know you've tried to do the work in the middle schools here, but there is so much more you could do as a principal. Why don't you at least mull it over?"

"When would you need my decision?"

"You have twenty-four hours," he said.

Twenty-four hours. I was rattled. I had given up seeking principal positions and had just started to feel positive about my work with the district as it was. But, to be honest, I was flattered to be asked, even encouraged, to do this internship. Maybe he saw something in me that I couldn't see myself. How much of my decision to not pursue a principalship had to do with fear and lack of confidence? Did I not want the job—or did I think I couldn't do the job? I wasn't totally sure.

But here was an opportunity staring me in the face, along with a vote of confidence from a tough boss. Was that the universe calling to me to take a risk? What was the real risk, anyway? If I didn't like it, I could always go back to my current position. After agonizing all night, I decided to go for it. I told the superintendent the next day.

"I'm delighted you accepted the offer!" he exclaimed.

A week later, I got a phone call from one of my trusted principals.

"Kathy," he said, "what's happened to your position?"

"What? What do you mean?" I responded quizzically.

"The new budget just came out. There is no line item for a middle school program developer. Your job isn't in the budget. Did you know that? What's going on?"

"Oh, the superintendent asked me to do the principal internship. And I said yes. I guess they just aren't going to fund the position this year," I explained.

"Really? Are you sure you're okay with this?" he persisted.

"I guess so," I said.

A few days later, a new budget came out. In this iteration, the principal internships had been eliminated. I was now out of a job. I realized I'd been bamboozled. This had all been a set-up. I made the first possible appointment to see the superintendent and was steaming when I entered his office.

"You had a plan, didn't you? How could you do this?" I demanded.

"Who the f—are you to say that?" he exploded.

I was speechless. I wasn't used to people shouting or swearing at me.

He continued to shout. "Who the f—is the one who stabs people in the back?"

I just sat there, in stunned silence.

"You thought I wouldn't find out, didn't you? You thought you have friends in this city, don't you? Well, your friends aren't so great after all! They told me what you said. They told me everything you said! I thought you were trustworthy. You are a backstabbing liar!"

I was struggling to stay calm and not to cry.

"I told my opinion," I managed to get out. "Two years ago, I stood up in public to defend you. But things have changed. When a School Committee member asked me my opinion in private, I shared it."

"You are so naïve," he sneered. I had to agree with him.

I left his office shaking, trying desperately to not start crying. *If I cry*, I thought, *he'll win*. I wasn't going to let him win. When I got back to my hermitic little office, I opened my computer and started looking for jobs. It was time to leave Cambridge, go somewhere else, expand my horizons. I needed a fresh start. Doing what, I wasn't sure.

And then, the perfect job showed up. The Harbor School in Boston was looking for a director of instruction. How serendipitous.

CHAPTER 16

THE HARBOR SCHOOL
2008–2009

The Harbor School (THS) was not on the harbor, at least not any-more. Founded in 1996 as an Expeditionary Learning[1] middle school, it was first housed in a community center near the Colum-bia Point Housing Projects in Boston. While students could not see Boston Harbor from their classrooms, they were within walk-ing distance of it, and the harbor was a defining part of the school's identity, curriculum, and activities.

But the school had recently moved to the former Grover Cleveland School building in the heart of Fields Corner in Dorchester, about three miles from the harbor. It was an imposing structure, built in 1920, looming directly across from the train tracks of the neighbor-hood T station ("the T" is Boston-ese for subway). It took up most of the city block and had the stolid appearance of its namesake. It was also in the center of what city officials had euphemistically called the Circle of Promise—the area with the highest murder rate in Boston.

One day in my first week at the Harbor, I had just parked outside the school and was unloading some boxes from my trunk. Out of the corner of my eye, I saw a young man, disheveled, shoeless, and clutching something—a coat? a bag?—streaking toward me. I was startled; it was still early in the morning. But I didn't panic; in fact, what was happening didn't really register in my brain. He sped right past me, weaving through the cars in the parking lot. Ten, maybe five, seconds later, two police officers appeared in hot pursuit. They too sped right past me, as I stood holding my box of books. *Yes, this is a different neighborhood than Cambridge*, I thought.

The Harbor School was the brainchild of Scott Hartl. I met Scott in 1995 when I worked with Expeditionary Learning as its first teacher-in-residence. Scott's office was down the hall. For many years, he had been both an Outward Bound instructor and a high school science teacher. He wanted to bring the philosophy and practice of Expeditionary Learning/Outward Bound (ELOB) into an urban environment.

At this time, Boston was looking to create some new schools with innovative programs. Scott started developing a proposal and recruited a planning group to work with him. He and I spent a number of hours talking about the middle school program at Graham & Parks. His new school would have a humanities curriculum; narrative progress reports rather than grades; portfolios and graduation review panels; and other key elements of the G&P program. It would also incorporate new approaches, inspired by ELOB, and would be located in a very different community than Cambridge.

I watched the seed of Scott's ideas grow into a reality as, a year later (1996), the Harbor School opened. One of the first teachers hired was my former G&P assistant teacher, Winston Cox. Winston, a young Black man, had worked with me for three years. I wasn't quite old enough to be his mother, but we had a strong, almost familial bond. I'd tried to convince Winston to take on a full-time teaching job in Cambridge, but he wanted to work in a school with more Black and brown children. He leapt at the chance to be in on the ground level starting a school like Harbor.

So the Harbor School was not an unknown place to me. I'd felt a strong connection to it, especially in its beginning years, and had watched its development over time. That was why it felt serendipitous when I opened my computer and saw the school was looking for a director of instruction, or DI.

Not only was I excited about connecting with the Harbor School, I also was interested in the position of DI itself. The DI is an administrator, part of the leadership team of a school. But the focus of the job is on supporting teachers with curriculum and instruction.

That seemed to be the perfect role for me. I wouldn't have the full responsibility of the school—budget, legal matters, politics, etc.—on my shoulders the way a principal does, and I wouldn't deal with student discipline, the way an assistant principal does. My passion was around teaching and learning and, in this position, I could concentrate on that. I sent my application in immediately and eagerly awaited a response.

Scott had left the school around 2004. Evidently, quite a bit of controversy had existed around the hiring of the principal to replace him. As a white male, Scott had made a strong effort to hire people of color. After all, of the 300 or so students, 93 percent of them were Black or brown. Discussions of race and racism were integrated into the fabric of THS, and the staff had a considerably higher percentage of people of color than the typical Boston public school. But, somehow, BN, a white woman, was selected as principal over an internal candidate, a Black man. This had definitely rankled a number of people. In addition, BN pushed for the school to become "full inclusion," meaning that students with special needs would be fully integrated into the mainstream classes, with little to no pull-out instruction. These changes in leadership and mission led to an exodus of many veterans. In 2008, when I started there, 70 percent of the teachers had been at the school for two years or less.

I didn't know any of this at the time. All I knew was that I felt a resonance with the Harbor School. And I desperately wanted to get out of Cambridge. When the school offered me the position a month later, I was elated. I was ready to jump across the Charles River, from Cambridge into Boston. I didn't bother to read the small print.

I hadn't realized that Harbor was an extended-day school. It started at 8:00 a.m. and ended at 4:00 p.m., an eight-hour—rather than the standard six-hour—school day. So my day would be considerably longer (plus, now involve a commute). *Oh well,* I thought. I didn't have kids at home anymore, and I was ready to put in the time. Then I found out that, as an administrator, I had to work an eleven-month year. No two-month summer! That was a blow. The summer was a time for RR&R: research, rest, and recovery. I had always taken courses or studied something for part of each summer, but it was on my own terms and schedule. *Oh well*, I thought. Working in the summer would probably feel less stressful than during the rest of the school year. Then I found out that, as a beginning administrator, I would start at the bottom salary tier. After thirty years in Cambridge, with my PRN experience, I was at the top of the teacher pay scale there. I discovered I would be earning at least $10,000/year less than I had been. *Oh well*, I thought. Money wasn't the reason I'd wanted the job.

But, basically, I'd taken a job where I had longer workdays, longer school years, less pay, and more responsibility. *Oh well*, I thought. *This is the kind of work I've been wanting to do for a long time.*

My new office was smaller than my previous office at Thorndike Street, and this time there was not even a window. The prior occupants had been reams of paper, file folders, and extra staplers: it had been a storage closet. I managed to fit in a desk, a chair for a visitor, and a filing cabinet. If someone wanted to come in to talk privately, we had to stand up and move the chair around to close the door. *Oh well*, I thought. *I don't need to spend a lot of time in my office anyway.*

Then I looked at the school's MCAS scores. I am not a big believer in test scores, but they can tell you certain things. Given the school system's general failure in regard to students in the Harbor's demographics—93 percent students of color; 85 percent of the students receiving "free or reduced" lunch, an indication of low socioeconomic status; and at least a third on an IEP (Individualized Education Plan)—I was not surprised that the scores weren't terribly high. But what worried me was the steady decline in student proficiency, especially in math, over the last three years.

Then I started talking with the teachers. They were effusive in their welcome. "We are *so* happy you have come to Harbor!" some said. "We are *so* excited that you are here!" others said. I was excited, too, but I started sensing that something was not being said. It was a little like when, as a parent, you come home and your kids are *so* happy to see you. You start to wonder what had been going on with the babysitter before you got there.

I soon started to understand just how much the school was in disarray.

To begin with, I started to notice the tension between the staff and administration. Teachers complained about poor communication from the principal and a lack of support in general. They frequently said they felt that the school leaders didn't listen to their needs and weren't "on the same page" with them. They wanted more support with students and consistency in follow-through. They felt that the principal made promises but did not keep them. They also desperately needed more support and guidance in curriculum and instruction. Which is why, I found out, the staff had pushed for my position to be created.

Teachers in Expeditionary Learning schools have both the privilege and responsibility to develop strong, integrated, purposeful, project-based units of study, called "expeditions." It takes training, skill, planning, research, coordination, and time to do this well. Some of the Harbor teachers had developed solid and engaging expeditions over the years, but the turnover in staff had seriously impacted the curriculum. The school had not documented these expeditions; when a teacher had left the school, their curriculum had left with them. Many of the new teachers didn't understand what Expeditionary Learning was, much less how to plan an expeditionary curriculum.

Developing an expedition is challenging enough, but when you layer a full-inclusion model on top of that, it becomes even more daunting. Harbor had worked with an exemplary K–5 school called the Patrick O'Hearn, just down Dorchester Avenue from Fields Corner. Bill Henderson led the O'Hearn. He was a visionary leader who had pioneered a model of full inclusion, which included a structure of co-teaching. (The O'Hearn was later renamed the Henderson in Bill's honor.) Each classroom was led by two teachers, one trained as a general education teacher and the other, as a special educator. They worked seamlessly together: the gen-ed teacher planned curriculum content while the special-ed teacher adapted the lessons to the specific needs of all the different children in the classroom. Clearly, this required considerable planning time, as well as strong collaboration skills.

The Harbor School had adopted this co-teaching model, but it was much more challenging to carry out in a middle school where students were not in a self-contained classroom, as they are in elementary school. The budget couldn't stretch enough for the school to hire a special educator to work with each academic teacher, so the former had to split their time between subjects. This meant that the special educators had to meet and plan with two different teachers in two different subject areas.

To be a true full-inclusion Expeditionary Learning school, teachers needed a lot of planning time. But at Harbor they didn't have it, or at least not enough of it. Too often, teachers' schedules conflicted, so there was no common free period. Sometimes a gen-ed and special-ed teacher would meet, but they would end up planning curriculum content together, not allowing the special-ed teacher the time s/he needed to create adaptations for students. Sometimes gen-ed teachers would send their lesson plans to their special-ed partner the night before or the morning of the next class, leaving her or him to scramble to put together something at the last minute. Even when these teams had a common planning time, teachers didn't always know how to use the time well. A few teams did have it down, though. They planned ahead, each one knew and understood his/her role and responsibilities, they collaborated well. They provided a model of how it could be done. But this was not the norm.

It is critical that internal structures be in place to support a school's mission. But so often this is not the case. People far from the classroom make decisions, like introducing an inclusion model or a new literacy program or a new math curriculum, without providing the time, resources, training, and ongoing support for teachers so they can truly embrace this change. I've seen this happen over and over again. It tends to lead to frustration, cynicism, resistance—and often failure of the initiative.

There were also school climate issues. This is not unusual for a middle school, when you bring new students together at the height of puberty, with their insecurities about themselves, their bodies, their friends, and their place in the world. But Harbor had a particular challenge. One third of the students had special needs that ranged from moderate reading disabilities to autism, Down Syndrome, and other more extreme physical problems and cognitive delays. The O'Hearn was a feeder school for Harbor; its students understood and accepted all kinds of differences. But Harbor also had students from other elementary schools in the city, and those students had not learned the same kind of inclusive kindness. A school climate survey at Harbor asked students if they felt that students treated *each other* with respect; seventy-eight percent said "no."

Many students lived in neighborhoods that were poor and suffered violence (remember the Circle of Promise). I spoke with my advisory group of twelve students about violence in their lives.[2] Every single one of them had a story: a cousin or an uncle killed, a brother or father shot, someone in prison, shots being fired in the night. One student had witnessed his neighbor being shot. It was traumatizing just to listen to these tragedies, much less experience them firsthand. And that didn't even begin to address the violence of poverty. Kids came to school hurting and angry. It was not surprising that tensions flared easily.

One day, a petite seventh-grade girl came in.

"Good morning, Zora!" I greeted her. She ignored me.

"Good morning, Zora!" I called, louder this time. She continued to ignore me. The principal and some other staff were standing nearby. I could feel their eyes on me. *Dang*, I thought, *I can't let this pass.* So I pursued her down the hall. When I caught up to her, I asked her to stop.

"Leave me the f—alone," she spat. Okay, now we are in a battle.

Luckily, Mr. B happened by and saw what was happening. Rob Bustamante was a cross between a disciplinarian and a social worker at the school. He tried to help students work out problems, while still holding them accountable. Kids trusted him. Rob asked Zora to come sit in his office, just to talk. "We'll get back to you," he said to me over his shoulder.

About an hour later, he and Zora found me.

"I'm sorry for disrespecting you," she said, looking down at the floor. Her apology didn't sound too sincere to me, but I was willing to accept it. He thanked her, sent her off to class, and then turned to me.

"Last night, around three in the morning., Zora's apartment was raided by the police. They were looking for her brother, who is a possible suspect in a murder case. He wasn't home, but they had her, her grandmother, and another sibling on the floor in handcuffs. Also, the police were all white. She isn't feeling too good about white folks right now. She's pretty upset, and exhausted."

I was lucky that I actually got the story behind Zora's anger. Many times, students don't have an opportunity, or even feel that they have the right, to explain themselves. Sometimes, they don't want to tell you about their personal lives. Sometimes they don't even know why they are so enraged. Good teachers know how to deescalate such a situation, but not all do. So kids blow up and, more often than not, adults react punitively.

One day, I was in the front office when I heard some commotion. I looked out into the lobby and saw Officer M leading one of our eighth-grade girls out of the school. In handcuffs. I was appalled. I didn't know what had happened, but I couldn't believe that a fourteen-year-old girl had been handcuffed in school.

Officer M was a fully uniformed Boston Police officer, which meant he wore a gun, a baton, and had handcuffs. I had been shocked at the beginning of the year that a police officer was stationed full time in our small middle school. I hadn't seen police in schools since Medford High School in 1980. Officer M was friendly enough. An African American man in his late forties, he had a laconic way of walking and talking. But why was he there? To protect us from the neighborhood (a few shootings had occurred at the nearby T station)? To guard the students?

When I'd first asked the principal why he was there, she said, "Oh, you'll come to be glad he's here."

When I asked why the girl had been handcuffed, she said something about the student having gotten "out of hand" in class.

"But handcuffs?" I asked.

"You don't know the circumstances, Kathy," she responded.

No, I didn't know the circumstances. What had triggered Taysha to get so upset? Had she, like Zora, brought anger and fear into school or had something happened here?

The next day I went to talk with Officer M about it. He was not happy about the situation. "It really didn't need to come to that," he said. "It could have been de-escalated, but they told me to cuff her, so I did."

I wasn't familiar with the concept of the school-to-prison pipeline at that point, but I couldn't help but wonder about the long-term impact of this incident on this girl. How could she ever trust us again?

I had been learning more about the impact of trauma on student learning, as well as its secondary impact on teachers working with traumatized youth. We can't expect children, or adults, to be able to function well when living in a heightened state of fear and anxiety. And yet, we do. Susan Cole, the mother of a former G&P student, was the primary author of a book—which one can download for free—called *Helping Traumatized Children Learn*, and she had been in touch with me about it. The book describes the way that traumatized children often behave in ways that schools interpret as disruptive rather than as a symptom of trauma. I shared copies with some teachers and other staff.

Interestingly enough, a few of the Black teachers pushed back.

"You are just soft," they said. "You come from leafy Cambridge. This is just our lives. You've got to toughen up if you're going to survive here." It was true that I was an outsider. But I wondered if these folks had become so accustomed to the trauma of violence and poverty that they couldn't feel outraged by it anymore.

In an environment in which so much trauma, so much hurt, and so much deprivation exists, having rules that are clear, fair, and consistently enforced is critical, as Geoff Canada, the director of the Robert White School, had wisely said. But this did not seem to be the case at Harbor. The rules generally seemed fair, but they were not clear to everyone, and they were certainly not consistently enforced. One small, but significant, example of this was the school-uniform policy.

The Harbor School uniform consisted of khaki pants and a dark blue shirt. You could wear an official THS shirt complete with logo, but just a plain blue polo or button-down was acceptable. I had never been a fan of uniforms, but I understood some of the rationales behind having them. Some young people don't have many clothes at all: a uniform is an equalizer. Also, as another staff member explained to me, if students wear a uniform, it makes them feel a part of something. It creates a certain kind of discipline. It sets a standard of conduct.

The students hated school uniforms, and they found innumerable ways to undermine the policy. Wearing their pants down around their knees was one popular expression for the boys. One day, I was walking up a flight of stairs directly behind an eighth-grade boy, his patterned boxers fully on view.

"Pull up your pants, Jamal," I said.

"Why you lookin' at my butt, Ms. Greeley?" he responded.

"Because I can't miss it, Jamal. Pull up the pants," I replied.

The girls liked to wear their shirts as tight as possible, sometimes with a plunging neckline. Other kids went in the opposite direction, wearing shirts and pants that were many sizes too big on them. Some wore hoodies or sweaters, and when a staff member challenged them, they would reveal their THS garb on underneath. It was a game. Some students would come to school in regular clothes, claiming their uniform was dirty.

The policy stated that the school would send students home if they were not in uniform. But some teachers didn't want to lose the kids from class, so they just kept them. Or they didn't want to take time from their class to battle with a kid, then send him or her to the office, and have to follow up on this infraction. The staff would give them something to put on over their "street" clothes. The policy was neither clear nor consistently enforced.

Teachers wanted more support from their administrators. They argued that their job was to teach their students. They wanted the principal and assistant principal to hold the students accountable for being in uniform. Couldn't those administrators monitor students as they came in each morning? Shouldn't *they* be the enforcers of this school-wide policy? The principal pushed back. "Students will not respect you if you don't enforce the school rules," she argued. "This is part of the way that you show you are the boss." Plus, she didn't have time to do a uniform check every day. She had other, more important things to do.

While I didn't particularly like the uniform policy, it seemed to me that if it was a school policy, we had to enforce it. I brought this up in one of our weekly Leadership Team meetings.

"Don't you think it sends the wrong message to everybody if we're lax about the uniforms?" I asked. "I mean, we make parents buy them and sign a pledge that their children will wear them every day. It seems like a slippery slope if we don't back up our word. I think the teachers would really appreciate it if Admin could take this on."

"Well, Kathy, if you think this is so important, then why don't you do it?" BN, the principal, shot back.

I really didn't think this was my responsibility as the director of instruction. I was already monitoring breakfast and lunch periods, as well as running the buses in the afternoon, spending nearly two hours a day with such administrative duties. I didn't mind the time with the kids; in fact, I liked seeing them outside the classroom. But that administrative work had impacted my ability to meet with teachers and observe them in their classrooms. I had raised this concern before but had been told that I needed to be a better team player.

Perhaps the principal was right. Maybe I should have taken it on. But this revealed another problem at the Harbor School. At the leadership level, we struggled as a team. To be fair, my position as DI was new, and we had just increased the size of the Leadership Team by 50 percent. We didn't have clearly defined roles. We didn't know how to work together. We also didn't have common expectations about how to work together.

In one of our early meetings, as we were discussing an issue, I disagreed with BN, offering a different point of view. At the end of the meeting, she asked me to stay for a few minutes.

After the assistant principal had closed the door, she turned to me and said, "Don't *ever* contradict me in public again, do you hear?"

Was the meeting public? I wondered. It was just the three of us. Isn't that what we were supposed to do with each other?

"No," she said. "Do not contradict me in front of anyone."

I was taken aback. To me, that was normal, to have candid, honest debate. At Graham & Parks, debate was an essential part of our culture. But I quickly learned the culture at the Harbor was quite different.

Nearly every time I entered BN's office, she was sitting at her desk, focused on her computer or some papers. I would knock, and she would glance up, pointedly look at the clock on her wall, sigh, look back at me, and then reluctantly invite me to come in. I'm not sure that this was personal; it seemed she did it with many people who wanted to speak with her, unless it was someone from Central Office, a funder, or an external agency. She was very good with these outside people. She was a great salesperson for the Harbor School and had managed to raise funds and bring in extra programs, like a special-needs arts project. She had also somehow secured a Boston School bus that was available all day, every day (with a driver who would take naps sprawled across the front seats). This was important for the school, as doing "fieldwork" is at the heart of an expedition. Without the ever-ready bus, our trips would have been severely limited.

But BN struggled with the internal operations of the school. Between the flagging school morale and declining MCAS scores, some serious issues faced the school. I didn't know what to do. BN and the assistant principal seemed resistant to even acknowledging the situation. I tried reaching out to Court Street (the Boston Public Schools central office) to get some curriculum support for the teachers. But that was a black hole. BPS had a new superintendent, and it seemed that the leaders of different BPS departments came and went like the latest flavor of the week. The whole school district seemed to be in tumult. I rarely had a phone call returned; when I did, I was told that they could do nothing to support us right now.

Luckily, Harbor was connected with two organizations that I thought might be able to provide some support: Expeditionary Learning (EL) and the Boston Pilot School Network. The pilot schools, of which Harbor was one, operated like in-district charter schools within the Boston Public Schools system. Staff were part of the Boston Teachers Union, but the schools had certain key autonomies that other Boston schools did not have—e.g., more control over budget, curriculum, and staffing. The Center for Collaborative Education (CCE), the organization that had also directed the Turning Points initiative, oversaw the pilot schools. I had friends at both EL and CCE, so I sent out private pleas for help. Both responded.

In November, CCE dispatched a staff member who would meet with the Leadership Team (the principal, assistant principal, and me) once a week or so for the rest of the year. Leah Rugen was just what we needed—a gentle and skilled facilitator who helped us identify both strengths and weaknesses of the school and of our team. It took several months of meetings, but she navigated us through tricky waters and eventually helped us develop a document that clearly articulated each of our roles and responsibilities. With her help, we were able to build some trust with each other, which enabled us to present a more clear and unified voice, particularly with staff. In addition, we were able to address how to work more effectively with other teams in the school, like our Planning and Management Team and grade-level teams.

That fall, an historic event took place. On Tuesday, November 4, 2008, Barack Obama became the first African American to be elected president of the United States. On Wednesday morning, the school was bubbling over with euphoria. It was a rare moment of unadulterated joy at THS. When Obama was inaugurated as president on January 20, 2009, the whole school gathered in the old auditorium to watch as the ceremonies were projected onto a large white bedsheet. As Obama held up his right hand to take his oath, I looked around the room. People were enthralled. Kids were giving each other high fives, staff were hugging each other, grown men were crying. Students came up to me and said, "Hey, Ms. Greeley, maybe I can be president some day!" We all felt a new day was dawning, and we welcomed it with chants of "Yes, we can!" The hope was palpable. Little did I realize then that, at least as far as school policies go, our days were about to get much darker.

Expeditionary Learning also stepped up. Two talented school "designers" (i.e., curriculum developers) worked with teacher teams to help develop new expeditions. This work was slow going, but we did see growth and progress. The seventh-grade science and math teachers worked on a geology unit that explored the concepts of glaciation, erosion, and deposition. Using Thompson Island in Boston Harbor as their focus, these teachers invited students to participate in solving a crime: Who stole the north end of the island? (Steep eroded cliffs rose up on that end of the island, and a spiraling deposited sandbar at the other end.) In their unit on systems of the human body, the sixth-grade team worked with students researching and writing pamphlets for local health clinics about common diseases in their neighborhoods, like asthma and diabetes.

As our Leadership Team came together, we agreed to form a few staff committees to address teachers' concerns. I worked with the School Climate Committee. In our first meeting, a dozen people showed up at 7:00 a.m. We asked each one to share what brought them to the meeting. They said:

- Want to be the school we could be, and used to be.
- Need a common vision.
- Feel like there are many different strands that don't integrate as much as possible (e.g., EL and inclusion).
- Need to be on the same page and have common systems that everyone follows to support student learning.
- Want respect from administration for both staff and students.
- Need to improve communication, but this starts at the top with admin. Need to do things in a timely manner and be better organized.
- Teachers have some voice, but big conversations/issues are not addressed.
- Need to respect norms.
- Should not use inclusion as an excuse.
- Need to improve connections to our families and community.

This was an impressive list. Teachers had clearly articulated many of the challenges facing the school, as well as the kinds of supports and structures they needed to do their jobs. While they did call on the school administration to up its game in certain instances, their comments came from caring, not anger.

I wondered where the school would have been if it had nurtured these open, honest, collaborative conversations earlier. It continually astounds me how rarely schools ask teachers and other staff for their input on what schools need. I don't mean, "Do you need a new whiteboard or more math books?" I mean, "What do you need to do your job to the best of your ability? What do underperforming students need to be successful? How would you address the 'achievement gap'? How would you prioritize these various initiatives?"

Toward the end of the year, the School Climate Committee presented recommendations to the whole school. These included approving a document we named "Common Expectations"—that we would share with students—revising the THS Code of Conduct, reviewing and improving a system for checks and rewards, implementing a one-binder system for all students (along with training and ongoing check-ins on using it), and more. People were excited about these proposals and enthusiastically endorsed them.

As the director of instruction, one of my first campaigns was to get kids reading. Early in the year, I had asked one class how many of them had read five books over the summer. One student raised her hand. How about three books? A few more raised their hands. One? Maybe another four or five hands. This was a bad sign. According to reading specialists like Richard Allington, reading *quantity* is critical. He advocates that students read up to two hours a day *in school*. Students who independently read at least fifteen minutes a day score in the top 80 percent and above on reading tests. So this was our first hurdle. I wanted our students to fall in love with reading. We needed to help them find books they liked and give them time to read. After all, the more you do something, the better you get at it.

Many schools have DEAR time: Drop Everything And Read. In my seventh- and eighth-grade humanities class, we had set aside fifteen minutes most days for independent reading. I loved this time because I got to read, too. But I discovered, as I'd look up from my book and scan the room, that not everybody was as engrossed in reading as I was. The kids who struggled with reading often had their books open, but they would be staring off into space. They weren't really reading at all. I learned from educator-researchers like Ellin Keene, Susan Zimmerman, and Cris Tovani that I had to play a more active role in supporting readers. I needed to make sure they had the "just right" book, that it truly engaged them, that I gave them strategies for when they got stuck, that we had conversations about their reading. *Just* "dropping everything and reading" was not enough. But first, we had to get books kids would want to read.

The Harbor School had a library. It was a large space, though sparsely resourced. But it was a place to start, and we scheduled weekly visits for each class so students could select books of their choice. One day I was visiting a seventh-grade humanities class during their independent reading time. I was circulating among students, trying to model for the teacher how to engage in quiet conversations with kids without causing a distraction or disturbance. I noticed a couple of boys avidly reading a book together, giggling under their breath. When I walked over to their desks to see what was entertaining them so much, one of the boys stuck the book inside his desk.

"What are you reading?" I asked curiously. The two boys looked at each other and didn't say anything. I repeated my question. "What are you reading? I'm interested in seeing it."

One boy pulled the book out of his desk and I took a look. It was a book from the Triple Crown series. The Triple Crown series is not like the series of books that have won Newbury or Coretta Scott King awards. Triple Crown books are soft porn.

I was shocked. "Where did you get this?" I asked the boy.

"The library," he responded.

"No way," I said. "Did you bring this in from home?"

"No, I got it from the library," he insisted.

"I don't believe you. I'm going to check with Ms.—."

"Okay," he shrugged. "Can I keep the book?"

"No!" I replied.

"But what am I going to read now?" he asked.

I took the book and headed up to the library. The school did not have a librarian, but we had a part-time library assistant. I still didn't believe the student, but I felt I had to check. When I showed Ms.—the book, she said, "Oh, yes! We have a bunch of them!"

"What? Are you kidding me?" I exclaimed.

"Yeah, we have maybe half a dozen," she said.

"I really don't think we should have these books in a middle school library," I replied.

"Why not? They're good! I've read most of them."

"But they are not appropriate for young adolescents," I argued.

"Isn't that censorship?" she argued back. "Who are you to say what kids can and can't read?"

I was frustrated. I was still new at Harbor and was still seen as an outsider. But all I could think of was what if the newspapers got a hold of this story? With all the other pressures on Harbor right now, we didn't need a scandal about giving our students porn. So I went to the principal.

I knocked on her door, she looked at the clock, sighed, and invited me in. I explained what had happened. "Can you back me up on this?" I asked.

"I agree that it is probably not a good idea to have these books in our library," she said. But if you're the one who wants to take them out, you should be the one to enforce it."

This was before we had done our work with Leah from CCE. I felt left hanging out to dry. *Okay*, I said to myself. *I will*. I went back to the library and told the library assistant that all the Triple Crown books had to come off the shelves. She could take them home with her if she wanted. She grumblingly gave in.

Over time, we started taking our students to the Fields Corner Public Library each week or so. Some librarians shudder when they see a group of young teenagers coming into their sacred space. But a fabulous librarian at Fields Corner welcomed us and introduced our students to a wide range of books, fiction and nonfiction. She gave wonderful book talks to get them interested in trying a book and was excited and encouraging when a student was ready for a new book. Gradually, reading started to catch on.

It wasn't until February that the Leadership Team started to strategize about the MCAS, which would take place in May. We should have started in September, but we were barely speaking to each other then, so we were certainly starting behind the eight-ball. The biggest cause for concern were the math scores. For four consecutive years, the school had failed to meet AYP (annual yearly progress) in math. About 62 percent of the students were in the warning (or failing) category. While their ELA scores were better, those, too, fell below the district average.

With Leah's help, we mapped out a plan. We wanted the teachers to feel a sense of urgency around this. We identified extra teaching time for students during the day, sacrificing some other classes. The principal met with the math team, and I worked with the humanities teachers. I reviewed the test with them (as much as we had access to) and mapped out all the skills being tested that they felt they needed to focus on most. We discussed how much to do test prep versus finding ways to embed skills in what we were already doing. Given how late it was in the year, we had to work primarily on teaching specific skills and helping students learn test-taking strategies. It was full-court-press mode. We were all nervous when the testing days finally arrived.

The MCAS takes several days to administer. Outsiders (that is non-school people) don't understand how it can utterly disrupt a whole school, even the students and teachers not taking the test. In a full-inclusion school like Harbor, it is even more complicated than in a typical middle school. Students with an IEP (Individualized Education Plan) usually have accommodations for testing, such as taking the test in a smaller group or sometimes even one-on-one, having a teacher scribe for them, or using certain assistive technologies like text-to-speech. Students with extreme special needs have the option to assemble a portfolio of work rather than take the test. The state must approve this, and it is extremely time-consuming for the special education teachers to pull together all the pieces of evidence required to get the state's go-ahead.

As director of instruction, I was assigned the job of organizing the MCAS. That meant devising a labyrinthian plan of staffing coverage and space (e.g., finding extra rooms and test monitors for small groups or one-on-one) and timing. It was up to me to train the teachers in test administration (the directions were about thirty pages long), organize all the test booklets and "bubble sheets" (this was before the MCAS became computerized) for teachers to pick up and return, make sure they were all accurately labeled, and ultimately return them to the state's MCAS Center. Simple enough, right?

Wrong. I still can't explain why, but running the MCAS took a full month out of my schedule. A full month. Counting tests, making sure kids had "bubbled" their names and other information correctly, rescheduling tests for kids who had been sick, finding staff and space to re-test, etc. At one point, the state told me that we had to test one of our students who was in a psychiatric ward on suicide watch. After multiple phone calls, the Department of Education (DOE) relented on that one. Plus, the DOE's directions came with threats of being fined, fired, or *arrested* if the DOE found any irregularities—like an instructional chart being left up in a classroom, a teacher helping a student who was confused by the directions, a bubble error, a missing test booklet, and, of course, any evidence of cheating. I was terrified.

Each afternoon, we locked up the tests in a storage closet (not in my office). Before storing the tests, I would assiduously count them, making sure we had the correct number of test booklets for each answer sheet. Then I would count them the next morning when I took them out to give to the teachers. Then I would count them again when the teachers returned the materials to me. One day around 4:00 p.m., when I was counting the booklets before putting them in the storage closet, I came up short. I was missing a booklet.

Frantically, I counted again. Still one booklet short. I started going through all the other piles of testing booklets (about 250 of them) to see if one had been misplaced. I counted multiple times, coming up with a different number each time. I took a deep breath, slowed down, and counted again. One short. So I locked the closet and started looking in each classroom in the whole school, in trashcans, on teachers' desks, inside students' tables. By this time, everyone else had gone home except the custodian. He asked me what I was doing. I explained and he went to look through trash bags he had already collected. Nothing.

It was nearing 7:00 p.m. by this time. I'd been looking for this test booklet for three hours. I went back to the student's homeroom and looked again on the teacher's desk. There it was, under some other papers. I should have been angry at myself for not finding it the first time or at the teacher for her carelessness, but I was just relieved I'd found the blooming booklet. I wouldn't get arrested for an MCAS crime after all. But it was only when I put the final packing tape on the boxes of test materials to send back to the DOE did I truly feel I could breathe easy.

Another part of being an administrator is evaluating teachers. I only remember being evaluated once or twice when I was teaching in Cambridge. I once said something to Len at Graham and Parks about this. I knew he evaluated certain other people in the building, but I could not remember him ever evaluating me.

"I don't need to evaluate you, Kathy," he said. "I know what you do. Every time I stop in to visit your classroom, I see what is going on there. I talk to kids; I talk to parents. I know what goes on in Room 304."

"But don't you need to tell me my strengths and weaknesses?" I pressed.

"Why? You already know what they are. You're always thinking about how to improve your practice," he replied. "I don't need to tell you what to do. I trust you."

I know I was not the only teacher in the school he felt this way about. Len knew his teachers well; he was a constant presence in the building; he nurtured a culture of reflection and growth. The teachers who did not rise to his expectations did not last long there.

The first time I do remember being formally evaluated was in one of my early years as the middle school program developer. My supervisor invited me into her office and handed me the three-page evaluation form for me to read through silently. She had checked every box as "Exceeds expectation," except for one that had to do with following the required curriculum.

I was puzzled. "Why did you check this as 'Needs improvement'? I don't teach a curriculum and I can't control what teachers in the middle school do with their curriculum."

"Oh, I know. I just couldn't check every box with 'Exceeds,' could I?" she laughed.

"But I'm not responsible for that!" I objected.

"It just wouldn't look good," she answered.

"But that's not fair."

"I guess that's true," she sighed. "I'll change it to a 'Meets expectation,' instead, but that's as high as I'll go."

Evaluating teachers is a hot topic. The stereotypical view promoted by corporate ed reformers is that we need rigorous evaluations of teachers to "weed out all the deadwood." Their mantra is that we have "failing" schools because we have failing teachers. If we could only get rid of the "bad" teachers and put "good" teachers into these places, everything would be fine! We wouldn't have to provide more resources or fix crumbling buildings or feed children or fix poverty, racism, and inequality. "The problems of our public school system rest on the shoulders of mediocre teachers," they say.

I do believe that having a high-quality teaching force is essential to good schools. I also know that some teachers should not be teaching. There are also teachers who may have started out strong and then, for any number of reasons, lose their way. Having a clear, fair, and consistent process (Geoff's advice again!) of evaluation is important. But what does that really look like?

At Harbor, I was faced with this question up close and personal when I suddenly found myself on the other side of the evaluation process. In November, the principal, the assistant principal, and I had divided up the staff; each of us would meet with, observe, and evaluate about ten teachers. That may not sound like a lot (some principals have twenty-five or more people to review), but if you follow the protocol correctly and if you write a thoughtful and thorough report, each evaluation is very time-consuming. I wanted to approach the task holistically and humanly. I wanted a conversation between the teacher and me. I wanted to use the process to provide support, guidance, and encouragement to my teachers. I wanted to give honest, specific feedback that they would find useful and would help them strengthen their teaching.

Because it was my first time doing evaluations, I asked if I could see some from the previous year, as a model. I also wanted to see what strengths and weaknesses had been identified for particular teachers, in order to assess how much growth they had made. I asked the assistant principal, who had evaluated a few of the teachers I was now assigned to, for these documents. He kept promising to get them to me, but that never happened. Finally, I went to the school secretary and asked her if she could pull some of the files (they were kept under lock and key). She brought out a few different folders; they were empty. I realized that some evaluations had never been done.

Two evaluations stand out for me. The first was with a special educator for eighth-grade humanities. Sarah, a young white woman, was smart, committed, hardworking, kind, and collaborative. But the students were running roughshod over her. Her strategy seemed to be to ignore bad and disruptive behavior, as if it weren't happening. Students would get up and leave the room without permission. I watched one student clean out his bookbag during the mini-lesson. Students teased and taunted each other in class. One day, a boy made fun of another student's name in front of the whole class and she ignored it. Sarah had strong ELA (English/language arts) skills, but she struggled with the social studies part of the curriculum. She was very supportive to her most struggling students but had low expectations for the class in general, tending to teach to the lowest level.

I met with Sarah in November. Out of the eight dimensions of the Teacher Performance Evaluation, I had given her a "Meets expectation" for only four of them. She was devastated. I'd tried to point out her strengths, but the challenges were many.

"No one has ever told me this before," she sobbed.

I was shocked. Sarah was in her third year as a provisional teacher at THS. Schools were supposed to evaluate provisional teachers every year until they gained professional status, at the end of year three. I felt terrible. I really liked Sarah, she contributed a lot to the school in many other ways, and I don't like to make people cry.

"Listen," I said, "this isn't your fault. You should have gotten this feedback much sooner. But we have time. I will work with you this year, at least once a week, if not more. You have so much potential to be a good teacher!"

She wiped her eyes and managed a small smile. "Okay," she sniffed. "I really want to do a good job."

"I know you do," I responded as I gave her a hug.

We met again at the end of February. She had clearly made some good progress in a number of areas, but she still struggled with classroom management, setting high expectations for all her students, using ongoing assessments to inform her instruction, and some of the social studies content. We had only been meeting for a few months, I reminded her, and I could point to a number of specific areas of growth.

As the time for Sarah's final evaluation drew near, I realized I had a problem. I had been coaching her. It is a big no-no to both coach and evaluate a teacher. Teachers have to feel totally trusting with a coach, so they can be open about their struggles, their worries, their weaknesses. Sarah had certainly done that with me. It would be unfair to then bring that perspective into an evaluation. I brought this up to the principal.

"I really don't think I can be her evaluator," I explained. "I think it crosses a line."

"Well, I'm already done with my evaluations," she responded. "I don't have time to take on another one. Plus you did her initial evaluation so you have to follow through with it."

"I think this is going to be really unfair to her. I'm willing to do more evals next time or take on some other responsibility if you would do this one."

"You should have thought about that sooner. You just have to bite the bullet."

I dreaded the meeting with Sarah. I had agonized over this. Lost sleep. After several months of work together, she had indeed developed more skills. She had welcomed feedback and tried hard to act on it. But she hadn't made as much progress as I would have hoped. And if I gave her a positive review, she would have permanent status. If only she had gotten effective feedback the whole three years she'd been at the Harbor School! But she hadn't. And I couldn't put my name to a paper saying that she was meeting or exceeding standards, because she wasn't.

There was a lot of crying and a lot of anger at our meeting. She was furious (rightly so) that I, as her coach, was evaluating her. She felt betrayed by me. I felt I'd betrayed her. But I'd had no choice.

"I've worked *so* hard," she wept.

"I know," I sighed. "I know it feels unfair. I'm really sorry, but I have to make these decisions based on what is best for our students."

Sarah moved from Boston at the end of the school year. She started teaching yoga classes in Washington, D.C. About a year later, I was at home when the doorbell rang. A man stood holding a beautiful blue hydrangea plant. "Special delivery," he said.

I was baffled as to who would send me something like this. It was from Sarah. Her note said something like this, "Thank you for pushing me. You were right. I've gone back to school and am learning a lot. Thank you for believing in me."

I heard later through the grapevine that she started teaching again in a D.C. school and eventually became the special-ed leader for the school. I was proud of her.

Most of my other evaluations that year were easier than the one with Sarah. Except for one. Greg was a young African American seventh-grade humanities teacher. He was in his thirties and was a single parent to a lovely nine-year-old girl, whom he adored. He cared a lot about his students and really wanted them to see education as a ticket out of their tough neighborhoods. He loved football and was studying to be a professional referee. Academically, he was the opposite of Sarah—strong in his knowledge of social studies, especially Black history, but weak in ELA. His two-hour humanities classes tended to be long lectures followed by random worksheets on parts of speech or vocabulary. I had been working with Greg to increase reading and writing with his students; it was his class where the Triple Crown books had surfaced. He also struggled with behavior management.

Like Sarah, this was Greg's third year at the Harbor School. And like Sarah, he had received hardly any feedback on his teaching. It was up to me to give him an honest evaluation, support him in developing his pedagogy, and decide whether or not he would still have a job by the end of the year. At first, when we would debrief a class, Greg made a lot of excuses.

"The kids don't usually act like that," he'd say. "I don't know what got into them."

But over time, we were able to talk openly about what was happening in his class and ways he could respond or prepare differently. He started to trust me, and I saw him trying out my suggestions and recommendations. But he also continued to be overwhelmed by the curriculum and couldn't keep up with the workload.

By the end of the year, when the final evaluation was due, I knew I could not endorse him. Again, I felt terrible. If he had had three good years of supervision and coaching, he could have been a decent teacher. But I asked myself the question: *Would I want my own child to be in his class? No.* If I gave him a positive evaluation, he would be a permanent teacher. I couldn't be responsible for giving professional status to a teacher who did not meet standards.

He came to meet with me, and I broke the news. He begged, "Please, Kathy, don't do this. Please. I have to support my daughter. What am I going to do if I lose my job? Please. I know I can do better."

"I wish I could, Greg," I said grimly. "I wish we had more time. You deserve better. But I just can't."

"Please, Kathy, how am I going to support my kid?" he pleaded, with tears in his eyes. "I'm sorry," I answered with a sigh.

I watched his slumping shoulders as he left my tiny office. Here was a young Black man who wanted to teach. He clearly needed more training and support, but do we just kick someone out like that? I wondered. It wasn't his fault that he hadn't gotten feedback and guidance that might have helped him grow as a teacher. Why should he be punished because other people didn't do their job? Aren't we supposed to be trying to recruit, and retain, teachers of color?

I picked up the phone and called Human Resources at Court Street. "I have a personnel dilemma," I said to the clerk, "and I need to speak with someone who can advise me." One of the high-ups got on the phone. I made my case.

"Look, we have had this young Black man on our staff. I feel I have to give him a negative evaluation, but I do think he has potential. This was the first year he really had a thorough eval. The problem is that this is his last year before permanent status. Couldn't we bend the rules a bit? Think outside the box? Don't we want people like him to be in our schools?"

I explained that it's challenging to teach humanities, especially at an Expeditionary Learning school. And we had the full-inclusion model on top of that! In a more typical school, I said, this teacher may be able to be very successful. I didn't expect to persuade the administrator. After all, I was talking to someone in the bowels of the bureaucracy.

To my surprise, she responded, "You've got a good point. Let me think about this and talk to some other folks. I'll get back to you."

It took a number of weeks, but one day she called and asked, "Do you think this teacher would be willing to meet with a coach on a weekly basis?" she asked.

"I think he would be willing to do anything if he could keep his job," I laughed.

"Well, I think we can extend his provisional status one more year. If he meets regularly with a BPS coach, we can assess his progress again toward the end of next year. He is really going to have to work hard and show significant improvement. But if he does, we will give him professional status."

"Awesome!" I exclaimed. "I can't wait to talk to Greg!"

Needless to say, he was thrilled to get another chance and pledged to work his butt off. Cut to the future. Greg did not stay at the Harbor School. But, to my knowledge, he is still working in the Boston Public Schools as a high school social studies teacher, where he is doing well.

So many teachers I know today dread being evaluated. In the corporate "ed reform" model, evaluation feels like a "gotcha!" But, to me, a critical evaluation should never come as a surprise. Good schools are based on positive, trusting relationships where there is transparency and mutual respect between administrators and staff. Good schools also have high expectations of both students and teachers, as well as ongoing reflection and inquiry that create fertile ground for both students and adults to learn and grow. This doesn't mean that staff never get hard or critical feedback. But hopefully, in this kind of culture, teacher evaluation can take on a very different feeling—and purpose. The goal becomes to help teachers do their jobs better, not to fire them if they are struggling.

We got through the MCAS and would have to wait until August for our scores. So we refocused our efforts on school climate, staffing, and professional development. We did ask a handful of staff to leave and were able to hire some new, promising young teachers. At the end of June, we held a two-day institute to focus on curriculum development. Teachers worked closely with coaches from Expeditionary Learning to identify clear learning goals and to plan rigorous and engaging lessons. At the end of August, teachers would come back for an additional three days to focus on integrating literacy strategies into their disciplines and on differentiating instruction.

In mid-August, we received our preliminary MCAS scores. The results were not good; we had failed to meet the AYP set by the Department of Education. I wasn't surprised. We had tried, but it was too little, too late. However, while we were disappointed, we felt that we were poised to turn things around. We held a daylong retreat with our Planning and Management Team to analyze the MCAS scores. This group of teachers, support staff, and administrators spent the day in small groups analyzing the scores and identifying areas of strengths (yes, there were some) and weaknesses. We developed a plan of action with specific goals, reasonable timelines, and lines of accountability, which we shared with staff in August.

We had accomplished a lot in the last year by putting structures in place that would support teaching and learning. Our leadership team was united, we had clear rules and expectations that everyone understood and bought into, we had a new structure for staff and academic discipline meetings, and we had teachers committed to working in a full-inclusion Expeditionary Learning school. Energy was high; the outlook was positive.

At our staff meeting just before the students returned, our assistant principal declared, "This is going to be the best year in Harbor School history!"

CHAPTER 17

CHEMOTHERAPY
2009–2010

The academic year 2009 started out strong. Morale was good. People felt energized. We were even consistently enforcing the school uniform policy. And BN, the principal, was pregnant—due in April. But we felt an undercurrent of anxiety. We had been hearing about a new government policy called Race to the Top, an initiative of Obama and his secretary of education, Arne Duncan. Many progressive educators had expected the Obama Administration to undo much of the damage of the No Child Left Behind Act. The overreliance on test scores, their unrealistic promises (all children will be "proficient" in reading and math by 2014), and other elements of NCLB had had a profoundly negative impact on public education. As more and more schools—especially in affluent white suburbs—failed to meet AYP (Annual Yearly Progress), the public began increasingly to question such a test-driven approach.

But Race to the Top (RTTT) was like No Child Left Behind on steroids. The Obama administration put $4.35 billion on the table in the form of a grant program to "encourage" states to adopt its new policies. Forty-six states, suffering from severe budget cuts during the Great Recession in 2008, were willing to jump in and fight like piranhas, ready to promise big changes to get the funding they needed.

What did a state have to do to win an RTTT grant? A number of things. First, states had to agree to adopt new "college and career-ready" standards; more specifically, the Common Core Standards. Although Obama didn't create the Common Core, he promoted its adoption across the country. The Common Core was quite contro-versial, and both the left and the right attacked it, for different rea-sons. Along with these new standards, states were "encouraged" to employ one of two testing consortia, either PARCC (Partnership for Assessment of Readiness for College and Careers) or Smarter Bal-anced, (this always sounded like a kind of margarine to me) which had received $350 million from the federal government to design tests for the new core standards. Massachusetts initially decided to go with PARCC, but that story comes later.

While RTTT did not hold states to the 100 percent proficiency goal of NCLB, standardized testing was still a critical part of the package. Now, not only would the tests evaluate students, but they would now assess teachers as well. This, too, was highly controver-sial (and later dropped) as students in more urban schools scored lower on the tests than their suburban (predominantly white) counterparts. People worried that teachers would choose to work in schools in wealthier zip codes for fear of losing their jobs if their students didn't do well on the tests.

Other parts of RTTT included the expansion of charter schools and the creation of "alternative" teacher-certification routes (like Teach for America). But the part that we had been hearing about was the idea of "turnaround" schools. The Boston Public Schools (BPS) had announced that they would be releasing a list of schools that would be targeted for turnaround. *What did that mean?* every-one wondered. *How was it decided who would be on the mysterious list? When would you know if you were being turned around or not?* These were all questions hanging in the air that fall of 2009.

In October, the phone call came. We were on the turnaround list. Then we were not. Then we were again. For a few days, we bounced back and forth between anxiety and relief. We still didn't know what it meant to be on the list, but we figured it probably wasn't good. But the final verdict was yes, we were a "turnaround school." While this was a blow given the work we had done the year before, I tried initially, naively, to be hopeful. Maybe we would get the help we needed to continue our own reform efforts. After all, BPS had been silent last year when we had asked for their assistance.

In mid-November, a team of BPS suits with clipboards descended on the school. They spent two hours visiting classrooms, and then they reconvened to share notes. They allowed a few Harbor School staff to be at the meeting, including the principal, the assistant principal, and me, but made it clear to us that we were only there as observers. They asked us nothing. Nothing about the history of the school, our analysis of the school's challenges, the efforts we had made to improve, resources we thought we might need. When we tried to interject, they told us to be quiet. After an hour of discussion, they made their own analysis and started to develop solutions. *We are here to help*, they assured us. They offered some extra planning time for teachers. They assured us literacy and math help. They left with promises to be in touch.

Why did the district only show up now? Where had it been when the scores started to decline four years ago? Why hadn't someone from BPS asked what was going on? Or even better, offered help? Why hadn't the district responded to our pleas for assistance a year ago? Doesn't a district have responsibility for supporting its schools when they are struggling?

The staff felt tremendous anxiety. What was going to happen next? What did it mean to be a "turnaround school"? No one seemed to have any answers. A heavy cloud settled over the school. Anxiety undermined the clear focus we had established at the beginning of the year on student achievement and staff development. Teachers started to worry about the future—the school's and their own. We tried to concentrate on the school-improvement goals we had identified that September, but people wondered if their work would just be undone. Decisions about scheduling, grading, future staffing patterns ground to a halt as people would ask, "Can we make decisions about this now?" "Will all the work we do just get changed next year?"

For three months, these questions hovered, coloring everything in the school. People did their best to stay dedicated to our original action plan. We were trying out new expeditions, continuing to do fieldwork in the community. Our various staff meetings were running smoothly. Our leadership team was getting along better. Always, though, uncertainty and apprehension gnawed at us.

Finally, at the end of February 2010, representatives from BPS came back to explain the implications of being named a turnaround school. The federal government had identified four levels of intervention. At the first level, a school would be able to extend the school day, make changes to the curriculum, have more control over staffing, get extra support. At the second, the entire staff (including teacher assistants, secretaries, custodians, cafeteria workers, etc.) would have to reapply for their positions; BPS could rehire a maximum of 50 percent of the staff. The principal would most likely be replaced. Level Three required a complete redesign by an "outside educational agency," i.e., a private institution. The final level meant closing the school. At this point, it was unclear which designation the Harbor School would receive.

Finally, on March 4, four months after the initial announcement, BPS told us our status. It also happened to be the day of our annual Exhibition Night, in which students presented their work for families and the community to see. As teachers were madly trying to set up their classrooms for the three hundred people who would show up that night, the principal called an emergency meeting. We had been designated as Level Two. She was being moved to another school in July, and everyone had to reapply for their positions.

People were stunned. Some started to cry. Small groups of folks hugged each other. A few just stood alone and shook their heads. Then the questions began again.

"Are we still going to be an Expeditionary Learning school?"

"Are we going to be a full-inclusion school?"

"Who will choose the new principal?"

"How do we reapply for our positions?"

"What is the timeline for all this?"

BN had no answers. We were all in the dark.

Then the anger started to build. *Why are they doing this to us? Don't they see all the good things we do here? Who are they going to get who would work any harder and care any more about our kids than we already do? Let one of them try to come here and teach my class!*

And then, something else happened. In about three hours, everyone realized, the school would be full of students and their families. The tears and the anger subsided, and a determination set in. "We need to be there for our kids," said one veteran teacher. "We can't go into Exhibition Night feeling defeated."

"We can't let them label us or our kids as losers," said another.

"Let's show everybody just what our kids have done this year," chimed in someone else. "We have to come together and make this a real celebration," added the next.

And, they did. That night, as parents came into the school, the only clue about the difficult news received that day was the television crew in the lobby that showed up to interview the principal and random parents about the school's fate. Teachers ignored the bright lights and camera in the school lobby and welcomed visitors into their classrooms, allaying people's fears and focusing them on the projects their children had done. Sixth graders shared their research on Ancient Egypt and displayed the pamphlets they had written on diseases that plagued their neighborhoods. Seventh graders taught their parents math games and explained their models of the inner structure of cells. Eighth graders read their "slave narratives" and explained the Pythagorean theorem to their younger siblings. One person from the Boston School Department attended. Just one.

The next week, the Human Relations director from the BPS came to answer questions about people's jobs. The meeting was tense, and confusing. While people wanted a clear process and timeline, it seemed as if the district was figuring out the plan as they went along.

"When will the hiring process for reapplying to the school begin?" a teacher asked.

"Maybe not until May or June," the HR director said. But the deadline to apply for the "excess pool"—in which people could apply for other teaching positions in Boston—was March 19, less than a week and a half away.

"Can we apply to the excess pool and still reapply for our positions at the Harbor?" asked another teacher.

"No," the director replied. "If you choose to reapply for your position, you cannot apply for any other job in BPS."

"That doesn't seem fair," someone said. "It's bad enough having to reapply for your own job—but then you have to wait until everyone else has gotten jobs before you can apply for one, with only a fifty-fifty shot at getting your old job back? That's like double jeopardy."

"You have a point there," the HR director admitted.

Would the school continue to be an Expeditionary Learning school? Inclusion? Will we have a co-teaching model?

"I don't know," he answered. "That all has to be figured out this spring."

"So—we have to make a decision in a week whether we want to take a 50 percent chance to be at a school that we don't know what kind of school it is going to be, we don't know who the principal will be, and we don't know what the structure will be?" one teacher summed up.

The HR director grimaced. "I know this is difficult, and we are operating on a very tight timeline. Maybe we can extend the excess pool deadline a bit."

I asked about the assistant principal and me. All the negotiations around the turnaround status, at this point, only involved people in the teachers' union. As administrators, DB and I were in a different position. We did not have protection through a union. We knew BPS was going to move BN to a different school, but no one had any answers for the two of us.

"You will have to wait until all this gets worked out with the teachers," the HR director said.

The deadline was extended one week, to March 23. The school department assigned a new principal to the school that week. He met with the staff and governing board. He seemed to listen as people spoke passionately about the school and what made it so special, in spite of the MCAS scores. They explained the changes we were making and the hopefulness they had felt at the beginning of the year. They declared their commitment to the school and the students and their families, pledging to work hard. Finally, Dr. M spoke. He was brief.

"You are the reason this school is failing," he said, pointing at the staff. "There are going to be major changes at the Harbor School." He did not say exactly what they would be.

This meeting shook people. Six decided to "excess" themselves; but the rest of the staff chose to reapply.

On April 15, the Thursday before April vacation, people received a letter from the BPS stating that they had to submit a written letter by Monday, April 26, declaring their intent to reapply for their positions at the school. It further explained that they had to agree to an open-ended contract, in which they could be asked to work a longer school day or an unnamed amount of extra days in the summer without extra compensation. If someone was offered a contract to return to the school and, for any reason, they turned it down, they were barred from seeking employment anywhere else in the Boston Public Schools. No one had told us any of this before. The letter ended by stating that people would be informed by Wednesday, April 28, as to whether they would be rehired or not. Not knowing whether or not this included me, I submitted my letter of intent. I really wanted to continue the work we had started at THS, in spite of my concerns about our new principal.

April 28 was a dark day at the Harbor School. Dr. M had scheduled ten-minute appointments in which staff would find out their fate. In reality, the meetings were often less than one minute. After all, how long does it take to say, "You're in" or "You're out"? Again, people felt hurt, angry, and confused. It was unclear how Dr. M had made these hiring decisions. Aside from staff members' written "letter of intent," no formal application process involving interviews or observations had occurred.

While the people who were invited back were relieved, no one felt good. As one teacher said, "I feel like the guilty survivor of a train wreck. Why did I survive and other people didn't?"

By the end of the day, 56 percent of the staff knew they would not be coming back the next year.

Our community was fractured. Our students had taken the news hard. Being labeled a "failing school" felt intensely personal to them. "People think we're losers," they said. "People think we're dumb."

Teachers tried to put a positive spin on things, even though they weren't feeling it. *Change can be good*, they said. *Maybe we're going to be an even better school*, they offered.

But the kids weren't having it. *Why should we even try anymore?* They were upset that certain teachers were returning and others were not. It didn't make any sense to them. These were young people who already felt labeled by their society as throwaways, easily expendable. The dismantling of their school just made it worse.

We still had two more months of school to go. The MCAS assessments were looming. How would we hold it together for the rest of the year? Would staff turn against each other? Would people start to call in sick? How would we keep the kids focused and working?

BN left the school in April to have her baby. The assistant principal and I were still in limbo, having not heard back about our jobs— but now we were in charge.

"I feel like I'm running a morgue," he said. He started looking for other positions, saying he couldn't imagine working under Dr. M. I was concerned, too, but felt torn. In spite of all its problems, I loved being at the Harbor School. I didn't want to give up on the progress we were making. But with not one word about my own fate, either from BPS or Dr. M, I wondered if I should start looking for other possibilities, too.

Then a friend told me about an opening in Cambridge. "You should apply," she said. "You would be great in this job. And you have no idea what's going to happen at Harbor. Maybe it's time for you to be in charge."

The Cambridgeport School was looking for a principal. Once again, I had an internal debate: *Do I really think I could be a principal? Am I scared of the responsibility?* After being at the Harbor for two years, though, I had a lot more confidence in myself. Furthermore, Cambridgeport felt like a good match. It had started in 1990, sharing the Graham & Parks's philosophy of constructivist education. "Cport" had a similar structure of a parent-staff steering committee and was committed to project-based learning and portfolio assessment. G&P and Cport had always considered themselves "sister" schools. Even though I felt like a traitor jumping ship, I decided to apply.

The hiring process for a principal, at least in Cambridge at that time, was long and arduous. After the Cport parent-staff hiring committee selected me as one of two finalists, I had multiple interviews with a variety of stakeholders, a visit by a Cport delegation to the Harbor School, a role-play with the current principal, and a community meeting with parents. Oddly enough, I was enjoying this interview process. Perhaps my ambivalence about leaving THS lowered the stakes for me; I'm not sure. But I loved the opportunity to talk openly about my philosophy, my beliefs about schools, my approach to leadership. How do you create a sense of community in a school? How would you handle a difficult evaluation? What role do you think parents should have in a school? Then, a question came up about my age. I was fifty-six years old at the time, and some people wondered if I was on the verge of retirement. I was shocked. Retirement had not even crossed my mind at this point! *On the contrary,* I explained. *I was energized and excited to step into this role. Why would I even apply for this job if I wasn't committed to staying for a while?* I felt I had been building up to this my whole career and was ready to put into practice my experience and beliefs.

I did not get the job. I was disappointed, of course, but I decided to see it as the Universe making a decision for me. Maybe I was meant to stay at the Harbor School—although I still hadn't heard anything official about my position. I did hear a lot in the press, though, about how Boston was looking for teachers who were "really dedicated to urban youth," people who were "willing to work hard," and "weren't driven by their own interests" (as opposed to those self-ish, lazy teachers in failing schools). These articles infuriated me. *Who do you think is working here now?* I raged.

It was a difficult time. A few staff did check out, but the majority acted with the utmost professionalism. People continued to work hard, continued to put in extra time to support kids, continued to work well together. People had to take time off to interview for other positions or to conduct sample lessons, but teachers covered for and supported each other. I was proud to be associated with this team.

By May, I still hadn't heard about my position. But I did get a different phone call. The new principal of the Graham & Parks School, Sarah Fiarman, was on the line. Sarah had been a student teacher at G&P years ago. She had gone on to be a highly regarded third- and fourth-grade teacher at the Cambridgeport School, and she had helped us at the Dr. Martin Luther King Jr. School as the Responsive Classroom trainer, the staff's choice of social competency curriculum. She was smart, passionate, energetic, enthusiastic.

"I know we probably can't pry you out of the Harbor School," she said, "but I have money to hire a coach. We've lost our way here over the years, with all the focus on the MCAS and new standards. People feel like the school isn't what it used to be. How can I convince you to come help G&P get back on track with project-based learning? I can't think of a better person to do it than you."

"Just ask," I replied. "I would love to come home."

I never did hear anything official from BPS about my role as director of instruction. Dr. M never even spoke to me, even though he started visiting the building on a regular basis. Oh wait. He did once. On the last day of school, he stuck his head in my office (literally, just his head) and said, "Uh, where are the eighth graders' portfolios?"

"We sent them home with their families after their graduation review panels," I answered.

"Oh, I see," he nodded, and left. That was it.

In mid-June, for the first time since the inception of the MCAS, we received our preliminary scores *before* the end of the school year. We were anxious to see these scores because we believed that, in spite of the major disruption of the "turnaround" process, we had made significant improvement by sticking to our target goals and plans we had set the previous summer. And indeed we did. In math, we reduced the number of students in Warning by 18 percent in the sixth grade, 14 percent in the seventh grade, and 25 percent in the eighth grade (fully one quarter of the class). Ten students scored "Advanced."

We also saw significant growth in our ELA scores. In the sixth grade, 13 percent more students were Proficient. In seventh grade, we had a 50 percent reduction in the number of students in Warning. In 2009, in the eighth grade we had moved 17 percent more students into Proficient. This year, we maintained that level of Proficiency and saw two more students score as Advanced.

We presented these results at a teacher luncheon the last week of school. People cheered. Whether they were returning to the Harbor School or not, they knew they had been part of a *real* turnaround process. As one teacher said, "At least I can leave holding my head high."

While our students had made progress in improving their MCAS scores, we saw student growth and learning in many other ways, too, that were not measured by a test. Sixth graders wrote and produced their own version of *The Odyssey*. Seventh graders researched, wrote, and illustrated children's books on the geology of Boston Harbor, which they read to students at the Henderson School—a model that Thompson Island Outward Bound started using with other BPS middle schools. Eighth graders visited and met with the curator of the John F. Kennedy Presidential Library and Museum to learn how to mount their own museum exhibit comparing the African and Irish experiences in America. All our eighth graders did community service work at sites like the Kit

Clark Senior Center and the Dorchester Multi-Service Center. Kids were reading more and talking about books they liked. Students led their own parent-teacher conferences; 85 percent of our families participated. All sixty graduating eighth graders orally defended a portfolio of their work to a panel of teachers, community members, and their parents.

But none of this mattered to the powers-that-be. They did not acknowledge even our MCAS improvement. We wrote a letter to the superintendent citing our data but heard nothing back. It bears repeating: We. Heard. Nothing. Back. We were on the Turnaround Train and could not get off. This infuriated me. Why were they not interested in our own efforts to turn things around? Why were they so determined to dismantle a school that had shown significant growth and progress in just one year?

Diane Ravitch writes in *Death and Life of the Great American School System*, "As we seek to reform schools, we must take care to do no harm." Schools are not factories. Teachers are not interchangeable parts, and educated children are not a product that rolls off an assembly line. Schools are complex institutions with a complex mission of educating all kinds of children from all kinds of families from all kinds of backgrounds with all kinds of learning needs and strengths. After decades of studying school reform, Ravitch warns against the quick fix. Because each school has its own unique conditions, history, and challenges, careful diagnosis of the problems a school is facing is essential. But, as one Harbor School teacher commented, "It is like we had appendicitis and they decided to give us massive chemotherapy."

Schools improve when they focus on key fundamentals and stick with them. We learned that at the Harbor School. We had needed help. When we asked for district help, we got none. But over the 2009–2010 year, rather than blanket layoffs of teachers, we pushed to do careful evaluations. We worked on clarifying and strengthening our curriculum. We improved professional development. We focused on a few targets and tried to maintain that focus throughout the year. That all made a difference. We knew we still had a lot of work to do, but we also knew we had been on the right road. But none of that mattered anymore.

The Harbor School ceased being an Expeditionary Learning school, its original mission, and became solely a full-inclusion program. After alienating a number of the special-needs parents, Dr. M was removed just before Thanksgiving in 2010. He'd been at the school less than four months. Two more interim principals served at Harbor to finish out that year. The next year, 2011–2012, Harbor again had three different principals. In 2012–2013, the K–12 Henderson Inclusion School absorbed the school. The Harbor School no longer exists.

CHAPTER 18
YOU CAN'T GO HOME AGAIN
2010 – 2012

Compared to Fields Corner, Cambridge is indeed leafy, especially in the area where Graham and Parks was now located. The school had moved in 2003 from the more dense and diverse neighborhood of Cambridgeport to a building across the street from the Radcliffe Quadrangle, part of Harvard University's campus. In spite of the improved amenities—a real playground with grass and space for children to run around, a full-sized gym, an auditorium with a stage, a cafeteria with windows and doors that opened onto a courtyard— the staff had fought this move. Our old building was filled with beautiful murals and a wide variety of art installations, most of these works created by students over the years. A tropical rainforest made with ceramic tiles brightened the basement cafeteria, an Egyptian sarcophagus guarded the entrance to a sixth-grade classroom, and a fiery mural depicting Jean-Bertrand Aristide of Haiti and Martin Luther King Jr. in their fights for freedom loomed over the stairwell. It was a living museum of student learning. But, even more importantly, from its founding the school had been dedicated to maintaining racial and socioeconomic balance. Teachers feared the move would lead to a significant shift in the student population, making it more white and more affluent. Which it did, at least for a while.

Student demographics changed for other reasons, too. In 2002, Ron Unz, a Silicon Valley multimillionaire, funded a referendum on the Massachusetts ballot to ban bilingual education and force schools to teach "English only" to new immigrant children.[1] Previously, the Haitian bilingual students studied math, science, and social studies in their mother tongue, while spending the rest of the day learning English. In spite of extensive linguistic research supporting the use of one's native language in teaching English-language learners, the referendum passed two to one. This ended the Haitian bilingual program at G&P, a defining part of the school's identity. In its place, we had a small Sheltered English Immersion (SEI) program, in which all subjects were—and still are—taught only in English.[2]

The G&P staff was also changing. Len Solo had been the principal for twenty-seven years when he retired in 2001. Over the next nine years, the school had four different principals, each with her own vision, her own roadmap for change. In addition, teachers who were beloved stalwarts at the school, working there for decades, had started to retire. Just like with the turnover at the Harbor School, fewer and fewer people worked at G&P who had a real understanding of and commitment to the original mission of the school.

This is where I came in. After Sarah extended her invitation to me to return to G&P, we took a long walk together. She had been excited to return to the school but had remembered a different kind of Graham & Parks from when she had done her student teaching there decades earlier. The district had been chipping away at the autonomies G&P had had as part of its original charter. The school had less control over its budget, governance, hiring practices, and certainly curriculum. As veteran teachers retired, the projects that had long characterized the school were disappearing. Sarah wanted to strengthen the hands-on, project-based learning that had been the hallmark of G&P's constructivist approach to teaching and learning. She was concerned about the newer teachers who didn't seem to understand how to develop curriculum, much less plan "an expedition."[3] She had reached out to Expeditionary Learning (EL) for professional-development support, but their involvement would be limited. She felt I could be a link between G&P's past and its future.

"People trust you," she said. "You can bridge EL's work with G&P."

There was one little glitch, though. The money she had to hire me came from the English/Language Arts (ELA) Department—and was meant to pay for a literacy coach.

"But isn't literacy closely entwined with an expedition?" Sarah argued.

I agreed. It is the central part of any curriculum. There is reading, writing, speaking, thinking in every discipline.

"That's what I thought!" Sarah exclaimed. "Ohh, I think this is going to work!"

I was excited. I thought back to my first years at Graham and Parks and our staff developer then, Isabel Hanelin. I remembered how she had helped me to rethink my pedagogy and gave me permission and encouragement to experiment in my classroom. She had asked insightful questions and helped me reflect on what was working and what wasn't working. She had helped me be a better teacher. I wanted to be the new Isabel Hanelin.

Although Sarah assured me I had the position, I still needed to follow the hiring process. So, in the spring of 2010, I met with a small interview committee that included Sarah, a teacher, a parent, and KT, the head of the English/Language Arts Department. I smiled at the group and they all smiled back, except for KT. She looked unhappy to be there. They took turns asking the scripted questions and I answered. Toward the end of the interview, KT spoke up.

"I want to know if you are going to follow the directions from the ELA office. You have a reputation for doing your own thing. Do you think you can be a team player?"

"I am definitely a team player," I responded, a bit taken aback. "I'm happy to follow the ELA Department, as long as it makes sense . . . which I'm sure it does." I smiled. She did not smile back.

"Are you willing to participate in training?

"Of course," I said. "I would welcome that."

"Are you willing to meet on a regular basis with other literacy coaches?" she continued.

"Of course!" I answered sincerely. "I believe in collaboration. It is great that the coaches all meet together. I'm sure I can learn a lot from them."

"All right," she concluded. "You know, you are not my preferred candidate." That was an unusual comment to make in an interview. "But Sarah insists that you are the right person for the job. I guess I will go along with her judgment."

So I actually had two bosses—my principal and the ELA Department. And they wanted me to do very different things. Sarah wanted me to focus on developing strong expeditions, but the ELA Department had adopted a particular approach to literacy that they wanted all teachers to use. Some G&P teachers were resistant to this model. They had been successfully teaching children to read and write for years. These teachers had developed an extensive toolkit, including some of the elements the ELA Department was now promoting, that put children at the center of their teaching. They couldn't understand why they should now abandon their own rich practice for someone else's model. When I'd asked that question at the district level, KT said it was important that everyone use the same approach.

"Why?" I asked. "Isn't the real goal to have kids reading and writing successfully?"

"We need to have a consistent approach in the district," I was told.

"But isn't it about the outcome?" I argued. "Aren't there many paths that lead to the mountaintop?"

Maybe these kinds of questions earned me my reputation of being a little difficult.

I spent most of that first year back at G&P (2010–2011) "in training." KT had mentioned this expectation, but I was surprised to discover that I was required, along with three other new school-based literacy coaches, to take a two-hundred-hour course in the Lesley Literacy Collaborative (LC) model developed by Irene Fountas and Gay Sue Pinell. We met for four full days during the year and once a month for two hours after school. In addition, I had to "student teach" in a third-grade classroom half the school day for the full year. Once I completed all this, I would be sent, like a missionary among heathens, to convince the recalcitrant G&P teachers to adopt the Literacy Collaborative system "with fidelity."

While it was a bit frustrating to be treated like a total novice (all four of us new coaches felt this way), I did learn a lot. I felt I could carry the LC banner without compromising my own beliefs. But I was never fully convinced that it was the one and only way to teach children reading and writing. There were other literacy gurus, like Lucy Calkins, Ellin Keene, Stephanie Harvey, and Nancie Atwell—not to mention our own veteran teachers—who also had a lot to offer. I did not understand the ELA Department's resistance to looking at good practices from many different sources. That's what we had done on the old G&P junior high team. We were not opposed to adopting a curriculum, but we felt we also needed to understand a variety of curricula and be able to draw from them when needed. It involved looking closely at what our students were actually doing, not just what the curriculum was telling us to cover.

Today, in many schools, I see this lack of ownership over content. Newer teachers learn to follow a curriculum or a series of lessons without really understanding the research and thinking *behind* what they are doing. Here is one tiny example. Good readers make connections between their own lives and what they are reading—that is, a "text-to-self" connection (there are also text-to-text and text-to-world connections). When we make a personal connection with a character or incident in a book, like the loss of a friendship or a revelation about a parent, we are able to develop a deeper insight into both the character's life and our own.

But I've heard teachers say to students, "Find a text-to-self connection in this chapter." And I've heard students respond, "Well, Carla has a red sweater and I have a red sweater too." And the teacher accepts that. But that is not a meaningful connection at all. Clearly, the teacher does not truly understand how identifying

personal connections in one's reading helps develop deeper understanding. She is just following directions.

It is a little like cooking. To be a really good cook, you need to
do more than just follow a recipe—you need to understand your
ingredients and how they interact with each other. You need to be
able to make adjustments—add a little more garlic (or a lot if you're
in my family), substitute kale for spinach, add in garbanzo beans
for more protein. To be a really good teacher, you have to know and
understand the ingredients of a good lesson and to whom you are
teaching it.

In carrying out my duties for the ELA Department, I tried to do
the work with sensitivity and respect toward the teachers, but when
I came to their team meetings I could see in their eyes a resistance,
or an exasperation at best.

"We have a big agenda today, Kathy," they would say. "And we
only have forty minutes. What do you need from us?"

"Uh, just checking to see if you've started the unit on personal
narrative yet?" or "Have you done the writing assessment yet?" or
"Have you started benchmarking yet?" or "Have you been able to
enter the test scores into the database yet?" or "Were you able to do
the post-assessment?" I didn't want to harass teachers, but the ELA
Department wanted this information and they regularly reminded
me that they paid my salary. Rather than becoming the new Isabel
Hanelin, who had nurtured inquiry and reflective practice, I found
myself in the role of district police.

As if there hadn't already been enough disruption to the school—a
new location, a stream of different principals, new teachers replacing veterans, changing student demographics—there was yet
another major change brewing that fall. Cambridge was in the
throes of a hot debate about abandoning the K–8 model and creating middle schools in the city, thus turning the city's twelve K–8
programs into K–5s and moving all the sixth, seventh, and eighth
grades into four "stand-alone" middle schools.

The G&P staff, parents, and students fiercely opposed the push for middle schools and testified over and over again at School Committee meetings to keep the school together. Our upper grades were an integral part of the school. Cross-grade relationships had been important for years, for both students and staff. We believed it was possible to have a high-quality middle school program within the K–8 structure. Our success in creating a rigorous academic program along with a developmentally appropriate one was reflected in the long waiting list to get into G&P's junior high.

How ironic, I thought, *to return to Cambridge now, in the midst of a debate about middle schools.* I had spent years trying to convince the superintendents and their people of a plan for improving the middle school programs. Although I was a strong supporter of the K–8 model, to me, the debate over K–8 versus independent middle schools was not the real issue. The real question was: how do you create a high-quality, developmentally appropriate program for young adolescents? According to extensive research on middle schools, both models could be effective (there was a slight bias for K–8 schools in more urban areas). What was more important was what went on *inside* the school. Was there a rigorous academic curriculum that was relevant to the concerns of adolescents? Was the schedule built around the academic core? Were teachers addressing the needs of all learners? Was there a caring and supportive environment that valued students? Were all students known well by at least one adult? Were young adolescents' developmental needs being met? These kinds of questions had guided us at G&P. They had also been the foundation for my strategic plan for the district.

I decided to dig out my files and share them with the new superintendent. As I entered his office, I flashed back to the last time I had been there—with JMG. I shuddered slightly, but knew that Dr. Y was a very different person. He was laid back, easygoing, personable. He gestured for me to sit at his table. I pulled out my file and handed it to him. As he skimmed through the many documents I'd brought, I described the structures and programs we had instituted at G&P over time. I explained what I had done in my role as Middle School Program Developer. I showed him the three-year plan I had developed with the Middle School Leadership Team. He read through the plan and looked up. "Who wrote this?" he asked.

"I did," I answered.

He looked surprised. "Hmm. This is impressive," he responded, his eyebrows raised.

"We learned a lot about middle school design over the years," I said enthusiastically. "We do need change, but we don't need to totally disrupt the whole district. There are many steps we can take to build strong middle school programs within our K–8 schools. I know, because we did it at G&P, and other schools have been moving in the right direction, too. I would be very happy to work on this with you and your team."

He nodded, thanked me warmly for coming, and I headed out. Did I actually see him stick the folder I'd brought into a drawer? Or was it the wastebasket? Or was I just imagining that? At any rate, we never spoke about the plan again. After months and months of testimony, debate, angry meetings, and a divided community, in the spring of 2011, the School Committee voted, on the Superintendent's recommendation, to create four new middle schools.

At Graham & Parks, the grief was palpable. People cried. I cried. Losing our sixth-, seventh-, and eighth-grade colleagues and students—a third of the school—was like having an arm torn off your body. Or even worse—a death. These teachers weren't just colleagues; they were friends, mentors, comrades. The students were our babies. They were all part of a family. This was yet another blow to the identity of the school. Posters appeared in the hallways: "G&P, RIP."

The district announced that the upcoming school year (2011–2012) would be dedicated to planning for these four new schools. They assured us that the process would be an inclusive one, gathering best practices for young adolescents from across the city and beyond. We had lost the battle, but we consoled ourselves with the idea that more students would be exposed to our good teachers, our strong curriculum, and our projects and initiatives that had developed over time. We would do what we could to help build effective and solid middle school programs across the city.

Although it mostly impacted the upper-grade teachers, the battle over the middle school question took a toll on the whole school. The K–5 teachers seemed stressed and overwhelmed. Just keeping up with emails from parents, the principal, the coaches (literacy and math), their various department heads, etc., was a gargantuan task. But it was more than that. There was a level of anxiety that seemed at odds with my own memories of being a teacher at G&P ten years earlier.

Gradually, I started to see that there had been another big, more insidious change at G&P: Education Reform. The MCAS, No Child Left Behind, and Obama's Race to the Top—all these had gradually but relentlessly forced changes in all schools, even the Graham and Parks Alternative Public School. The consequences for failing to "meet AYP" (Annual Yearly Progress), even by a percentage point or two, could be enormous—and terrifying. No one wanted their school to be taken over by the state, much less closed down.

In Cambridge, the worry about MCAS scores and the consequences of not meeting AYP had spawned an increasing number of district assessments. There were tests given to students to measure what we needed to teach to prepare them for the tests. Tests to prepare kids for the tests. Tests to give kids practice to take the tests. At one point, elementary teachers were giving twenty-two district or state assessments a year! Even the CPS administration hadn't realized how much time students were filling in bubbles. These tests basically told good teachers what they already knew—actually, the tests often revealed far less than what teachers already knew. But these assessments resulted in numbers—"hard" data—and people, at least those in charge of educational policy, seemed to trust numbers more than they did teachers.

The new buzzword was "data-driven instruction." Spreadsheets and data analysis ruled corporate America, and the ed reform gurus believed that this was the way to fix our "failing schools" and "close the achievement gap." There was even a book called *Driven by Data* that you could find on almost any principal's desk at the time, including Sarah's.

According to proponents, "Data Driven Instruction and Inquiry (DDI) is a precise and systematic approach to improving student learning throughout the year."[4] In my experience, though, improving student learning was never precise nor systematic. According to Data Driven Instruction, if schools just collect data, analyze the data, develop an action plan, implement the action plan—voila, the problem is fixed!

To be fair, this process has value, although it does not solve all problems. At G&P, under Sarah's tutelage, we conducted "inquiry cycles" at each of the grade spans (1/2, 3/4, etc.) using a similar process. These inquiry cycles (also known in an earlier decade as "action research") proved to be useful, especially when the teachers themselves identified an issue of concern, decided what data should be collected, had time to analyze and discuss what the data revealed, did research on the issue to deepen their own knowledge base, and had time to try out new ideas, with impunity.

But this wasn't always how people used the data-driven approach. Schools started to assemble "data walls" and "data dashboards." We spent hours creating them and then more hours staring at them. They were often displayed in staffrooms or put up during a team or staff meeting, with the intent of "holding ourselves accountable." These data displays seemed to shout, "Look at these five kids in your class who aren't reading on grade level. What are you doing about that, huh? HUH? *HUH*?" People would surreptitiously compare their students' data to those from their colleagues' classes. Sometimes they would feel relief. "Oh, my kids aren't doing as bad as _____'s are." Other times, they would cry. "I don't know what else I can do to help Jaiyana! I've tried everything!" People began to dread these meetings, and often left in tears.

Don't get me wrong. It *is* important to look at data. Teachers are responsible for their students' growth and learning. But there are problems with the data-driven reform model. First of all, who defines what kinds of data we're looking at? Is it a standardized test score, like the MCAS from the year before? Is it a computer-based test or a teacher-designed assessment? Furthermore, even when we use data from more finely tuned assessments than the MCAS, there are a lot of "data" we don't pay any attention to. For example, maybe Jaiyana is reading below grade level, but did we note that she has started to develop more confidence in decoding words? Or that she is asking more questions about what she is reading? Or that she is getting excited about reading? Did we know that she completed a whole book on her own for the first time? Those facts are important data, too, but they are rarely measured.

That's the second problem with our practice being driven by data: we start focusing on numbers instead of children. Twenty years earlier, we had talked about our students, not their numbers. We might reference some assessments, but that was not our starting or ending point. As a team, we would raise questions about a child, share information about him or her, look at examples of their work. Instead of compiling spreadsheets, I could have been observing children in classrooms. A teacher could have said, "Come into my classroom. Could you observe what Jaiyana is doing? Could you read with her and tell me what you think is going on? Could we have a conversation about what to do to support her?"

Today, we've stopped seeing the human beings in front of us. Yet seeing children, really *seeing* them, is the foundation for good teaching. Pat Carini, the legendary teacher and cofounder of the Prospect School in Vermont, spoke about the centrality of looking carefully at our students and their work: "The aspiring teacher commits herself or himself to relatedness to children. That is, to be a see-er of children."

Inspired by Pat Carini, Steve Seidel, my Project Zero mentor, leads monthly meetings ("rounds") for teachers to look at student work together. Up to fifty educators gather in a large circle in the Eliot Lyman Room of Longfellow Hall at the Harvard Graduate

School of Education to carefully look at one piece of student work. *One.* Sometimes it is a poem, other times a painting. We have looked at essays, stories, and math problems. A few times, we watched a video of a dance or theater performance. Whatever the piece of work, Steve leads the group through an hour-long protocol that helped us all to truly see the child and what s/he was working on. I would often feel impatient at the beginning of this process because I was used to being on the fast track of school life. But by the end, I was always amazed by how much we could learn, not only about this one child, but about teaching and learning in general.

This kind of looking at student work is not practical to do all the time. But it is a critical exercise in looking carefully and thus seeing the deep dimensions of a child's learning process. These monthly gatherings were an antidote to the number crunching I spent so much of my day doing. They were the antithesis of scoring a standardized test in which people are paid to read an essay a minute. Steve's practice of "rounds" helped us all to see children instead of numbers.

Third, this kind of focus on data encourages us to blame teachers. I loved the teachers at G&P. I knew how hard they worked and how deeply they cared about their students. And yet, in our data meetings, I found myself judging these same people, thinking that if they just worked a little harder, or were just a little bit better at their job, they wouldn't have five kids reading below grade level. But I was looking at data, not people. I would forget how hard it is to teach a class of twenty or twenty-five children (in some districts, many more) with many different learning needs. I would forget that these children were growing in all sorts of other ways. My periodic lapses in empathy would surprise me. I prided myself on being the teachers' advocate, speaking up for them whenever I could. They were the ones in the trenches. They were the ones who were trying to figure out how to reach, instruct, inspire students. How could I so easily lose my perspective? If *I* could get sucked into a myopic view of student achievement, so would many people much further away from the frontlines of the classroom. And that is dangerous.

At times, looking at data is extremely productive for teachers, especially when it is rooted in children's real work, not in standardized tests. Analyzing student writing—as we did in my first few years as a literacy coach at the school—is a good example.

During that period, three times each year, teachers across the district gave their students a common writing prompt. Then, released from their classes for a day, they gathered together to read these essays. Part of my job as the literacy coach was to facilitate these meetings. We used a rubric to assess six traits of writing: idea development, organization, voice, word choice, sentence structure, and writing mechanics (that is, spelling, punctuation, and grammar). While this rubric wasn't perfect, it did give teachers a focus and a common vocabulary to look at student writing. Teachers read and scored other students' essays (not their own students'). Ideally, two teachers scored each paper. If there was a discrepancy between them, they would talk about it together and come to a consensus on a final score. "You gave Hakeem a five on topic development? I only gave him a three."

Teachers benefitted from this writing-assessment process in many ways. First, they were exposed to the writing of children outside their own class. I heard teachers say things like, "Wow! How did you get your kids to write such great opening lines?" Or, "Wow! Your kids are using a lot of rich language. How have you been working on that?" Teachers would spontaneously share practices that others might put into practice the very next day. Also, discussing a scoring discrepancy helped develop better analysis skills. ("*Why* did you give Hakeem a five?") Another positive outcome came from mapping the data (which I happily did). If several students were scoring particularly low in one area, like organization or writing mechanics, that signaled the need to spend more instructional time on that skill. Sometimes we even noticed trends across a whole grade level. Then we could talk about working as a team on a particular trait.

This was a good assessment. It informed both curriculum and instruction. It helped teachers grow. It provided immediate and relevant information about what to work on in class, both as a whole and with individual students. The problem was that, after a few years, this process did not always happen in the right way: the district stopped funding substitutes, so teachers could no longer meet to analyze and discuss their students' writing. Teachers had plenty of their own students' work to correct; reading a whole other set of essays on their own time became quite burdensome, so they began to score just their own class's writing. Now only one set of eyes was reviewing each essay. Thus, the chance to look more deeply and more objectively at students' work was lost. Scoring the writing assessments became yet another task to check off the list rather than a purposeful practice.

Benchmarking, a reading evaluation, was another useful district assessment. Teachers read one-on-one with a student with a certain level book (ranging from A as a beginning reader to Z, a proficient eighth-grade reader), listening to the child read aloud and noting any errors in decoding and fluency. Then they asked the student questions about what they had just read. This gave teachers an enormous amount of important information about students' reading ability. Did they decode words by sounding them out, or were they figuring out words from the context of the sentence? Were they reading with confidence and expression, or were they just reciting the words they saw on the page? Did they understand what they were reading at just a literal level, or were they able to infer deeper meaning?

Contrast this to a standardized test in reading, such as the MCAS exam. If a student answers a question incorrectly, why? Was there a key vocabulary word they did not understand? Did they read a passage about which they had no prior knowledge or context? Did they bubble-in B when they meant to bubble-in C? Did they read the question wrong? Was it a confusing question? How long did they try to figure out the correct answer? Did they reread any of the passage, or were they just rushing to get through it? Had they had breakfast and a good night's sleep? Did they have a fight with a friend? All these can be reasons why students get an answer wrong. If we don't know why a child makes a mistake, we don't know how to help them.

As I started my second year back at G&P, staff morale was low. So much so that it was the first item of business for the Instructional Leadership Team. The ILT was made up of a representative from each grade-level team, plus the principal, the literacy coach (me), and the math coach. This group was charged with developing a school improvement plan (required now by the district), but the teachers felt they could not even begin to think about that before addressing the climate of the school. Sarah, the principal, put aside her planned agenda and invited the teachers around the table to speak. They did not hold back.

"We are just in survival mode."

"It seems like people are feeling overscheduled and overwhelmed with trainings, committees, and other meetings."

"We need time to think deeply about our lessons and we don't have it."

"A lot is required of new teachers in the district." (They had to attend mandatory new-teacher training, meetings with mentors, meetings with coaches, meetings with curriculum coordinators—on top of teaching their classes.)

"People want to feel more grounded. Right now, we're just getting by, day to day."

"Our meetings are structured and directed by other people. We'd like to have more freedom about what and how we run them."[5]

I could see how many external demands teachers were dealing with. Demands that I hadn't experienced when I was in the classroom. No one had told me to teach a particular curriculum or administer a particular assessment, especially at a particular time. No one had told me to enter student test scores into a database (both tedious and time-consuming, and totally unhelpful as to how to teach a child the next day). More and more was being put on teachers' plates, and nothing ever came off. It was like speed-up on an assembly line.

This was in stark contrast to the meetings I remembered with my junior high team. Granted, there was never enough time, there was always too much to do, we rarely got through a whole agenda. But we had been in control. We were not responding to the demands of people far from our classrooms, be it district, state, or federal overseers. We were responding to our students and families.

The ILT had little power to really address teachers' concerns. We did what we could, like scaling back our inquiry cycles for the year (from two to one), but we could not excuse teachers from district-mandated meetings or curriculum changes. We did agree that we could do three things that would improve morale: build community, articulate "who we are," and build a sense of ownership of the school's mission. How we would do those things was not clear. But before we could even begin to think about that, another juggernaut was about to hit.

Dubbed the "Innovation Agenda," the district launched its planning for the four new middle schools that fall of 2011. This change was going to affect every school in the city. Just figuring out physical space and other basic logistics was a huge challenge, much less developing a clear educational vision. The district established a task force of planners, including several teachers from each building, and people were hopeful that this group would develop a truly innovative plan. But the committee rarely met. It seemed like decisions were being made in back rooms. Teachers became frustrated.

Finally, one day in the spring, middle school staff were invited to give their input on the design. They were excited that, at last, they would be able to share their thoughts, experiences, concerns, and suggestions. A few hundred teachers gathered on an early release day. The first hour involved a presentation. Eventually, participants began getting restless. "How are we going to have time to share our ideas?" the teacher next to me wondered, echoing my own concern. During the next hour and a half, teachers cycled through different "workshops," with about thirty minutes in each to comment. Given that each workshop had a good twenty to thirty participants, few people had a chance to share their views or ask questions. That was the extent of teacher input into the Innovation Agenda.

This was not the first time I'd heard the promise of "teacher input" in developing a new initiative, nor would it be the last.

Usually, when the district (or the state or the Common Core) claimed that it had involved teachers in the planning stages of a new venture, like with the Innovation Agenda, that effort was simply token. Or perhaps there would be one teacher-member on a committee of ten or twenty. Or perhaps the district asked teachers for their input on curriculum *after* it had already ordered the new textbooks (this happened with the Math Department in Cambridge). The superintendent and other administrators would tell parents and School Committee members that teachers had been an integral part of the process. Because people generally trust their teachers, they would feel confident that the new program, curriculum, assessment, whatever—had genuinely incorporated teacher input. But this was, and is, rarely the case. I've learned to look closely when education reformers claim that changes have incorporated teacher input.

Rather than assessing the strengths of existing middle school programs, both in the city and beyond, and building a vision based on research and successful practices, the district opted for a new middle schools approach that appeared to be a throwback to the 1950s. There would be no block scheduling (there would be seven 48-minute periods a day). No multigraded classes. No humanities curriculum. No interdisciplinary curriculum of any kind. No interdisciplinary teacher meetings. No narrative progress reports. No portfolios or graduation review panels. The Innovation Agenda was, in fact, anything but innovative.

After having watched our work at the Harbor School go down the tubes with the "turnaround" debacle, I again felt bereft. It was a sucker-punch in the solar plexus. So much hard work, thoughtful reflection, conversations and debates, creative curricula and various projects (taking years of tweaking and revision)—not to mention strong working relationships—were wiped out in this transition.

As the district prepared for the opening of the middle schools in 2013, I was faced with a personal dilemma. Would I go with the middle school teachers to the new Vassal Lane Upper School or stay with the K–5 teachers at Graham & Parks? In some ways, it made the most sense for me to go to the middle school. My background was firmly in that arena, and I felt like my literacy skills were most helpful to teachers in the older grades. I'd had no training with teaching beginning readers and writers. But the more I heard about the Innovation Agenda, the less I thought I could tolerate being a part of it. I decided to stay "home" at G&P.

This move to a citywide middle school structure spawned yet another significant change for G&P. With the sixth, seventh, and eighth grades leaving, there was now physical space for something else: the majority of the Sheltered English Immersion (SEI) program. (The program had been housed at one of the schools that would now be a middle school.) We already had a couple of SEI classes and, before that, a strong history with the Haitian bilingual program; the school community felt the consolidation of the SEI program would be a good fit with G&P. In addition, the district assigned a multigraded self-contained special needs class and a special needs preschool to the school.

This meant that one third of the staff would be new. And they had not chosen to come to the Graham & Parks Alternative Public School—they had been assigned. Some of the teachers resented being yanked out of their own familiar communities and plunked down into a new one. Furthermore, these new programs answered to different bosses in the district and had many external constraints on what they could and could not do. Tension and mistrust simmered. Now the school's vision was even less clear, much less embraced by a cohesive staff. The need to "build community, articulate 'who we are,' and build a sense of ownership/mission of the school" became even more urgent. But, once again, forces far beyond us would derail our efforts to address what the school really needed.

CHAPTER 19

RACE TO NOWHERE
2011–2016

MCAS, all its preparatory assessments, and all the structural changes to the school cast a long shadow over Graham & Parks. Had we met our AYP? What was our SGP? What did CPI mean again? I didn't think the pressure could get much worse on teachers and students, but I was wrong.

The brunt of Obama's Race to the Top (RTTT) was about to kick in, on a number of fronts.

In 2011, Massachusetts adopted the Common Core State Standards (CCSS), with a few minor amendments. While RTTT did not require states to adopt the Common Core, most states adopted some form of them, knowing that would give them an edge in the competition for the Race to the Top prize money. Released in 2010, seemingly out of nowhere, the CCSS's English/language arts (ELA) and math standards allegedly emphasized critical thinking and evidence-based arguments and were supposed to prepare K–12 students to be "college and career ready." The Gates Foundation funded the Common Core to the tune of $200 million—along with a few other billionaires who generally leverage their wealth to control public policy (dubbed the "Billionaire Boys' Club" by Diane Ravitch). Two organizations, the National Governors Association (NGA) and the Council of Chief State School Officers (CCSSO), developed its standards, initially written by university professors, leaders of education-advocacy groups, and experts from testing companies. Later, under pressure from teachers' unions, Common Core organizers added a few teachers to the working group (however: remember my warning about "teacher input").

To me, having broad common standards was not a bad idea. What do we want students to know and be able to do? This gives educators guidance about what to teach. However, the Common Core went far, far beyond this. No subject area was left untouched by the standards movement. There were state standards for music, art, and physical education as well as all the academic subjects. And along with required standards came required assessments. More and more of them. And assessments drive instruction.

Teachers, particularly in K–5, were aghast when they looked at the Massachusetts Common Core Standards. For kindergarten, there are nearly seventy standards in English/Language Arts alone. For first grade, there are nearly eighty. They get more complex as you move up in grade levels. Here is an example of one of the writing standards for first graders:

> *Write opinion pieces that introduce the topic or name the book they are writing about, state an opinion, supply a reason for the opinion, and provide some sense of closure.*

Below is one writing standard for fourth graders:

> *Write narratives in prose or poem form to develop experiences or events using effective literary techniques, descriptive details, and clear sequences.*
>
> a. *Orient the reader by establishing a situation and introducing a speaker, narrator, and/or characters; organize an appropriate narrative sequence.*
> b. *Use dialogue and description to develop experiences or events or show responses to situations.*
> c. *Use a variety of transitional words and phrases to manage sequence.*
> d. *Use concrete words and phrases, figurative language such as similes and metaphors, and sensory details to convey experiences or events precisely.*
> e. *Provide a sense of closure appropriate to the narrated experiences or events.*
> f. *For poems, use patterns of sound (e.g., rhyme, rhythm, alliteration, consonance) and visual patterns (e.g., line length, grouped lines as stanzas or verses) to create works that are distinctly different in form from prose narratives.*

Before the state adopted the Common Core standards, we had started a new round of inquiry cycles at G&P. Each grade-level team was exploring an issue (based on data and observations) that they had identified among their students. For example, the first- and second-grade team was delving into a study of reading fluency because they were concerned that students were weak in that skill. Fluency is a critical part of being a strong reader. If a student is a fluent reader, she can read with speed, accuracy, and expression, which also indicates comprehension to an important degree. The teachers had been reading and discussing the latest research on fluency in their team meetings. They were listening to tapes of students reading aloud, in order to develop a consistent baseline for assessment. They were sharing lessons with each other to improve student fluency. But with the adoption of the Common Core, this all ground to a halt. We had to shift our focus to poring over the Common Core.

As our teachers met to review these new standards, they wondered if the developers of the Common Core had ever been in an elementary classroom. Had they ever met a six-year-old? How about a child that was just learning English? Did they *really* expect first graders to write an opinion piece that 1) introduces a topic, 2) states an opinion about it, 3) supplies a reason for the opinion, and 4) provides some sense of closure? What did it mean for a fourth grader to "use concrete words and phrases, figurative language such as similes and metaphors, and sensory details to convey experiences or events precisely?" How were we going to *teach* this stuff?

When my children were in first grade, they were learning how to write their upper- and lowercase letters. So, if a first grader was expected to write an opinion piece, she would have to begin to learn how to write a year earlier—in kindergarten. Fairly rapidly, the traditional first-grade curriculum became the new kindergarten one. And the second-grade curriculum moved to first grade, and so on up through all the grades.

One day I was visiting the kindergarten class next to my office. As I walked around the little round tables, I watched the children diligently trying to make uppercase As. Some of them were holding their pencil with a fist, rather than between their thumb and fingers. The teacher gently showed them how to hold the pencil correctly. As soon as she left, though, many of them went back to holding it with their fist. I mentioned this to our occupational therapist, who worked with the primary classes on handwriting.

"They are not ready to be doing this," Regine said. "In kindergarten, they should be working with clay and gluing tissue paper and finger painting. Those are the activities that will build their hand and upper-body strength so they *will* be able to write. Developmentally, many of them are not ready. But this is what they have to do now because of the new standards."

The same held true with reading. Children used to begin to learn to read in first grade. Some children started earlier, but many others didn't. My own daughter didn't "crack the code" of reading until the end of first grade (she is now a teacher). My nephew didn't start reading until the end of second grade (he is now a lawyer). In Finland, famous for its high-quality schools, reading isn't formally taught until a child is seven years old. But pressure is now on for students to enter first grade knowing all their letters, the sounds they make, and how to blend them together to make a word. Here is an example of a text that a child should be able to read at the *beginning* of first grade:

> Kate played with her tooth at lunch. She wiggled it and wiggled it. "Don't wiggle your tooth," said Ben. "I want to eat my lunch."

One outcome of this pressure to teach specific skills earlier and earlier is a spike in student anxiety and depression. We started seeing more meltdowns, more acting out, more temper tantrums, more resistance to school. Also, as schools make more academic demands on children, there is less time for other things in school. One of the biggest tragedies of ed reform's impact on elementary school children is the loss of play. Walking into a kindergarten class twenty years ago, you would see children building structures with blocks, playing make-believe in the house area, smearing paint with their hands at a big easel, and experimenting with waterwheels. Through this kind of play, children were learning important skills preparing them to become readers, writers, scientists, mathematicians, and more.

Children also learned how to get along with each other, how to negotiate differences, and how to be part of a group. Do you remember the poster that said, "All I really need to know I learned in kindergarten?"

> Share everything. Play fair. Don't hit people. Put things back where you found them. Clean up your own mess. Don't take things that are not yours. Say you're sorry when you hurt someone . . .

And so on. Now, all too often, kindergartners sit at a table filling in worksheets. The younger-grade students are not the only ones suffering from these developmental mismatches and the speed-up on the learning assembly line. We can see these problems throughout the grades.

Along with these new standards, Massachusetts had to have a Common Core–aligned assessment system. Although the MCAS was one of the most rigorous standardized tests for public schools in the country (as well as being the most punitive: a student cannot get a high school diploma without passing the test), it was not "Common Core-aligned." Initially, in 2014, the state invested heavily in the Partnership for Assessment of Readiness for College and Careers (PARCC), one of the testing consortia supported by the Obama administration. The PARCC promised to measure "critical thinking" and "higher-order thinking skills" and be "much more rigorous" than the MCAS.

Now we had to learn about the PARCC. Instead of working with teachers in their classrooms, I attended at least three separate workshops, each of them close to two hours, replete with PowerPoint presentations, so I could bring information about the PARCC back to our staff. At one of these sessions, I was sitting next to a principal from another school. A district coordinator droned on as she walked coaches and administrators through a byzantine series of charts and diagrams. At one point, the principal leaned over to me and whispered, "This makes the MCAS look like cupcakes. My kids are screwed." Everyone in the room had that deer-in-the-headlights look.

How was the PARCC different from the MCAS? In some significant ways. First, the PARCC, in its claim to test "higher-order thinking skills," had a different format than the MCAS. Some reading-comprehension questions had a Part A and then a Part B. Part A was your typical multiple-choice question, like: "Based on the reading passage, what will Roy and Willie **most likely** do the next evening?" The student selects A, B, C, or D. Then, in Part B, the student is supposed to select the best *evidence* for their answer to Part A. This is supposed to measure more critical thinking and the ability to support an argument.

At one literacy coaches' meeting, we were discussing how to introduce the new test to our teachers. What kinds of skills are embedded in the test? What do we need to emphasize with students more? What do we need to focus on less? We decided to try out the test ourselves. We broke into small groups to look at different grade-level tests. Four of us huddled together, looking at the fifth-grade test. We read the passage and then came to the first question with a Part A and Part B.

"I think the answer is B," said Sarah.

"I don't know," responded Jo. "C also makes sense."

"I know, I thought it was C," chimed in Liza.

"C does make sense," said Sarah, "but I think they want us to answer B. Maybe we should look at Part B and that will give us a clue." So we went on to Part B.

"It could be any of these!" Jill exclaimed.

"I agree," I chimed in. "If you really think carefully and critically about the passage, each of these could apply."

"But there is only one right answer," Jo reminded us. We spent about forty-five minutes trying to figure out the correct answers. We were all literacy coaches with master's degrees, and we couldn't get past the first question. What were our students going to do?

Another important difference between the MCAS and PARCC was that students had to do more writing. Not only did they have a separate writing prompt, but they had to write responses to their reading. In particular, they had to read different passages and then compare them. One fourth-grade prompt, for example, was based on L. Frank Baum's book *The Wizard of Oz*. After the students read two different passages, they had to answer this question: "Based on her words and actions in both passages, describe two of Dorothy's qualities. Think about the person that Dorothy is. How do those qualities affect her adventures? Support your response with details from both passages."

Finally, the PARCC was designed to be taken on a computer. When I first learned that all students, beginning with third graders—who are eight years old—would be taking the state assessment on a computer, I couldn't believe it. Was this developmentally appropriate? Nor did I believe it would ever happen. Our school (and most others) didn't have enough computers for more than one or two classes to use at a time. Where would we get all the computers? Then what about broadband and connectivity issues? How would students throughout the state of Massachusetts take the test at the same time?! (The state insisted on this for the ELA writing test as they didn't want students to "cheat.")

Furthermore, if students had to compose an essay on the computer, they would have to know how to type. In our district, students didn't begin to learn to type until fifth grade (I learned in ninth grade). Would we have to start teaching third graders how to type so they could take the test? What about equity? Wouldn't children with access to a computer at home have a greater chance of developing better typing skills than those without such access? Would we have to start teaching them in second grade so they would be ready and comfortable to compose on the computer by third grade? If we have to teach children how to type, whether it is in second or third grade, what will we have to give up in order to make the time for keyboarding skills?

Back at Graham & Parks, we once again—in the middle of the year—had to drop our original professional-development plan to introduce teachers to this new style of test. This time, we had been focusing on vocabulary development as a whole school. Teachers had chosen to read one of four different professional books on vocabulary. We had worked together in small, cross-grade groups to discuss the different texts, and then we developed a common framework for our approach to teaching vocabulary. Teachers had decided which strategies they wanted to work on and shared progress and challenges at team meetings. Just as we were starting to feel like we were really accomplishing something, we had to interrupt our PD work to focus on PARCC.

There was tremendous pushback against the Common Core standards and PARCC. Hearings were held around the state; hundreds of people came out to testify against one or the other, or both. The education commissioner was getting squeezed on all sides. Critics from the Right did not like the top-down imposition of standards from the federal government. People on the Left opposed standardized testing and believed that the standards and the test were both developmentally inappropriate and racist.[1] The commissioner defused the growing resistance by declaring that Massachusetts would not adopt PARCC. Instead, he announced at a big press conference, the Department of Education would design its own test: MCAS 2.0. Not surprisingly, when the new test came out in 2017, it looked an awful lot like the PARCC.

In 2012, the conservative Pioneer Institute estimated that the implementation of the Common Core—including testing, professional development, textbooks and instructional materials, and technology—would cost close to $18 billion across the U.S.[2] I'm not sure how much was actually spent, but I do know the amount of time and money invested in this could have been spent a lot more wisely. This Race to the Top reform diverted real efforts to strengthen teaching and learning. Instead of looking closely at our students and their work (which is what assessment is), we were spending time trying to figure out an awkward computer platform and scrambling to teach kids how to type.

In addition to the Common Core and its requisite testing, Race to the Top also required "performance-based" evaluations of teachers and principals. These would be based on "multiple measures of educator effectiveness (tied to targeted professional development and feedback)." While not specifically linking teacher salaries to test scores, as had been tried in the past (and had failed), this new initiative was based on a corporate, market-based model.

As many districts did, Cambridge adopted an online evaluation tool. The system had multiple steps and a particular format. Once again, administrators and coaches attended workshops to learn how to navigate the website and its expectations. It was so complicated that the Human Resources Department put out a fifteen-step timeline to help both teachers and principals know what they needed to do and when; and then HR had to revise it because it created so much confusion. Once again, we had to use precious meeting time to explain this new form of evaluation to staff. Once again, we had to put other work, work focusing on teaching and learning, on hold.

As part of this new online evaluation system, at the beginning of the school year teachers had to fill in a Self-Assessment Form and identify a Student Learning SMART Goal and a Professional Practice SMART Goal. By November, there would be an Educator Plan Form. In January, and then again in March, teachers had to complete their Collection of Evidence Form, uploading test scores, student work, and any other proof of reaching their goals. Then there was a Formative Evaluation Form and, finally, a Summative Evaluation.

If this seems like gobbledygook to you, it did to us too. What is a SMART goal? teachers asked. (SMART stands for "Specific and Strategic, Measurable, Action-oriented, Rigorous, Realistic and Result-oriented, and Timed and Tracked.") What if my goal isn't SMART? they asked. What does it mean to be "action-oriented" or "timed and tracked"? Where do I find the district performance rubric? Does my individual goal need to be the same as the school's

School Improvement Plan (SIP) goals? What if the SIP doesn't apply to me (e.g., a music or physical education teacher)? What kinds of assessments should I include? What can I use as evidence? We spent hours with teams and individual teachers trying to answer these questions and helping them fill in these forms. It felt more like working in a sales department than in a school.

The corporation that developed this evaluation tool also serves industries like engineering, construction, mining, oil and gas, facilities management, pharmaceuticals, casinos, and public safety (such as law enforcement and fire departments).[3] But, as much as ed reformers would like schools to be the same as a corporation or a factory, they are not. Good schools are based on relationships, not a collection of data points and SMART goals. Teaching and learning are complex and multifaceted. That doesn't mean that we don't need to have a system of evaluation and accountability, but that system must be aligned with the mission and goals of educating our young people.

With the Race to the Top demands, the onslaught of district assessments, the change from K–8 to middle schools, and the Sheltered English Immersion and special ed programs moving into the G&P building, I could understand why our teachers were so stressed, anxious, and exhausted. They were bouncing around like marbles in a pinball machine, from one new "reform" to another. They grew increasingly cynical about our professional-development plans, as one plan after another had had to be abandoned because of district, state, or federal mandates.

"That work on vocabulary was good," one teacher said to me. "It's just too bad we never finished it. We never seem to finish anything."

CHAPTER 20

GOOD STUFF
2010 – 2018

In looking back at those years at Graham & Parks from 2010 to 2018, it felt like a big jumble of chaos. Teachers were constantly assaulted by initiatives, assessments, federal and state mandates, politics, and the ever-present Test. There was a lot of crying. At times, it seemed that the best way I could support my teachers was to simply offer a shoulder to cry on. But in spite of all these demands, and I do mean in spite of them, we managed to do some wonderful work with children. Somehow we were able to carve out time to develop new interdisciplinary projects and improve ones that classes had done for years.

One of the first projects I worked on was during my "student-teaching" with the third-grade team. According to the Massachusetts social studies frameworks, students in third grade are supposed to learn about their own city. The teachers had discussed creating a guidebook to the city for kids. When I went to the local bookstores to find some models, we discovered there weren't any guidebooks at all for just Cambridge. So we decided to make our own. We developed an expedition that we called "Constructing Cambridge," in which we asked two big questions: How was Cambridge developed? and What makes Cambridge unique? We met with local experts, took trips to historical sites (Cambridge is full of them), met with city leaders, scientists, and business owners. Finally, we wrote our guidebook: *Cambridge: From Alewife to Zuzu—The Best (and Only) Guide to Cambridge Written by Third Graders!*

To launch this project, we taped a long stretch of blank paper on the corridor wall, stretching about twenty feet between two

333

classrooms with the letters of the alphabet on it—A to Z. Passersby could write down their favorite places, people, or things in Cambridge under the appropriate letter. The third graders excitedly watched as our list grew. We had Julia Child under C; *Good Will Hunting* (the movie that Matt Damon and Ben Affleck, native Cantabridgians, wrote and acted in) under G; Kendall Square (once a saltmarsh but now the biotech center of the world) under K; Passim's (the folk-music club where Joan Baez and Bob Dylan played) under P. We didn't get an X, but we did get a Q—for Qwirkle, a game that was produced in a factory in Cambridge! It was a wonderful way to draw on our community's knowledge, and we learned a lot about the city that we hadn't known before.

Each student "adopted" a topic (or two or three, depending on their skill levels) and researched it, either by visiting the location (students argued over who would get Bartley's Burger Cottage), reading about it on the internet, or talking to adults who were experts in Cambridge history. They then wrote a paragraph based on their research. In addition, each student wrote an "opinion" piece about their favorite spot in the city. These ranged from the Cambridge Public Library to soccer fields to restaurants. One girl wrote about home.

Because we were publishing the book, the writing had to be high quality and error-free. It was sometimes a torturous process, making third graders go back and correct yet another draft or look for more information. But we repeated the mantra: Quality work takes quality time. Keep at it! And they did.

A parent (heroically) helped us put the book together, and the day the box arrived from the publisher we had a true celebration. The students gathered around Meg, one of the third-grade teachers, as she ripped off the tape.

"Drum roll, please!" she announced, and pulled out their books.

Kids squealed with excitement and pride. Parents beamed. Years later, a parent told me that the Cambridge A–Z book had been the project her son had been most proud of in all his years at the school.

The first graders' study of vertebrates was not a new expedition. But each year, it got better and better. The teachers kicked off the unit with a whole-class study of owls, beginning with a visit with live owls. Students could hardly contain their excitement the day the "Owl Lady" came. She brought her specimens in covered cages; sixty first graders gathered on the rug in one of the classrooms in utter awe. She explained to them that the owls were skittish and the students had to be very quiet so as not to startle them. You could hear a pin drop in the room. For an hour, they listened to her describe the habits of each owl, quietly raising hands to ask questions. While the children were looking at the owls, I was looking at the children. Every one of them, even the most squirmy, was glued to the presenter and her magnificent beasts.

After the Owl Lady visit, the classes dove into their study on owls. They read stories about owls, both fiction and nonfiction. They learned about owl feathers, claws, and beaks; owl habitats; and what owls eat. They dissected owl pellets. They drew pictures of owls. Then, together as a class, they wrote a story about an owl. But the project didn't end there.

The next step was for the students to pick their own vertebrate to study—another kind of bird, or a fish, or a squirrel, something they might find in their own backyard in Cambridge. A local park ranger visited the classes with pictures and stories of all the kinds of vertebrates they might find in the city. The class read the Smithsonian's Backyard Books like *Chipmunk at Hollow Tree Lane* and *Cottontail at Clover Crescent*, and analyzed the writing of professional authors.

"What do you notice about how the writer begins the story?" Debra asked.

"They tell us what time of day it is and where the animal is!" students observed.

"Yes, that helps us learn about their habitat. What else do you notice?" she continued.

"I notice how the author doesn't just say it's morning. She describes the colors in the sky as the sun comes up."

"What are some really juicy words that you notice?" Debra stood poised at her easel, ready to take notes. Together, the class built lists of words that they liked: *slither, burrow, cuddle, snuggle, scurry,* and *swoop*. They also learned words like *nocturnal, diurnal, amphibian,* and *habitat* and developed a common template for organizing their own stories.

Each child wrote a nonfiction story about their own animal modeled after the Smithsonian books, complete with a scientifically accurate illustration. All the stories were compiled in a beautiful book of which each child received a copy. They also created dioramas of their animal and its habitat from clay that were done in great, careful detail. Finally, the class wrote a field guide, sharing the information they had learned in yet another format.

A couple of years later, the first-grade teachers were told to drop this expedition. Why? The Science Department was changing its curriculum, adopting the Next Generation Science Standards (NGSS). First graders weren't supposed to talk about habitat anymore; they would learn about that later, in third grade. They could still study vertebrates, but this had to be done at the beginning of the year, not at the end. And remember: No talking about habitats! The teachers knew that a vertebrate study would not be possible at the beginning of the year; the children wouldn't have developed the necessary reading and writing skills for it. So they pushed back. But "The Department" told them that they were giving assessments across the district on each unit, and therefore they all had to be done at the same time, in the same sequence.

"How are these assessments going to be used?" the teachers asked.

"We're not sure yet," was the response.

The Next Generation Science Standards is the science version of the Common Core. They were also controversial, both on the Right and the Left. States like Wyoming and Texas have refused to adopt NGSS because it includes the teaching of evolution and human-caused climate change. More progressive educators have questioned how developmentally appropriate the standards are. The NGSS Core Practices are not bad. On the contrary, they include critical science skills like asking questions, developing and using models, analyzing and interpreting data, planning and carrying out investigations, and engaging in argument from evidence. But the devil was in the details. Here is an excerpt from the first-grade NGSS:

FIRST GRADE

The performance expectations in first grade help students formulate answers to questions such as: "What happens when materials vibrate? What happens when there is no light? What are some ways plants and animals meet their needs so that they can survive and grow? How are parents and their children similar and different? What objects are in the sky and how do they seem to move?" First grade performance expectations include PS4, LS1, LS3, and ESS1 Disciplinary Core Ideas from the NRC Framework. Students are expected to develop understanding of the relationship between sound and vibrating materials as well as between the availability of light and ability to see objects. The idea that light travels from place to place can be understood by students at this level through determining the effect of placing objects made with different materials in the path of a beam of light. Students are also expected to develop understanding of how plants and animals use their external parts to help them survive, grow, and meet their needs as well as how behaviors of parents and offspring help the offspring survive. The understanding is developed that young plants and animals are like, but not exactly the same as, their parents. Students are able to observe, describe, and predict some patterns of the movement of objects in the sky. The crosscutting concepts of patterns; cause and effect; structure and function; and influence of engineering, technology, and science on society and the natural world are called out as organizing concepts for these disciplinary core ideas. In the first grade performance expectations, students are expected to demonstrate grade-appropriate proficiency in planning and carrying out investigations, analyzing and interpreting data, constructing explanations and designing solutions, and obtaining, evaluating, and communicating information. Students are expected to use these practices to demonstrate understanding of the core ideas.

So many details. How do you teach all these different concepts in a way that is engaging and makes sense to a first grader? In Cambridge, the introduction of these new science standards caused yet another upheaval in teachers' lives. For grades 1–5, these new curricular demands became particularly onerous as teachers were already coping with the new ELA and math standards. For people teaching interdisciplinary units or expeditions, this change upended their entire curriculum.

The Science Department decided to test out a new NGSS curriculum and our fourth-grade team joined in as "pioneers," along with the fourth-grade team from the Cambridgeport School. Soon, most of the teams' meeting time was taken up with the district science coach. The teachers were struggling to learn the science themselves. They didn't understand wave properties, electromagnetic radiation, conservation of energy and energy transfer, or energy in chemical processes, much less how to teach these concepts to ten-year-olds. Plus, the standards involved the teaching of so much content, teachers found they had to give up other parts of their overall curriculum to have time to cover the science.

"I had to give up my read-aloud time," said one fourth-grade teacher.

"We're still working on our personal-narrative essays that were supposed to be done a month ago," said another. "There just isn't enough time in the day to do it all."

When I asked what they were thinking about for their spring expedition, they sighed. "I can't develop an expedition on this stuff when I am just learning it myself. Right now, I'm just going day to day."

"What about your American geography expedition?" I asked. "We were going to rethink that this year."

"I haven't taught social studies at all yet," said another. It was now January.

"I can't think about planning anything new," declared the first.

Periodically, one of them would come into my office and cry. We were hearing similar stories of distress from the Cambridgeport teachers, too. Everyone was overwhelmed.

The solution to all this seemed obvious. We needed to integrate the curriculum. The pressures of the MCAS had pushed each department into its own silo, making demands on the schedule that teachers couldn't possibly meet. If we could step back and look at the essential skills and habits of mind in each of these disciplines, we could teach and practice them holistically. Asking questions is critical to being a scientist, but strong readers and good mathematicians also ask questions. Engaging in argument from evidence is not just a science skill; it is critical thinking. Analyzing and interpreting data is not only part of science, but it is also a mathematical and social science practice. What if we could bring the departments together, agree on essential skills and practices for each, look at how they overlap and reinforce each other, and develop a framework to teach these things that have meaning and purpose for students?

Luckily, the principals of both schools agreed and they requested a meeting with the district curriculum coordinators. At this meeting, the "pioneer" teachers from both schools described their frustrations. They were scrambling to keep up with the curriculum demands from each department. They didn't know what *not* to teach in order to make time to teach the new content. They felt the new standards had no context, and, as one said, they "struggled to prevent instruction from becoming a frantic forced march from one topic to the next or a collection of isolated facts." Everyone in the room could hear the strain and distress in their voices.

For once, the district listened seriously to its teachers.

"We see this is a problem," said the director of elementary education. "How do you think we can fix this?"

"By developing an interdisciplinary, project-based approach to the curriculum," we answered.

"What do you need to do that?" she asked.

"We need to bring the departments together to plan. They can't be competing against each other. We need to work together. We need a chance to look at all these different demands, find commonalities, identify priorities, and develop an integrated curriculum that will engage our students."

"I have an idea," piped up the science coordinator. "The Museum of Science [in Boston] has offered the Cambridge Public Schools a week-long 'sabbatical' for teachers. They provide the space [at the museum], materials, and experienced facilitators along with some of their science educators to help teachers work on a project of their choice. No one has asked to use this yet. Would you be able to free your fourth-grade teachers to do this?"

"Yes!" both principals jumped at the opportunity. "We absolutely will commit to and support this project!" This was the beginning of one of the best interdisciplinary, cross-school, full-year curriculum projects I'd ever seen in my nearly forty years in Cambridge. In fact, maybe it was the only one.

The Museum of Science (MOS) literally straddles the Charles River. It is perched above the Charles River Dam that was built in 1910 to keep seawater out and control floodwaters. The top floor of the building, where the resource library and meeting rooms are located, has a spectacular view of downtown Boston, the golden dome of the State House, and the rising metropolis of Kendall Square in Cambridge. It might have been distracting—except for the fact that we were all so excited to get to work. The district curriculum coordinators, along with the math and literacy coaches from the two schools, met with the MOS staff in advance to map out the parameters of the project—what standards, including essential skills and content, had to be included. It took a few days of mapping these out across disciplines and negotiating, but we eventually came to agreement. That in itself was a huge accomplishment.

Then the classroom teachers joined us. Even though we had a week, we all knew that wasn't nearly enough time to develop an entire unit, much less a yearlong curriculum. But first we wanted to find the story, a throughline, that could tie all these bits and pieces of curriculum together. This is never easy work. You have to spend time mucking about in the content, and, gradually, clarity will emerge. The first day we felt like we didn't get anywhere. The second day, people had come back with proposals—very different ones. At one point, we were all sitting around the big conference table—the teachers, the coaches, the district coordinators—arguing heatedly, when the MOS facilitator held up her hands.

"Everybody stop," she said quietly.

We all turned to look at her in surprise.

"Anyone who is *not* a classroom teacher, please move your chair away from the table," she said.

Those of us in this category pulled our chairs back, making an outer circle.

"And now," the facilitator said, "only the teachers may speak. Everyone else needs to be silent for a while."

Some of us were a bit taken aback, but the teachers were pleased. Now they truly had a voice. They sat up a little straighter, leaned in, and gradually began to unravel the tangled strands into a clear narrative.

While the curriculum would integrate language arts and science (and a bit of math), the Massachusetts fourth-grade social studies standards—focusing on the geography and people of the five regions of the United States—would frame their story. They would look at each region through the lens of the people who lived there and the ways they fought for a better life. They would also examine some of the profound scientific and technological changes that shaped both the land and the people of each region.

In an article for *Educational Leadership* describing this process, Karen Engels, one of the fourth-grade teachers who designed the curriculum, gives an overview:

> During the first quarter of the school year, we studied the science of changes to the earth's surface and the resulting variety in landforms across each region of the United States. As we studied the varied topography and geography of different regions, we concurrently studied the experiences of indigenous people in these regions prior to European settlement. Then, for the remainder of the school year, we delved into the technological and social history of the 1830s–1930s, primarily through the lenses of the following groups:

- *The Lowell Mill Girls during the 1840s who campaigned for a 10-hour work day.*
- *Enslaved African Americans during the 1850s and the abolitionists who fought for emancipation.*
- *The European and African-American pioneers who moved West after the Homestead Act of 1862.*
- *The Navajo during the Long Walk of 1864.*
- *Chinese immigrants working on the Transcontinental Railroad who went on strike in 1867.*
- *The Lakota who fought back against the U.S. government during the 1870s.*
- *The Dust Bowl and the Great Depression survivors of the 1930s.*[1]

The teachers pulled together primary sources, maps, photographs, read-aloud texts, historical fiction and nonfiction, and documentary films, and brainstormed possible field trips and guest speakers for each case study. Science was woven in at key points. For example, as students learned about the Industrial Revolution, they studied different kinds of energy, including waterwheels and the kinetic energy of the Merrimack River that powered the factories.

Of course, this did not all happen in five days. But the teachers established the framework, identified the threads that tied the fabric of the story together, and began to flesh out the opening unit. It would take many, many more hours of work (some paid and much unpaid) by the teachers, but by that fall they were ready to launch their study of "Our Changing Nation."

"How's it going?" I asked as I entered Jocelyn's classroom. It was October and the students were fully immersed in their study of the changing earth. They were just about to start digging into the experiences of the Indigenous people in each different region before the Europeans arrived.

"It's amazing!" Jocelyn exclaimed. "The kids really seem to get this stuff! The way we are teaching it this year makes so much sense to them. They seem so excited about it!" Each time I checked in with one of the teachers, the report was similar. Students were excited. They were making connections. They were motivated. They were building real understanding.

At the end of the year, "exhausted but exuberant," teachers marveled at the energy and investment their students displayed. To conclude a year of rich learning, students chose between creating and curating a science museum and writing and performing in a historical play comprised of monologues from the perspectives of people they had studied. In both the museum and the play, students showed a deep mastery of the content they had learned, and, more importantly, the connections between their learning and their lives today, from issues of police brutality to the scourge of climate change.

In addition, teachers noticed that their students' writing was much stronger.

"Did you change your approach to writing? I asked.

"No, not really," they responded.

"Then why do you think the students' writing has improved?" I pressed.

"They know more about what they are writing about; they have a deeper understanding and 'own' it in a different way than they did before. Having a storyline helped them make sense of it all."

This curriculum was a product of *real* teacher involvement, not the token or phony "input" that so many projects claim. While the district had had important and critical input in defining parameters, the teachers had been empowered to design a truly rigorous and engaging yearlong interdisciplinary study. They were given time and support. They were allowed to experiment and make adjustments. Most importantly, they were able to take the lead.

The first-grade teachers caught wind of this, even a few from other schools.

"Wait. The district let you work with all the departments to do a full-year integrated curriculum? We want to do that, too!"

But for some reason, in spite of its resounding success, the curriculum coordinators at the time were not willing to engage in this experiment again.

"We can't afford it," seemed to be the main excuse.

Or, "We don't have time," was the other.

This was profoundly disappointing to all, especially in light of past decisions. The district had been willing to spend thousands of dollars on new textbooks—that teachers did not want to use. A few years earlier, the ELA Department had hired outside consultants to lead a curriculum redesign effort, spending at least $250,000. It fizzled. The fourth-grade project had cost a tiny fraction of that and had resulted in a high-quality curriculum that could be used across the city.

I do not understand why more curriculum is not developed in this way. Not only do you end up with a stronger product because people who know the children well are the ones who are writing it, but the process of creating it is a kind of professional development in itself. When you bring teachers together to discuss standards, pedagogy, content, skills, lesson plans, resources, projects, assessments, and more, they themselves are building a deeper understanding of the content they are teaching. In the beginning of the fourth-grade curriculum design project, most of the teachers did not have a clue how waves work or what kinetic energy is. Some of them knew little about the Transcontinental Railroad or the Dust Bowl. But, by the end, they had a strong knowledge of all the content, not to mention how to present it well to children.

One day, as I was checking my email, I saw I had a message from Chris, one of the G&P humanities teachers who had moved to the middle school. I hadn't heard from him in a couple of years. It had been a hard transition for Chris. He'd hated giving up the two different humanities curriculums that we had developed at G&P over more than a decade, along with the projects, portfolios, and graduation review panels. But the middle school now had a new principal and things were beginning to shift. Chris was inviting me to a performance of student monologues.

I was thrilled! As a humanities teacher, my students had done monologues each year, and, after I'd left, Chris had embraced this project. It involved research on a particular person (my class had focused on resisters and rescuers during the Holocaust), writing a script in the voice of that person, memorizing it, and performing (in costume) before an audience of other students, parents, and community members. At the new middle school, Chris had initially been told he could no longer do this project. With new leadership, though, teachers were encouraged to be more creative, to try new things. Or, in this case, an old thing.

It was about 6:00 p.m. when I arrived at the school, and the event had already started. The halls were crowded with excited and jittery young teens and their families. Because so many students were performing, they had been divided up and were presenting their monologues in four different classrooms. Everyone had a program, explaining where to go to see which student and the historical person they were representing. You could tell who had already performed; they were the ones whispering encouragement to other students:

"You're gonna be great!"

"Don't worry. Once you get going, you'll be fine!"

"Just take a few deep breaths before you start, and focus."

"You'll feel so proud of yourself when you're done!"

I didn't know any of these students so I randomly picked a room to go into. All the desks had been pushed aside and rows of chairs faced an open space, with two large swaths of muslin cloth hanging behind to define a performance area. I smiled. I knew that muslin cloth. We had used it for backdrops for all our plays two decades earlier. I had wondered if those long drapes had been lost in the move to the middle school. But there they were.

There were about thirty people in the room, with adults and small children sitting in rows while the middle schoolers were gathered in the back of the room, perched on desks. A tall, slender girl stood in the improvised spotlight. She had on a peasant skirt and apron, her long hair pulled back in a prim bun, and she was holding a mixing bowl.

The teacher announced, "Next we have Annalee presenting Magda Trocmé."

A hush fell over the room, the teacher nodded at Annalee, she took a deep breath, and then transported the audience back to occupied France, 1944.

When Annalee finished her monologue, everyone burst into applause. But it was not over yet. She stayed in her character as Magda, a Huguenot woman who, along with her husband, André, saved over 5,000 Jewish children's lives.

"Questions for Magda?" asked the teacher.

"Yes," one parent piped right up. "Magda, why did you put yourself in danger like this? Did you ever worry about being caught?"

"Mais, oui," Magda replied. "But it was part of our religion. As Huguenots, we knew what it felt like to be persecuted. We knew we could not stand by and do nothing when so many innocents were being killed."

Another parent raised a hand, and another, and even some of Annalee's classmates ventured to question Magda. Finally, the teacher stepped in, thanked Magda for sharing her story, and she quickly transformed back into an American thirteen-year-old girl as she scurried out of the room. Her friends followed her out, hugging her (the girls) and patting her on the back (the boys).

I stayed to watch other performances. They were not all as stunning as Annalee/Magda, but many were. Even those students who stumbled or struggled a bit seemed proud of themselves. I wondered how I would have felt as a twelve- or thirteen-year-old delivering a monologue to a group of adults, most of whom I did not know. Would I have been able to write such a script, memorize those lines, answer those questions? I know I would have wanted to run away. But each of these students (*every* student in the seventh grade did a monologue) had been supported and prepared over time to meet this challenge. *That's what rigor is*, I thought. *That's what school should be about—setting high expectations for all students, and then providing the scaffolding and support to ensure they succeed in meeting them.*

John Lewis, the legendary civil rights leader, spoke about "good trouble." To me, this kind of project generated good anxiety. Not the anxiety that hours and hours of a standardized test creates for many students but, rather, the kind of anxiety that comes from presenting authentic, purposeful work in public. The kind of anxiety our plays had generated as we were waiting for the lights to come up. The kind of anxiety our seventh and eighth graders felt as they were going off to their first day of work during City Sites. Or the kind of anxiety students had felt when they presented their graduation review portfolios.

By the time I left the school that night, it was dark. I found my car, got in, and started to cry. Thinking about the battles we'd fought, and lost, for so many years to preserve the kind of education that had meaning, relevance, and rigor for children made me sad. Did I feel bitter? Yes. But seeing Chris resurrect this project made me so, so happy. We hadn't lost all that good work, after all. The seeds were still out there, lying dormant, ready to grow and sprout when the conditions were right.

So, mostly, I cried with joy.

CHAPTER 21

THE END . . .
2013–2018

Graham & Parks had another transition to get through. Just before Thanksgiving 2013, Sarah, the principal, announced she would be leaving the school in January. Harvard University had made her an offer she felt she couldn't refuse. She would be gone from January through April, and be back for the last two months of school before resigning permanently. An interim would take over during the winter months, and then there would be a search for a new principal.

People were shocked, and confused. We had all expected Sarah to be there for many years. She was so committed, passionate, and dedicated to the school. How could she abandon us? But Sarah, it turned out, was burnt out.

She wasn't the only one. Evidently the average tenure of principals is four years.[1] Thirty-five percent of them work two years or less in any one school. This is in stark contrast to a generation earlier, prior to NCLB and the corporatization of schools. Len Solo was the principal at G&P for twenty-seven years. Other legendary principals, like Deborah Meier, Linda Nathan, Joe Petner, and Bill Henderson, all worked in their schools for decades.

It isn't just school leaders who don't last in their jobs. Teachers are burning out, leading to a growing teacher shortage crisis facing the country.[2] Veteran teachers are retiring (the rate has been accelerating during the COVID-19 pandemic), and fewer young people are choosing the profession. Even more disturbing, nearly 50 percent of new teachers leave the profession within their first five years.[3]

What does it matter if people only teach for four or five years and then leave the profession? The negative impacts of constant turnover are many. It is expensive to recruit and train new teachers all the time. Turnover is highest in our neediest schools, so those children have the most inexperienced teachers. But most critically, we are not developing a new generation of master teachers. Most highly skilled educators I know feel that they only started to hit their stride *after* four or five years of teaching. But now, instead of hitting their stride, new teachers are hitting a wall.

Why don't people want to be teachers and principals anymore? Various studies point to a range of reasons: poor working conditions, insufficient resources, low pay, seemingly infinite demands on one's time. But these factors are not new. Schools, especially in poorer areas, have traditionally been under-resourced, teachers have traditionally been underpaid, the work load has always been daunting. So those reasons don't explain the exodus from the profession over the last decade.

Educators are leaving because of *two decades of corporate-driven education reform policies of standardization, testing, competition, speed-up, teacher bashing, and punishment*. Why? Maybe because teachers (and administrators) don't want to continue to be told to do more with less. Maybe because teachers don't want to be blamed by corporate reformers for struggling public schools, at the very same time that funding has been cut, along with many other parts of the social safety net, like food and housing assistance. Maybe because teachers are required to train as professionals and yet have no voice in professional decisions. Or because teachers are paid a fraction of what other professions earn that require a similar level of education. Or because non-educators continue to impose policies, practices, and new initiatives that often fly in the face of what teachers know is best for kids. Teachers know that poverty, racism, and the huge inequities of wealth in this country are the real problems facing our schools and communities. As one forty-two-year veteran mused, "Why would anyone with any brains and imagination *ever* want to be a teacher?"[4]

Suzi Sluyter, the highly respected Cambridge kindergarten teacher I quoted in the introduction, left her job in 2014. In another part of her letter explaining her difficult decision published in the *Washington Post*, Suzi wrote, "Each year I have had less and less time to teach the children I love in the way I know best—and in the way child development experts recommend. I reached the place last year where I began to feel I was part of a broken system that was causing damage to those very children I was there to serve. . . . I began to feel a deep sense of loss of integrity. I felt my spirit, my passion as a teacher, slip away. I felt anger rise inside me. I felt I needed to survive by looking elsewhere and leaving the community I love so dearly. I did not feel I was leaving my job. I felt then and feel now that my job left me."[5]

Sarah also left in 2014. The staff was crushed. Yet one more transition. They worried about who would replace her. Would the new principal understand and accept the culture of this alternative community? Or would we end up with a corporate-style leader who was ready to impose his or her own vision on the school? I had witnessed more than one school destroyed by an incoming administrator who was ready to "fix" things. The superintendent hired a young man in his early thirties, with a PhD in early childhood psychology and six years experience teaching kindergarten. Graham & Parks would be his first principalship. While he seemed awfully young to some of us, we were at least relieved to know that Tony was drawn to the school *because* of who we were. Tony believed in the importance of play and hands-on, integrated curriculum. He welcomed the multiple challenges facing our community. He wanted to continue Sarah's mission of restoring the best parts of the "old" Graham & Parks and was particularly committed to connecting the disparate programs in the building (gen ed, Sheltered English Immersion, self-contained special needs, and a special needs preschool).

One important step that Tony initiated, with support from the Instructional Leadership Team, in uniting the school was conducting "learning walks." Although we would change the structure of these "walks" from year to year, the basic purpose remained the same—to invite teachers to observe in each other's classrooms (one of the proposals our School Within teachers at Tufts had made to the administration in 1980). I was surprised when some staff pushed back on this plan. As a G&P teacher in the 1980s and 1990s, people had frequently visited my class, and I'd welcomed that. But it seemed that in the era of "ed reform," teachers were much more wary about opening their doors, even to their colleagues.

"Why are you doing these learning walks?" they asked suspiciously.

"What are you looking for?"

"Am I being evaluated?"

"Are people going to report me for something?"

This level of fear and resistance revealed just how much teachers were feeling scrutinized and judged.

So our first "walks" were voluntary, for the host teacher, that is. Other staff were required to visit at least one other classroom. We created structures that encouraged people to be neutral observers: "What do you see?" and "What do you wonder?" Then, after the visit, we would debrief as a group. The vast majority of teachers were excited and enthusiastic about this new practice, while offering lots of ideas to improve the next round.

These learning walks helped to begin breaking down barriers. Our gen ed teachers noticed how scaffolded the SEI teachers' instruction was. They observed the carefully designed mentor charts hanging on the walls. They remarked on all the visual supports throughout the SEI room. They developed a new respect for teaching English language learners. "No wonder the bilingual students struggle when they mainstream into a gen ed class," commented one teacher. "I don't provide half of that scaffolding for them."

The SEI teachers also had epiphanies. "So *this* is what you are expecting a fourth grader to do?" asked one teacher in surprise. "I need to amp up my game!" But most importantly what happened was a beginning dialogue about how to provide supports to struggling learners while being rigorous and holding high expectations for all children. Teachers were talking to teachers about teaching.

The learning walks were an exciting part of my coaching job. I loved helping teachers share their observations and reflections. These visits to other classrooms provoked more introspection and energized dialogue about pedagogy than many of my "coaching" sessions. But I was still caught between this kind of work in my school and the district leadership which was mandating standardized curriculum and assessments. I was still spending much of my time policing teachers about what curriculum unit they should be doing, administering "screeners" and computer-based skill tests, and compiling and sorting data charts.

One of the screeners required us to read one-on-one with the three hundred and fifty or so students in the school, first- through fifth-grade to test them for their fluency, three times a year. Students had three different passages that they would read aloud as we timed them. While there were some first graders who were able to do this in the beginning of the school year, others could not even get through the first sentence. These six-year-olds would look at the page blankly, then look up at me pleadingly, trying to sound out a word, occasionally recognizing a sight word like "and" or "the." It was torture. At the other end of the spectrum, fifth-graders, who had been practicing reading their own memoirs aloud for the local cable TV station, would read with phrasing and expression. Which was lovely, but it slowed their pace so their scores went down. It was a classic example of why data can be misleading.

Another ELA screener administered three times a year was supposed to measure comprehension. Students read various passages and answered multiple choice questions. It was a computerized adaptive test (CAT) meaning that the computer adjusted the reading level higher or lower depending on the test takers' answers. One day I noticed a second grader still laboring over the test after forty-five minutes. I was surprised because she was a very strong student. I looked over her shoulder to see how much more she had to do. She was in tears, painfully parsing her way through a passage by Joseph Conrad. I couldn't believe it. "I thought I was a good reader," she sniffled. I assured her she was and explained how the test worked. But even with that information, this seven-year-old continued to plug away at the passages. After all, she had been taught to persevere through tough tasks. She finally finished and rejoined the rest of her class who had left the computer lab fifteen minutes earlier. Outraged, I called both the district administrator in charge of this screening and the testing company itself. *This was a glitch*, they told me. *It will be rectified.* But it never was.

We also had the same battery of screeners for math, not to mention other district assessments in math, reading, writing, and science. Teachers complained that their students were being tested to death. One teacher commented, "We're spending so much time weighing the cow, we don't have time to feed it." The level of stress in the building was high, and frazzled teachers continued to appear at my door, needing a shoulder to cry on. I was feeling worn down by it all.

Throughout my years of teaching, I had run into people who counted the days to summer vacation. Once, a teacher said to me on the first day of school, "One hundred seventy-nine days to go!" I was appalled by that. I loved my work and felt privileged to be in a profession that felt more like a mission, a calling, than just a job. I couldn't imagine why people would stay in education if they didn't feel the same way. The work is just too hard.

But I found myself paying more and more attention to the calendar. How many more days to Thanksgiving? Winter break? Maybe this is a natural progression in all careers. After all, I'd been in education for nearly forty years. But I wasn't just tired. Like Suzi Sluyter, I felt defeated. I didn't believe in what I was doing, too much of the time anyway. I didn't want to be one of those bitter, angry, burnt out teachers. I had promised myself that if I ever got to that point, I would leave. So, after thirty-nine years in the profession, I announced in February 2018 that I would be retiring at the end of June.

That spring, teacher morale hit a new low. The Instructional Leadership Team (ILT) had been discussing school climate all year. The learning walks had been successful, but, just as in previous years with other truly useful initiatives like our teacher-driven inquiry groups, we had trouble sustaining them with any kind of consistency because of so many external and extraneous demands on teachers' time. Once again, people asked the questions, *Who are we as a school? What do we stand for? What do we value?* It was enough of a crisis that we felt we needed outside intervention. With financial support from the district, Tony hired a consultant to help the staff answer these questions together.

We gathered in the library on a Monday afternoon. The book stacks had been moved out of the way to make room for everyone. The consultant introduced herself and explained the purpose of the meeting. To start the process of re-envisioning ourselves as a school, after lots of change, upheaval, and pressures, we would make a "history-gram." She asked us to organize ourselves into a chronological line according to what year we came to work at Graham & Parks.

I knew I was the most veteran staffer there, but there were a handful of others—Claudie, Debra, Mary G, Christina. We smiled at each other, with pride, saying "Remember the good old days?" Then the consultant asked us to group ourselves into clusters of different "eras" and to write down what stood out most from our "era." The veterans dove in with delight. We talked about joy and community and excitement and innovation and challenge and purposefulness. We laughed out loud, but also with a tinge of ruefulness. Other teachers were looking over at us.

"There's an awful lot of laughter coming from over there," someone said.

"Yes!" Claudie shouted back. "School used to be fun!"

Things were so different now. As we listened to the other groups report out, they increasingly talked about stress, anxiety, discouragement, and fear. It was clear that something very special had been lost. *How did we get to this place?* everyone wondered.

The last few days of June were hot and humid, typical weather in the Boston area for the beginning of summer. Unlike seventeen years earlier when I had left my seventh and eighth grade classroom without packing much of anything, thinking I would be back in a year or two, I knew I was gone for good this time. I had to pack all my papers, books, files, supplies, photos, posters, and the various kitschy knickknacks teachers collect over time. I put duplicates of books that had guided my practice in the hallway, free for aspiring teachers to take—*Mosaic of Thought, An Ethic of Excellence, Hidden Gems, The Art of Writing, Playing for Keeps.* I hoped a new generation of educators would read these important books and see what treasures they were. But I was doubtful. The pressures to toe the line were too great for most novice teachers. Or they just didn't have the time.

I loaded the boxes in my car and then made a last visit to the office to turn in my keys and say goodbye. It didn't feel that different from any other year. We all say goodbye in June, looking forward to some time to rest and restore ourselves before gearing up for a new start in the fall.

"You'll be back in September, I bet!" laughed Cheryl, our wonderful office manager.

"You won't be able to stay away." I smiled and hugged her. But I knew I wouldn't be back. As Suzi Sluyter said, I didn't feel so much that I was leaving but that my job had left me.

CHAPTER 22

... AND MAYBE A BEGINNING?

Corporate education reform has failed miserably. Untold billions of dollars have been wasted on the Bush-Obama-Trump programs of testing, standardization, competition, and punitive accountability. This money has served mainly to enrich the pockets of private corporations like Pearson, Teach for America, and all sorts of other entrepreneurial ventures more interested in making money than in educating children, and to seriously threaten the existence of public education in this country.

Even the so-called reformers are admitting defeat. In a 2017 *Forbes* magazine article, senior contributor Ethan Siegel wrote: "[P]ublic education is more broken than ever. The reason, as much as we hate to admit it, is that we've disobeyed the cardinal rule of success in any industry: treating your workers like professionals."[1] In 2019, Van Schoales, president of A+ Colorado and a proponent of corporate ed reform, wrote, "The education reform movement as we have known it is over." He admitted that "[r]eformers (myself included) led an unneeded assault on the existing educator force, with ham-handed teacher evaluations and a focus on getting rid of poor performing teachers. In an attempt to modernize the profession, we ended up losing the hearts and minds of a generation of educators."[2]

In 2021, the Rennie Center for Education Research and Policy, a Massachusetts think tank that has advocated for high stakes standardized testing, charter schools, Common Core standards, and Race to the Top initiatives, issued a report called "Reimagining the MCAS: The Need for an Accountability System that Supports Deeper Learning." In it, the authors admitted that the high stakes standardized test has driven schools towards test prep rather than deeper learning. They acknowledged that the voices of students and teachers *"backed up by decades of research on how children learn* [my emphasis], are pushing educational leaders to prioritize instruction that fosters creativity and critical thinking." They conceded that the MCAS has had "unintended consequences that affect instructional decisions in nearly all districts, with a disproportionate impact on economically disadvantaged communities and communities of color."[3]

Really? Are you kidding me? You have finally figured this out? These milquetoast *mea culpas* have enraged me. Yes, we have had *decades* of research that has greatly expanded our understanding of how children learn. And none of it, *none of it*, has supported the policies inflicted on our public schools by corporate reformers and politicians. Teachers and their unions, parents and their organizations, university researchers and their institutions have been challenging these damaging and disrupting practices from the very beginning. Furthermore, we have decades of data (that beloved holy grail of corporate reformers) that have shown just how bankrupt these policies have been, too. Yet they still have a stranglehold over the daily lives of our students and teachers. Our schools are not significantly better in any way. If anything, with the huge wealth gap that continues to widen unlike any other time in our nation's history, our schools and our students are suffering even more.

So if these punitive policies have failed, what *can* we do to support and strengthen our schools?

When people have asked me this, I share my experience at Graham & Parks in the 1980s and 1990s, before corporate ed reform undermined the school. What made it work? Why did teachers want to be there? Why did staff stay for twenty and thirty years? Why did it have a long waiting list of students trying to get in? Why did it spawn other similar "progressive" schools in Cambridge and other places? Why did people come from all over the world to visit us? It was not rocket science. We had a clearly articulated vision of who we were. We were committed to being a democratic community and teachers had a real voice in all matters that impacted the school. We worked with parents, not for them. We were respected as professionals and saw ourselves as lifelong learners. We had considerable autonomy, including flexibility in developing curriculum, creating meaningful assessments, and designing developmentally responsive structures. We were encouraged to pursue our passions. We could experiment, create, and sometimes even fail without fear. Our community trusted us and we trusted each other.

But that's just one school, people would say to me. There are a number of excellent public schools, I would counter. *Yeah, but they are the exceptions not the rule* was the response. *You can't do that with all schools.* Why not? I wondered. And then I learned about Finland.

The tiny country of Finland (population of 5.5 million) was an international sensation in 2000 when their schools were rated as number 1 in the world in reading according to PISA (Program for International Student Assessment). In 2003, Finland scored at the top for math and then, three years later, they scored first in science[4]. It hadn't always been that way though. In the 1960s and 1970s, Finnish schools had been, at best, mediocre. Everyone wanted to know: What did those Finns do to improve their schools so dramatically?

Pasi Sahlberg was one of the architects of Finland's authentic education reform. In his book *Finnish Lessons*, he describes the decades-long process that they undertook in order to make their schools truly ready for the twenty-first century. The first step was to build a common vision in the country. *What do we want our schools to do?* they asked everybody, gradually building a consensus that has remained remarkably consistent and stable over time. Interestingly enough, one of their main goals was not to make it to the top of the PISA scores, but rather to make schools joyful places of learning. Yes, joyful because they knew a certain secret. *Children learn more when they are happy than when they are stressed.*

They researched practices in education from many different countries. "Some of our best ideas come from the U.S. and the U.K.," Sahlberg said at a forum held at Harvard's Graduate School of Education. "We don't understand why you Americans don't design your schools based on your brilliant educational leaders, like John Dewey, Eleanor Duckworth, Howard Gardner, and others."

Rather than undermining and denigrating the voices of teachers, Finland raised them up. Teaching is one of the most sought-after professions in the country. Educators are well paid, have a strong voice in determining curriculum and assessment, and are highly respected in their communities. All student assessments, except a final high school exit exam, are developed at the local level by teachers themselves.

Strong teacher training has been foundational to Finland's success. The Finns recognized that if they wanted to elevate student learning, they had to elevate teacher training. Highly selective, teacher interns participate in a five-year master's degree program (paid for by the state) which is balanced between the study of educational theories, research methodologies, and hands-on practice.

I was thrilled to learn about Finland's schools. I'd heard about interesting practices in other countries, like Japanese lesson studies and vocational education in Germany. But here was evidence that high quality, child-centered, democratic institutions could exist *at a large scale*. In Finland, they really did turn their schools around! But, almost inevitably, when I have shared this with other people, they have said, *That wouldn't work here. The U.S. is not Finland. Finland is a small country and much more homogeneous than we are.* That is true (although Finland is more diverse than people think and some parts of our country are not exactly diverse either). But wouldn't it be possible to apply Finland's lessons at a state level? Public education in the U.S. has historically operated primarily at the state and local level. There are thirty states that have the same or smaller population as Finland. Massachusetts, the sixteenth most populous state in the country, is only slightly larger. Reform at this level is certainly conceivable.

Furthermore, I am not advocating that we copy Finland's education system. Copying any system is not the answer. But we could learn from their *process*:

- Collaboratively create a vision.
- Research best practices that will support that vision.
- Invest in high quality teacher training.
- Empower education professionals with decision-making around curriculum, instruction, and assessment.

Imagine if we had committed the last twenty-five years and the billions of dollars wasted on the corporate reform model to an approach that is based on trust, professionalism, and shared responsibility. What would our schools be like now?

There is one more critical piece to Finland's plan to develop excellent schools for all their children. According to Pasi Sahlberg, it was the most foundational reform of all: equity. As a society, the Finns committed to reducing the income gap and developing policies that supported increased equity, not just in education, but in healthcare, housing, a clean environment, and more. They now have one of the smallest income gaps in the developed world.

In contrast, the U.S. has one of the biggest gaps in the world. The wealthiest 1 percent of Americans holds 32 percent of household wealth in the U.S. The top 10 percent have 70 percent of the wealth, while the *bottom half of the population holds just 2 percent.*[5] And this gap continues to grow.

For many, many years, we have known that the most important predictor of test scores is zip code. Children who live in wealthy communities and comfortable middle class ones will do better in school and on standardized tests than children from poor neighborhoods, be they urban or rural. And yet for the past twenty-five years as social programs have been relentlessly cut, we have been told that poverty is not the issue. Bad teachers are the real problem. Stop making excuses, the corporate reformers sneered. Teachers are just out for themselves. Do you really believe that all children can learn or don't you? Just because children are coming to school from neighborhoods wracked with violence doesn't mean they can't do just as well as a kid from a tony suburb. Just because there is lead in the water. Just because children are hungry. Just because there aren't enough desks to sit at or enough textbooks to go around. Just because they don't have a computer in the family (much less their own). Just because parents are working two jobs, or three. Just because a parent is incarcerated. Just because a family doesn't speak English. Just because children don't have a quiet space at home to study or maybe don't even have a home. If teachers just worked harder, they could overcome all these problems. After all, isn't education the great equalizer?

No. Education can not be an equalizer when children are starting school from such grossly unequal places. Some schools have tried to address this on a very individual level by providing "wraparound services." Geoffrey Canada's Harlem Children's Zone (HCZ) may be the largest and most famous example of this. I laughed out loud when I saw on the HCZ website that their goal was to "systematically break the cycle of intergenerational poverty" by addressing "all of the issues children and families faced—crumbling apartments, rampant drug use, failing schools, violent crime, and chronic health problems." This is an admirable goal and I imagine they have met with some degree of success, but we will never "systematically break the cycle of intergenerational poverty" in our country through the efforts of a few non-profits. Rather, we need to implement policies at city, state, and federal levels that support a living wage, affordable housing, universal early childhood education, equal access to high quality healthcare, criminal justice reform, and address other forms of inequities so we can better level the playing field *before* the game begins.

Inseparable from the current crisis around increasing poverty and wealth inequality is our history of racism. The deaths of George Floyd and Breonna Taylor (and too many others both before and after 2020) sparked a remarkable racial reckoning in the U.S. As Black communities rose up to demand justice, many white people were shocked out of their complacency and naïvete.[6] Schools, already dealing with an unprecedented global pandemic, were forced to deal with children's confusion, fear, questions, and grief around these brutal murders. Many school communities who had previously avoided discussing issues of racism were seriously caught off-guard for this difficult conversation.

Nearly 55 percent of public school students in the U.S. are of color, but over 80 percent of teachers are white. While it is critical to recruit and retain more teachers of color, all teachers need to have a deep historical understanding of the fundamental roles that race and racism have played and continue to play in the development of this country, whether they teach first grade or twelfth, whether they teach history, math, or music, whether they teach Black, white, brown, Indigenous, or Asian children. Teachers need to understand the ways that race and racism continue to impact policies in education, housing, policing, employment, food, healthcare, criminal justice, and pretty much every aspect of our society.

It is also essential that white teachers take a hard look at ourselves. I am not talking about feeling guilty about a past that cannot be changed. I am talking about being aware of the privilege white people have now. I am talking about recognizing and acknowledging just how much whiteness permeates, indeed defines, our institutions and our everyday lives. I am talking about accepting our own racism, be it intentional or not.

Years ago, Imani, an African American seventh grader, was telling me about being followed when he went into a store.

"Really?" I asked, naïvely. "That's never happened to me."

"Kathy, it doesn't happen to you because you're white!" he retorted, frustrated with my ignorance. *Oh,* I said to myself. *Right.* I thought back to my Robert White School students telling me how white women clutched their purses when they walked by. I had never noticed that before. But once the boys pointed it out, I saw this "dance" regularly. Teacher training programs as well as schools need to create spaces for teachers of all races and ethnicities to explore these complex and sensitive issues. If we don't, we will be woefully unprepared to deal with the students in front of us and the society around us.

These are huge tasks: reversing wealth inequality and addressing the racism that is so deeply embedded in the fabric of our nation. Especially in the present political climate, they are daunting ones. But we must take these steps if we want to create excellent schools that truly leave no child behind, not to mention a healthy society for us all.

With the bankruptcy of corporate ed reform exposed and the crisis of the COVID-19 pandemic in schools, more and more people are suggesting it is time to rethink education in this country. What can be done to improve educational opportunities for all our children? We can take the billions of dollars spent on standardized testing, standardizing curriculum, teacher testing, charter schools, and vouchers and commit this money to fully and fairly funding our public schools. We can also:

- treat teachers as professionals by paying them what they are worth and giving them an important voice in what they do;
- develop educational practices based on what we know about how children best learn;
- invest in high quality teacher training;
- examine our curriculum scope and sequence to be inclusive and representative of the people who make up our country;
- ensure that all schools have the computers and broadband, books and libraries, nurses and health centers, social workers and counselors that they need;
- repair old schools and building new ones so they are healthy, happy environments for children and adults.

This is a big order. But change can start even on a very small level, in a single district or even a single school. For example, because of the chaos created by the pandemic, teachers in Cambridge were finally able to have a significant voice in curriculum development. As administrators and politicians were fighting over whether or not to open schools in person, educators were scrambling with the day-to-day challenge of teaching remotely. A group of teachers, inspired by the fourth grade curriculum project with the Museum of Science (see chapter 20) working with their union, made a proposal to the district. *Give us some stipend money and let us work together to develop meaningful, integrated curriculum that can be shared across the district.* No one else had offered help to teachers struggling to teach online, so the superintendent accepted the offer. Grade level "collaboratives" met throughout the year to write digitally-based lesson plans that their colleagues could use. While some were stronger than others, these units were a lifeline for many teachers.

Research into successful schools has shown that reflection and collaboration are key to creating a culture of excellence. Transforming the culture of a school from one of fear and discouragement to one where teachers have a voice, feel trust in each other and their school leaders, and are encouraged to be thoughtful and reflective practitioners is another place to start.

Recently, I was talking with a friend who is a middle school principal. "Kathy, you'd be so excited! We are really changing the culture of the school," Julie said. "Teachers are beginning to work more collaboratively."

"That's awesome!" I responded. "How were you able to do that? I know some of those teachers and a few of them can be pretty resistant to change."

Julie explained. "When I first started there as principal, I interviewed every single staff member. I asked them three questions: *What do you need me to know about you and the school? What makes you proud? What do you hope for?* I listened carefully, took notes, and then shared everyone's comments with the whole staff (anonymously, of course), reflecting back to them their own accomplishments, hopes, and concerns."

"So instead of you telling everybody what needed to be fixed, it was the staff who identified issues the school needed to deal with?" I noted.

"Yes! I had some of my own concerns too, but I just added them in with the others. We discussed all the suggestions, and then, collaboratively, decided on just one to focus on as a school. The staff voted to work on race bias, but it could have been something else. The point is we chose it together and we've stuck to it. When people asked about the other challenges facing the school, I just responded, 'One thing at a time. We will get to those things, but we aren't going to jump around from one issue to the next. We won't ever get anything done if we do that.' People liked that. We had a real focus and we weren't going to let other things distract us. I think the teachers felt I was truly listening to them and that has helped to build a culture of mutual respect."

As I listened to Julie, I thought about how simple her approach had been. She asked her teachers what they thought and cared about. She communicated to her staff that she valued them, respected their opinions and perspectives, and wanted their input. She had asked them what issue they wanted to focus on together. She targeted one project at a time so as to not overwhelm people and to actually accomplish something. She treated them like the professionals they were. She was creating a culture where teachers could talk to teachers about teaching, where real change, the kind that truly benefits our students, could happen. It was a small step, but a deeply significant, even transformational, one.

Simple does not mean easy. But this can be a place to start. If we choose to. What is holding us back? As the author Toni Cade Bambara once wrote, "The dream is real, my friends. The failure to make it work is the unreality."

EPILOGUE

Since finishing this book, some other crises, in addition to the ongoing destruction of corporate ed reform, are profoundly affecting public education.

The first is the continuing challenge of the COVID-19 pandemic. While adults have worried about "learning loss," students from kindergarten to high school are suffering from depression, stress, and other mental health issues at rates never seen before in our country. Not just their education, but children's health and nutrition (schools are a primary source of food for some families), mental wellbeing, physical safety, housing, and more have been affected. The exodus of teachers and administrators leaving the profession feeling demoralized, overwhelmed, and undervalued has surged. School districts are struggling to fill teacher vacancies at all levels. It is important to remember, however, that while COVID-19 has exacerbated these critical matters, it did not cause this crisis. The pandemic has only shed new light on problems that have been festering for decades as the testing mania has increasingly dehumanized school.

Another development, perhaps even more disturbing, has been the growing right-wing assault on public education, particularly with regard to teaching about race and gender issues. So far, forty-four states have introduced bills or taken steps that would restrict teaching "critical race theory" or limit how teachers can discuss racism and sexism.[1] A New Hampshire chapter of the group called Moms for Liberty (which operates in thirty-five states) sent out this tweet: "We've got $500 for the person that first successfully catches a public school teacher breaking this law."[2] The governor of Florida is heralding the passage of his "Don't Say Gay" bill and trans students increasingly feel unsafe. The level of book banning has reached epic proportions.

But there are a few positive signs, too. A major one is the resurgence of unions, especially teacher unions. Teachers are finding their voice—and using it. In 2018, 22,000 teachers across the state of West Virginia walked off their jobs demanding a living wage and better working conditions. While they didn't win all their demands, they did win a five percent increase in pay, and sparked other teachers in states like Oklahoma and Arizona to do the same. In 2019, nearly 30,000 teachers and staff, with strong support from parents and the community, went on strike in Los Angeles calling for smaller class sizes, more support for nurses, social workers, and librarians, better pay, and fewer charter schools. In the 2022–2023 school year, there have been at least half a dozen teacher strikes in Massachusetts alone. Organizing around the slogan "Our teaching conditions are our students' learning conditions" is building unity with families and communities.

Teachers have been fighting to be heard in other ways, too. In 2016 in Massachusetts, pro-charter groups funded mostly by donors outside the state introduced a referendum calling for an expansion of charter schools. Question 2, as it was known, was defeated by a nearly two-thirds vote. Even though the pro-charter advocates spent millions of dollars in TV ads, the victory was a result of thousands of teachers, with the leadership and backing of their unions, knocking on doors and talking to people in their own communities about defending public education.

And in 2023, the Massachusetts Teachers Association, the American Federation of Teachers Massachusetts, and a coalition of other groups are taking on the MCAS directly with legislation to defang the test. The Thrive Act calls for an end to using the MCAS as a graduation requirement and prevents the undemocratic state takeovers of school districts. While this will not totally pull the plug on the corporatization of schools, it is a good start.

In spite of the attacks on public education, a clear majority of Americans continue to believe in this critical institution. Polls continually show that parents are happy with their children's teachers. Even with frustrations about school closures during the COVID-19 pandemic, many parents have articulated a profound respect and admiration for the work that teachers do.

Public education is the bulwark of our democracy. Building a strong public school system begins with a common vision of what we want for our children and our society. That was the starting place of reform in Finland, and it has been at the heart of all successful schools. But it is difficult to see, in these times, how to build a common vision for anything. Good grief, we couldn't even agree on wearing a mask to protect ourselves and others from a deadly disease, much less acknowledge the reality of systemic racism. How do we create spaces for honest dialogue and reflection about what kind of education we want for our children? How do we transform a culture of fear, anger, and suspicion into one of trust and collaboration?

Perhaps one way to do it is to look for commonalities. When you ask different groups of parents what they want their children to learn in school, they have surprisingly similar answers. Everyone wants their child to have strong academic skills—reading, writing, and 'rithmatic. But then, people begin to talk about a whole range of other things they want their children to learn: perseverance, critical thinking, independence, curiosity, collaboration, creativity, confidence, kindness, compassion, courage, and more. No one wants to send their children to an institution that tries to squeeze every student into the same size box (or test bubble). If we can find consensus in a vision that incorporates these skills, qualities, and values, we can begin to create, or recreate, schools that nurture them.

While I truly believe that we have the knowledge, wisdom, experience, and resources to create strong, rigorous, engaging, loving, inclusive, democratic schools throughout this country, I'm not so naïve as to think that that transformation is just around the corner.

Or even around a far corner. It may not even be on the block at the moment. But I do believe change is possible. We have to look around us and see what we can impact, what we have the power to affect. We find allies and open up conversations. Like Julie did, when she asked her teachers to talk to her. What do you want me to know about you and the school? What are you proud of? What do you hope for? Maybe that's a starting place.

What do you hope for?

ACKNOWLEDGMENTS

There is a lovely cafe down the street from my house. It was there, sitting with my friend Barbara Hedges, that I started to write this book. Once a week, we would meet for coffee and pastries. We would first talk about our lives, as we have been doing for over forty years, and then we would start writing. That structure, routine, and Barbara's support launched this project.

I also had the great privilege to be part of an amazing book group of educators. These women had all been leaders in their various fields of education: Betty Burkes, Nancy Carlsson-Paige, Ginny Chalmers, Brenda Engel, Lynne Hall, Jessie Wenning, and Sheli Wortis. The first book we read together was Diane Ravitch's *The Death and Life of the Great American School System*. We were trying to understand where the attacks on public education were coming from, and we learned a lot. I brought my manuscript to them and they provided great feedback and encouragement.

But it was Nancy Carlsson-Paige who was my rock. She spent hours reading and re-reading drafts. She spent hours on the phone with me and at my kitchen table. She was a cheerleader when I got discouraged, insisting that I had an important story to tell, and a tough editor when something just wasn't working. I'm pretty sure I would never have finished this project without Nancy.

I also had another group of people who were instrumental in the writing of this book—my teacher team from the Graham and Parks Alternative Public School. Twenty years after I had left my seventh and eighth grade humanities position, we had a couple of reunions in my kitchen. Steve Barkin, Ellen Gaies, Len Solo, and Laura Sylvan talked for hours about the "junior high" program we had built together (unfortunately Susan McCray couldn't make either gathering). These reflections and reminiscences were incredibly helpful to me. It was Len, our principal, though, who read the entire manuscript and gave me both useful feedback and told me even more about the school that I hadn't known. Len is a talented writer and poet himself, and I trusted him to be honest and direct, as he had always been.

Other people have also given me helpful feedback and encouragement, including Debbie Meier, Jackie King, Susan Markowitz, Ginny Christensen, Leah Rugen, Karen Engels, Jeanne Maxwell, and Dan Brooks. Many thanks to Leslie Cohen, a parent of former students at Graham & Parks, who edited a draft of the book, constantly warning me about using the passive voice. I also want to acknowledge some folks who did not read this manuscript, but were very influential in the story it tells: Ron Berger, Steve Seidel, and Dan French.

Writing a manuscript is one thing. Getting a publisher is quite another. I have to thank Sam Seidel, Bill Schecter, Ellen Ziskind, and Jonny Lerner for giving me advice and contacts for various publishers. But my eternal gratitude goes to Matt Becker and the University of Massachusetts Press staff. I wasn't sure if UMass Press would be interested in a book like mine, but unlike many publishers, they made it easy to ask. From the very beginning, Matt has been enthusiastic, supportive, accessible, and just about anything you could ask of an editor.

Finally, I have to give a shout-out to my wonderful daughters, Megan and Zoë, who have always encouraged me to trust in myself and use my voice.

SUGGESTED READING

These are some of the books that my esteemed book group read together over the years to try to better understand the assault on public education. It is far from a definitive list, but it's a great place to start.

Alexander, Michelle. *The New Jim Crow: Mass Incarceration in the Age of Colorblindness*. New York: The New Press, 2010.

Baptist, Edward E. *The Half Has Never Been Told: Slavery and the Making of American Capitalism*. New York: Basic Books, 2014.

Coates, Ta-Nehisi. *Between the World and Me*. New York: Spiegel & Grau, 2015.

Darling-Hammond, Linda. *The Flat World and Education: How America's Commitment to Equity Will Determine Our Future*. New York: Teachers College Press, 2010.

Delpit, Lisa. *Multiplication is for White People: Raising Expectations for Other People's Children*. New York: The New Press, 2012.

Ewing, Eve L. *Ghosts in the Schoolyard: Racism and School Closings on Chicago's South Side*. Chicago: The University of Chicago Press, 2018.

Fabricant, Michael and Fine, Michelle. *Charter Schools and the Corporate Makeover of Public Education: What's at Stake?* New York: Teachers College Press, 2012.

Farley, Todd. *Making the Grades: My Misadventures in the Standardized Testing Industry*. San Francisco: Berrett-Koehler Publishers, 2009.

Fruchter, Norm. *Urban Schools, Public Will: Making Education Work for All Our Children*. New York: Teachers College Press, 2007.

Goldstein, Dana: *The Teacher Wars: A History of America's Most Embattled Profession*. New York: Anchor Books, 2015.

Hagopian, Jesse (Ed). *More Than a Score: The New Uprising Against High Stakes Testing*. Chicago: Haymarket Books, 2014.

Horton, Myles and Freire, Paolo. *We Make the Road by Walking: Conversations on Education and Social Change*. Philadelphia: Temple University Press, 1990.

Kirp, David L. *Improbable Scholars: The Rebirth of a Great American School*

System and a Strategy for America's Schools. New York: Oxford University Press, 2013.

Kuhn, John. *Fear and Learning in America—Bad Data, Good Teachers, and the Attack on Public Education.* New York: Teachers College Press, 2014.

MacLean, Nancy. *Democracy in Chains: The Deep History of the Radical Right's Stealth Plan for America.* New York: Penguin Books, 2018.

Meier, Deborah and Gasoi, Emily. *These Schools Belong to You and Me: Why We Can't Afford to Abandon Our Public Schools.* Boston: Beacon Press, 2017.

Nelson, Steve. *First, Do No Harm: Progressive Education in a Time of Existential Risk.* New York: Garn Press, 2016.

Oakes, Jeannie. *Keeping Track: How Schools Structure Inequality.* New Haven: Yale University Press, 2005.

Palmer, Parker. *Healing the Heart of Democracy: The Courage to Create a Politics Worthy of the Human Spirit.* San Francisco: Jossey-Bass, 2011.

Ravitch, Diane. *The Death and Life of the Great American School System: How Testing and Choice are Undermining Education.* New York: Basic Books, 2010.

Ravitch, Diane. *Reign of Error: The Hoax of the Privatization Movement and the Danger to America's Public Schools.* New York: Vintage Books, 2014.

Ravitch, Diane. *Slaying Goliath: The Passionate Resistance to Privatization and the Fight to Save America's Public Schools.* New York: Alfred A. Knopf, 2020.

Rooks, Noliwe. *Cutting School: The Segrenomics of American Education.* New York: The New Press, 2020.

Russakoff, Dale. *The Prize: Who's in Charge of America's Schools?* New York: Mariner Books, 2016.

Sahlberg, Pasi. *Finnish Lessons: What Can the World Learn from Educational Change in Finland?* New York: Teachers College Press, 2010.

Schneider, Jack and Berkshire, Jennifer. *A Wolf at the Schoolhouse Door: The Dismantling of Public Education and the Future of School.* New York: The New Press, 2020.

Solo, Len. *Making an Extraordinary School: The Work of Ordinary People.* Baltimore: PublishAmerica, 2010.

Taylor, Keeanga-Yamahtta. *How We Get Free: Black Feminism and the Combahee River Collective.* Chicago: Haymarket Books, 2017.

Zhao, Yong. *Who's Afraid of the Big Bad Dragon? Why China Has the Best (and Worst) Education System in the World.* San Francisco: Jossey-Bass, 2014.

NOTES

INTRODUCTION: WHY WRITE THIS BOOK?

1. Looping is when students stay with the same teacher for more than one year.
2. For the complete letter, see Valerie Strauss, "Kindergarten Teacher: My job is Now about Tests and Data—Not Children. I Quit," *Washington Post*, March 23, 2014, https://www.washingtonpost.com/news/answer-sheet/wp/2014/03/23/kin dergarten-teacher-my-job-is-now-about-tests-and-data-not-children-i-quit/.
3. In 1990, Admiral James Watkins, the Secretary of Energy, commissioned the Sandia Laboratories in New Mexico to document the decline in the *Nation at Risk* report with actual data. When the systems scientists broke down the SAT test scores into subgroups, they discovered that the data did not support the claims of the report. Wikipedia, s.v. "A Nation At Risk," last modified March 21, 2023, https://en.wikipedia.org/wiki/A_Nation_at_Risk.
4. Leo Casey, "Is There a 'Corporate Education Reform' Movement?," April 10, 2013, accessed April 1, 2023, https://www.shankerinstitute.org/blog/there-corporate-education-reform-movement. For more discussion on the elements of corporate education reform, also see Valerie Strauss, "A Primer on Corporate School Reform," *Washington Post*, October 27, 2011, https://www.washingtonpost.com/blogs/answer-sheet/post/a-primer-on-corporate-school-reform/2011/10/26/gIQAyWrUKM_blog.html.

CHAPTER 1: TEACHER EDUCATION

1. Teach for America has basically operationalized this belief. See Jason Edwards, "The Problem with Teach for America: How to Fix Urban Teacher Problems in America," June 20, 2019, https://medium.com/@JasonPEdwards/the-problem-with-teach-for-america-7bedb463260a.
2. Sadly, this kind of trip could not happen in today's world. First, GM moved out of Massachusetts a couple of years after our visit, as did other industrial jobs. Plants moved south, either to North or South Carolina or further to Mexico. Second, even if there were an assembly line nearby to visit, there would be all sorts of liability issues on the part of the factory and school

regulations prohibiting such trips. Third, we could not have afforded to take this field trip. At that time, we all piled into a small fleet of cars and hit the Mass Pike. This would be *verboten* today. Teachers aren't even allowed to drive a student home who missed the bus. We would have had to rent a bus, which, at $200 an hour, would have prevented us from going.

3. Now it is all too common to see armed police officers in schools. They are called "School Resource Officers." They are not only in high schools, but in middle and elementary schools as well. For further information on this, see the ACLU report, "Bullies in Blue: The Origins and Consequences of School Policing," April 2017, https://www.aclu.org/report/bullies-blue-origins-and-consequences-school-policing.

CHAPTER 2: FIRST JOB

1. Many of these programs were never restored. How many of our students take shop or home economics anymore?

2. "See "Teacher Layoffs, Seniority, and Affirmative Action," Massachusetts Advisory Committee to the U.S. Commission on Civil Rights, August 20, 1981, https://files.eric.ed.gov/fulltext/ED226457.pdf.

3. Read Geoff Canada's *Fist, Stick, Knife, Gun* (Boston: Beacon, 1995) for a powerful description of the impact of these two issues on the Black community.

CHAPTER 3: FINDING HOME

1. As Len later said, "the teachers were, in a way, the curriculum. A teacher was the mediator between the world (what is to be learned/curricula) and the student." This did have a downside, however. Some topics were taught in multiple grades. In fact, teachers joked about how many times students could learn about the Wampanoag. It took time to remedy this as people were reluctant to give up complex and engaging units, but eventually the school developed its own kind of scope and sequence.

CHAPTER 4: WINDOWS INTO STUDENT THINKING

1. The previous fall (1985), Len had submitted a proposal to the Massachusetts Department of Education (under Mass. General Laws, Chapter 188, Dropout Prevention); this grant provided funding for a junior-high dropout-prevention program for the 1986–1987 school year.

CHAPTER 6: RECONSTRUCTION

1. "Overview: The Seven Developmental Needs of Early Adolescents," accessed April 3, 2023, https://arbetterbeginnings.com/wp-content/uploads/Overview-Seven%20Developmental%20Needs%20of%20Early%20Adolescents.pdf.

2. For a full description of each principle, see Coalition of Essential Schools, "Common Principles," accessed April 3, 2023, http://essentialschools.org/common-principles/.

3. I found out later that the principal of Shutesbury Elementary, Les Edinson, had been a teacher in the early days of the Cambridge Alternative Public School, CAPS. He and Len were good friends and colleagues.

4. See Ron Berger's book *An Ethic of Excellence: Building a Culture of Craftsmanship with Students* (Portsmouth, NH: Heinemann, 2003), for a lot more detail on Ron's classroom.

CHAPTER 7: REAL ASSESSMENT

1. Dr. Mitchell Chester, "Building on 20 Years of Massachusetts Education," Massachusetts Department of Elementary and Secondary Education, November 2014, http://www.doe.mass.edu/commissioner/BuildingOnReform.pdf .

2. This Common Core of Learning is not the same as the Common Core State Standards that came out in 2010.

3. All Massachusetts frameworks have been revised since that time, particularly in light of the new federal Common Core State Standards.

CHAPTER 8: TEACHING OTHER PEOPLE'S CHILDREN

1. Note: I don't list specific years here because this chapter spanned almost all my years at the school.

CHAPTER 9: THE REAL WORLD

1. I learned that studying family histories can be complicated and need to be approached sensitively. First, while many of our African American students knew why their ancestors had come to the U.S., they did not know where these people had come from originally. This was often a difficult conversation and eventually led to some study of internal migration. Secondly, for students who had been adopted or were living with foster families, this could be a triggering activity. We had to work closely with families in how we approached this.

2. "Making Theater, Making Meaning, Making Change," in *Journeys Through Our Classrooms*, ed. by Denis Udall and Amy Mednick (Dubuque, IA: Kendall/Hunt, 1996); and Kathy Greeley, *Why Fly That Way: Linking Community and Academic Achievement* (New York: Teacher's College Press, 2000).

CHAPTER 10: ED REFORM CREEPS IN

1. "MCAS Tests of Spring 1998 Percent of Students at Each Achievement Level for Massachusetts," Massachusetts Department of Elementary and Secondary Education, accessed April 3, 2023, https://profiles.doe.mass.edu/mcas/

achievement_level.aspx?linkid=32&orgcode=00000000&fycode=1998&orgt ypecode=0&.

2. Gail Russell Chaddock, "Adverse Impact? Tougher Tests and Zero-tolerance Discipline are Hitting Minorities," *Christian Science Monitor*, November 30, 1999, https://www.csmonitor.com/1999/1130/p14s1.html.

CHAPTER 11: EXIT: GRAHAM & PARKS, ENTER: NO CHILD LEFT BEHIND

1. There is much research on the importance of teaming now, including building "professional learning communities" or PLCs. As a place to start, see Rebecca Dufour, Richard Dufour, and Robert Eaker, *Getting Started: Reculturing Schools to Become Professional Learning Communities* (Bloomington, IN: Solution Tree, 2002).

2. The complete version of *The House* is in Cris Tovani, *I Read It But I Don't Get It: Comprehension Strategies for Adolescent Readers* (Portsmouth, NH: Stenhouse Publishers, 2000).

3. Dr. Mitchell Chester, "Building on 20 Years of Massachusetts Education Reform," Massachusetts Department of Elementary and Secondary Education, November 2014, http://www.doe.mass.edu/commissioner/BuildingOn-Reform.pdf.

4. Teachers at the school were not allowed to provide these services, even though they were the ones who knew the students well and understood what help those students needed. The implication was that the student struggled because the teacher was incompetent.

CHAPTER 14: IS THIS WHAT A PRINCIPAL DOES?

1. Pasi Sahlberg, *Finnish Lessons: What Can the World Learn from Educational Change in Finland?* (New York: Teachers College Press, 2011), 84.

CHAPTER 15: SILVER BULLETS

1. Jack Schneider, "Small Schools: The Edu-Reform Failure That Wasn't," *Education Week*, February 9, 2016, https://www.edweek.org/leadership/opinion -small-schools-the-edu-reform-failure-that-wasnt/2016/02.

CHAPTER 16: THE HARBOR SCHOOL

1. Expeditionary Learning, now known as EL Education, was a model for school reform that developed out of a partnership between the Harvard Graduate School of Education and Outward Bound in 1991.

2. Every staff person supervised an advisory group that met 3–4 times per week. There wasn't any curriculum or guidelines for these meetings so they ranged

significantly in quality, depending on how much each staff person was willing, or able, to put into planning.

CHAPTER 18: YOU CAN'T GO HOME AGAIN

1. Unz had initiated a similar ballot question in California in 1998, then in Arizona in 2000, and in Colorado in 2002.
2. According to the Massachusetts Department of Education, "Massachusetts law defines SEI as 'an English language acquisition process for young children in which nearly all classroom instruction is in English but with the curriculum and presentation designed for children who are learning the language. Books and instruction materials are in English and all reading, writing, and subject matter are taught in English. Although teachers may use a minimal amount of the child's native language when necessary, no subject matter shall be taught in any language other than English, and children in this program learn to read and write solely in English.'"
3. "Expeditions" are a term used by EL to describe a long-term, in-depth interdisciplinary study, lasting from six to twelve weeks. They involve students in research, field work (as opposed to field trips) and usually result in an authentic performance of understanding. While many expeditions were driven by science or social studies content, they were always rooted in strong literacy skills, as well.
4. "EngageNY Resources," New York State Education Department, accessed April 3, 2023, http://www.nysed.gov/curriculum-instruction/engageny.
5. Recently, I showed this list to a G&P teacher, and she laughed. "That list could have been from 2023. Not much has changed."

CHAPTER 19: THE RACE TO NOWHERE

1. There is a strong connection between modern-day standardized testing and the eugenics movement of the late nineteenth and early twentieth centuries. See John Rosales and Tim Walker, "The Racist Beginnings of Standardized Testing," *NEA Today*, March 20, 2021, https://www.nea.org/advocating-for-change/new-from-nea/racist-beginnings-standardized-testing.
2. "National Cost of Aligning States and Localities to the Common Core Standards," *Pioneer Institute and American Principles White Paper*, February 2012, https://pioneerinstitute.org/education/study-estimates-cost-of-transition-to-national-education-standards-at-16-billion/.
3. "TRAIN. PREPARE. MANAGE. Learning Management Technology, Courses, and Operational Software Built for You," Vector Solutions, accessed April 3, 2023, www.vectorsolutions.com.

CHAPTER 20: GOOD STUFF

1. For a more in-depth description of the curriculum see Karen Engels, "The Story of Us," *Educational Leadership*, November 1, 2017, https://www.ascd.org/el/articles/the-story-of-us.

CHAPTER 21: THE END . . .

1. Stephanie Levin and Kathryn Bradley, "Understanding and Addressing Principal Turnover: A Review of the Research," Learning Policy Institute, March 19, 2019, https://learningpolicyinstitute.org/product/nassp-understanding-addressing-principal-turnover-review-research-report.
2. Emma Garcia and Elaine Weiss, "U.S. Schools Struggle to Hire and Retain Teachers," Learning Policy Institute, April 16, 2019, https://www.epi.org/publication/u-s-schools-struggle-to-hire-and-retain-teachers-the-second-report-in-the-perfect-storm-in-the-teacher-labor-market-series/.
3. Alexandra Neason, "Half of Teachers Leave Their Job After Five Years: Here's What to Do About It," *The Hechinger Report*, July 18, 2014, https://hechingerreport.org/half-teachers-leave-job-five-years-heres/.
4. Quote from Mary Ginley, former Massachusetts Teacher of the Year, in *Why We Teach Now*, ed. Sonia Nieto (New York: Teachers College Press, 2014). She then answers her own question, "It's because somehow, even today, even with all the insanity, all the rules, all the poorly designed textbooks, all the directives to teach to the test, there are kids out there who need good teachers."
5. Valerie Strauss, "Kindergarten Teacher: My Job is Now about Tests and Data–Not Children. I Quit," *Washington Post*, March 23, 2014, https://www.washingtonpost.com/news/answer-sheet/wp/2014/03/23/kindergarten-teacher-my-job-is-now-about-tests-and-data-not-children-i-quit/.

CHAPTER 22: AND MAYBE A BEGINNING

1. Ethan Seigel, "How America is Breaking Public Education," *Forbes*, December 6, 2017, https://www.forbes.com/sites/startswithabang/2017/12/06/how-america-is-breaking-public-education/?sh=1fb626f67f18.
2. Van Schoales, "Education Reform as We Know It Is Over. What Have We Learned?," *Education Week*, April 26, 2019, https://www.edweek.org/policy-politics/opinion-education-reform-as-we-know-it-is-over-what-have-we-learned/2019/04.
3. "Reimagining the MCAS: The Need for an Accountability System that Supports Deeper Learning," Rennie Center Policy Brief, Spring 2021, https://www.renniecenter.org/sites/default/files/2021-06/Reimagining%20MCAS%20Policy%20Brief%20Final.pdf.

4. PISA is administered once every three years.

5. Editorial Board, "The U.S. is Growing More Unequal. That's Harmful–and Fixable," *Washington Post*, July 16, 2021, https://www.washingtonpost.com/opinions/2021/07/16/us-is-growing-more-unequal-thats-harmful-fixable. According to the same article, "A 2018 study of 28 countries in the Organization of Economic Cooperation and Development found that, on average, the top 10 percent of households owns 52 percent of wealth, while the bottom 60 percent owns 12 percent. But in the United States the top 10 percent held 79.5 percent and the bottom 60 percent held 2.4 percent."

6. Sadly some people have been shocked into a defensive reaction as evidenced by the false flag of so-called critical race theory.

EPILOGUE

1. Sarah Schwartz, "Four States Have Placed Legal Limits on How Teachers Can Discuss Race: More May Follow," *Education Week*, May 17, 2021, https://www.edweek.org/policy-politics/four-states-have-placed-legal-limits-on-how-teachers-can-discuss-race-more-may-follow/2021/05.

2. Moms for Liberty (@Moms4LibertyNH), "We've got $500 for the person that first successfully catches a public school teacher breaking this law. Students, parents, teachers, school staff . . . We want to know! We will pledge anonymity if you want," X (formerly Twitter), November 12, 2021, 6:28 a.m., https://twitter.com/Moms4LibertyNH/status/1459166253084467205.

KATHY GREELEY has an MA in education from Tufts University. She attended Harvard Graduate School as a Conant Fellow where she worked as the first "teacher-in-residence" for Expeditionary Learning. Kathy is a retired educator from Cambridge and Boston public schools and author of *Why Fly That Way: Linking Community and Academic Achievement.* She lives in Cambridge, Massachusetts.